MySQL™ Weekend Crash Course™

Jay Greenspan

Hungry Minds™

Best-Selling Books • Digital Downloads • e-Books • Answer Networks • e-Newsletters • Branded Web Sites • e-Learning

Cleveland, OH • Indianapolis, IN • New York, NY

MySQL™ Weekend Crash Course™

Published by
Hungry Minds, Inc.
909 Third Avenue
New York, NY 10022
www.hungryminds.com

Library of Congress Control Number: 2001093437

ISBN: 0-7645-3634-6

Printed in the United States of America

10 9 8 7 6 5 4 3 2 1

1B/SQ/QT/QS/IN

Distributed in the United States by Hungry Minds, Inc.

Distributed by CDG Books Canada Inc. for Canada; by Transworld Publishers Limited in the United Kingdom; by IDG Norge Books for Norway; by IDG Sweden Books for Sweden; by IDG Books Australia Publishing Corporation Pty. Ltd. for Australia and New Zealand; by TransQuest Publishers Pte Ltd. for Singapore, Malaysia, Thailand, Indonesia, and Hong Kong; by Gotop Information Inc. for Taiwan; by ICG Muse, Inc. for Japan; by Intersoft for South Africa; by Eyrolles for France; by International Thomson Publishing for Germany, Austria, and Switzerland; by Distribuidora Cuspide for Argentina; by LR International for Brazil; by Galileo Libros for Chile; by Ediciones ZETA S.C.R. Ltda. for Peru; by WS Computer Publishing Corporation, Inc., for the Philippines; by Contemporanea de Ediciones for Venezuela; by Express Computer Distributors for the Caribbean and West Indies; by Micronesia Media Distributor, Inc. for Micronesia; by Chips Computadoras S.A. de C.V. for Mexico; by Editorial Norma de Panama S.A. for Panama; by American Bookshops for Finland.

For general information on Hungry Minds' products and services please contact our Customer Care department within the U.S. at 800-762-2974, outside the U.S. at 317-572-3993 or fax 317-572-4002.

For sales inquiries and reseller information, including discounts, premium and bulk quantity sales, and foreign-language translations, please contact our Customer Care department at 800-434-3422, fax 317-572-4002 or write to Hungry Minds, Inc., Attn: Customer Care Department, 10475 Crosspoint Boulevard, Indianapolis, IN 46256.

For information on licensing foreign or domestic rights, please contact our Sub-Rights Customer Care department at 212-884-5000.

For information on using Hungry Minds' products and services in the classroom or for ordering examination copies, please contact our Educational Sales department at 800-434-2086 or fax 317-572-4005.

For press review copies, author interviews, or other publicity information, please contact our Public Relations department at 317-572-3168 or fax 317-572-4168.

For authorization to photocopy items for corporate, personal, or educational use, please contact Copyright Clearance Center, 222 Rosewood Drive, Danvers, MA 01923, or fax 978-750-4470.

 is a trademark of Hungry Minds, Inc.

 is a registered trademark of Hungry Minds, Inc.

 is a trademark of Hungry Minds, Inc.

About the Author

Jay Greenspan is a New York based writer, editor, and Web application developer. He served as senior editor and producer for Wired Digital's Webmonkey where he wrote articles on XML, databases, and programming and provided editorial direction for many areas of the Webmonkey site. The co-author of *MySQL/PHP Database Applications*, he has written for O'Reilly, Apple Computer, and many other companies and publications. He runs Trans-City Productions, a firm that provides writing and editing services for high-tech companies.

Credits

Acquisitions Editors
Debra Williams Cauley
Terri Varveris

Project Editor
Andrea C. Boucher

Technical Editor
Brad Bulger

Editorial Managers
Kyle Looper
Ami Sullivan

Senior Vice President, Technical Publishing
Richard Swadley

Vice President and Publisher
Mary Bednarek

Project Coordinator
Nancee Reeves

Graphics and Production Specialists
Beth Brooks, Sean Decker, Laurie Petrone,
Jacque Schneider, Betty Schulte

Quality Control Technician
Carl Pierce, Linda Quigley

Permissions Editor
Laura Moss

Media Development Specialist
Angela Denny

Media Development Coordinator
Marisa E. Pearman

Proofreading and Indexing
TECHBOOKS Production Services

Cover Design
Clark Creative Group

Preface

I'm imagining you, the reader, standing in an aisle of a bookstore thumbing through this and other tomes trying to find the one that fits your immediate needs. It can be a painful process, choosing a book. If you take a minute and read the rest of this Preface, you should have an indication of whether or not this book is for you.

MySQL is a great database, and developing with it can be quite a bit of fun. If you choose to buy this book, with its fetching blue cover, I think you'll have a pleasant couple of days, during which you'll pick up knowledge you can use for the rest of your technical life.

Who Should Read This Book

This crash course was designed to provide you with a set of short lessons that you can grasp quickly — in one weekend. The book is for two audience categories:

1. Those completely new to the world of relational databases. This book spends some time explaining relational theory and explains how to use SQL (the Structured Query Language) from the ground up. If you've never written a single query, or if you don't know exactly what a query is, this book can be your guide.

2. Those who have done some work with relational databases but are new to MySQL. Even if you've spent a good deal of time working with databases like Access or FoxPro, MySQL can be a bit daunting at first. This book helps you apply your knowledge to this new application.

You should know that MySQL is only one tool needed to develop applications. If you want to deliver database applications to an audience over the Web, you need other tools. Some of these are covered in this book.

What You Need to Have

To make the best use of this book, you need

- An Internet account. I reference Web pages throughout the book, and you'll want to read most of these as you go along.

- Any text editor. On Windows, this could be as simple as Notepad or as sophisticated as HomeSite or EditPlus. On Unix, feel free to use vi or Pico or emacs. On a Mac OS X, BBedit is a great choice.
- Patience. You will spend a lot of time working on a command line, which is similar to a DOS prompt. This can take some getting used to if you're accustomed to clicking and dragging.

Any computer running a modern version of Windows (Windows 98 or later), Unix/Linux, or Mac OS X should be fine. Sorry, MySQL will not run on Mac OS 9.

What Results Can You Expect?

Believe it or not, in the course of a weekend you can learn most everything you need to know to be a competent user of MySQL. With database servers, there are two general areas of knowledge you may need to learn. The first area concerns using MySQL for applications development. If you're looking to create Web sites or other applications that use a MySQL database on the backend (perhaps using Perl or PHP for middleware), you can expect this book to cover just about everything you need to know.

The second general area concerns administration of the database server. This is a very broad and important topic and is not covered in exhaustive detail in this book. Most of the major concerns a MySQL administrator will have are covered. You will find instructions covering backup, recover, and configuration, but not every topic related to administration is covered.

The Weekend Crash Course Layout and Features

This book follows the standard Weekend Crash Course layout and includes the standard features of the series so that you can be assured of mastering MySQL in a weekend. Readers should take breaks throughout. Drink liquids and stretch. The book presents 30 sessions that last approximately one-half hour each. The sessions are grouped within parts that take two or three hours to complete. At the end of each session, you find "Quiz Yourself" questions; and at the end of each part, you find part review questions. These questions test your knowledge and let you practice your newfound skills. (The answers to the part review questions are in Appendix A.)

Layout

This Weekend Crash Course contains 30, one-half-hour sessions organized into six parts. The parts correspond with a time during the weekend, as outlined in the following sections.

Part I: Friday Evening

In this part, you learn about the theories that govern database servers. Then you see how to install and work with MySQL. You end the evening seeing how to create databases in MySQL.

Part II: Saturday Morning

This part consists of six sessions that take you further into the world of MySQL. You learn a good deal of the Structured Query Language (SQL). By the end of this portion of the book, you've learned much of what you need to know to create MySQL-driven applications.

Part III: Saturday Afternoon

In this afternoon session, you develop your MySQL knowledge by applying advanced SQL features. By the end of the afternoon, you've learned techniques that help you write durable applications. Then you see how to apply all the previous lessons by creating Web-based applications written in PHP.

Part IV: Saturday Evening

Your evening starts with a look at using MySQL with Perl. It then moves on to showing some optimization techniques. The evening ends as you go through your first session on the vital topic of security.

Part V: Sunday Morning

You spend Sunday morning concentrating on topics related to MySQL administration. You learn how to apply all sorts of configuration options and see how to back up and restore MySQL data. There are many utilities that ship with MySQL, and in this session you see how to use most of them.

Part VI: Sunday Afternoon

The last sessions of the book attempt to broaden your MySQL horizons by giving you some potential uses for MySQL and food for thought. You learn about some clients that can be used with MySQL, how you can improve the performance of your server, and how to research difficult questions.

Features

First, as you're going through each session, look for the following time status icons that let you know how much progress you've made throughout the session:

30 Min.   **20 Min.**   **10 Min.**   **Done!**
To Go   **To Go**   **To Go**

The book also contains other icons that highlight special points of interest:

This is a flag to clue you in to an important piece of information that you should file away in your head for later.

This gives you helpful advice on the best ways to do things or a tricky technique that can make your HTML programming go smoother.

This states where related material can be found in the other sessions.

This gives a note of caution and will keep you from making commonly made mistakes.

Other Conventions

Apart from the icons you've just seen, only three other conventions appear:

1. To indicate programming code or an Internet address within the body text, I use a special font like this: The Web site appears at www.hungryminds.com.
2. Pieces of the SQL language are presented in all caps. For example, "To get information from a table you must use a SELECT statement."
3. To indicate a programming example that's not in the body text, I use this typeface:

   ```
   mysql> select * from table_name;
   ```

Accompanying CD-ROM

This Weekend Crash Course includes a CD-ROM in the back. There you find a sample database for use with the book, code listings, and a self-assessment test. See Appendix B for more information on the CD-ROM.

Reach Out

The publisher and I want your feedback. After you have had a chance to use this book, please take a moment to register this book on the www.hungryminds.com/events/reg/registr.html Web site.

I have created a Web site for this book: www.mysqlwcc.com. You can check in at the site if you have questions, complaints, or want to view errata information.

Also, please let me know of any mistakes in the book or if a topic is covered particularly well. Write to: jay@trans-city.com.

Acknowledgments

First I need to thank everyone involved with the creation of this book. I'm appreciative that Terri Varveris and Debra Williams Cauley at HMI gave me the opportunity to write this, my second book. Andrea Boucher's editorial direction and Brad Bulger's technical acumen assured that what you have in front of you is readable and accurate. Liz Warner's Perl expertise was much needed, and I thank her for her contribution.

Any book on open source software owes a debt of gratitude to the creators of these great tools. Thanks to everyone at MySQL AB and everyone else involved with MySQL development.

Finally, to Melissa: your love and support are part of everything I do. Thank you.

Contents at a Glance

Preface vii
Acknowledgments xi

FRIDAY 2

Part I—Friday Evening 4
Session 1–Why MySQL? 5
Session 2–MySQL Installation and Post-Installation Review 15
Session 3–Creating Databases: Governing Principles 25
Session 4–Creating Databases in MySQL 37

SATURDAY 50

Part II—Saturday Morning 52
Session 5–Viewing and Altering Databases and Tables 53
Session 6–Inserting, Updating, and Deleting MySQL Data 63
Session 7–Getting Data from MySQL, Part I: The Basic SELECT 75
Session 8–Getting Data from MySQL, Part II: Using SELECT with Multiple Tables 83
Session 9–Basic Functions in MySQL 95
Session 10–Date Functions in MySQL 105

Part III—Saturday Afternoon 116
Session 11–Other MySQL Functions 117
Session 12–Beyond LIKE: Using Regular Expressions and FULLTEXT Indexes 127
Session 13–Transactions with MyISAM and BDB Tables 137
Session 14–Using Gemini and InnoDB Tables 147
Session 15–Working with MySQL and PHP 157
Session 16–MySQL and PHP: Best Practices 169

Part IV—Saturday Evening 182
Session 17–Using MySQL with Perl 183
Session 18–MySQL and Perl: Best Practices 195
Session 19–Optimizing MySQL Queries 207
Session 20–Securing MySQL, Part I: The GRANT Tables 217

SUNDAY 228

Part V—Sunday Morning 230
Session 21–Securing MySQL, Part II: Your Unix Environment 231
Session 22–Advanced Configuration Options 241
Session 23–MySQL Client Applications 253
Session 24–Backing Up and Exporting MySQL Data 263
Session 25–Transferring and Importing Data into MySQL 273
Session 26–Replication 283

Part VI—Sunday Afternoon 296
Session 27–Diagnosing and Repairing Table Problems 297
Session 28–MySQL GUI Clients 305
Session 29–Optimizing MySQL 315
Session 30–Answering Remaining Questions 325

Appendix A–Answers to Part Reviews **333**
Appendix B–What's on the CD-ROM? **339**
Index **341**
End-User License Agreement **360**
CD-ROM Installation Instructions **362**

Contents

Preface vii

Acknowledgments xi

FRIDAY 2

Part I—Friday Evening 4

Session 1–Why MySQL? 5

   SQL Servers in the Development Process 5

     Developing Web applications 5

     The SQL server 6

       What an SQL server can do 7

       What an SQL server cannot do 7

     Developing desktop applications 11

   MySQL versus the Competition 12

     The advantages of MySQL 12

       It's fast 12

       It's relatively easy to use 13

       It's widely used 13

       It's open source 13

     The disadvantages of MySQL 14

Session 2–MySQL Installation and Post-Installation Review 15

   Linux Installation 16

     Installing from tarballs 16

     Installing from RPMs 17

   Installing on Windows 17

   Installing on Unix/MacOS X 17

   Installing from Source 18

   Make Your Life Easy with the NuSphere Install 19

   Post-Installation Review 20

     Scripts and applications 20

       Starting the MySQL server 21

       Interacting with the server 21

     Databases and files 22

     Libraries 22

   Configuring Unix/Linux to Initiate MySQL at Startup 23

Session 3–Creating Databases: Governing Principles 25

   Why We Don't Use the File System for Data Storage 26

   Working with Tables 26

   Problems with a Basic Table 27

     Update anomaly 27

     Delete anomaly 28

     Insert anomaly 29

Fixing Anomalies through Normalization 29
1st normal form 30
2nd normal form 31
3rd normal form 31
Relationships 33
One-to-many 33
One-to-one 33
Many-to-many 33
Other Important Database Concepts 33
Null 34
Indexes 34
Referential integrity 34
Session 4—Creating Databases in MySQL 37
CREATE DATABASE Statement 37
CREATE TABLE Command 38
Column types 39
Text column types 39
Numeric column types 41
Date and time types 43
Table types 44
Creating indexes 44
Creating foreign key constraints 46
Loading the Sample Database 46

SATURDAY 50
Part II—Saturday Morning 52
Session 5—Viewing and Altering Databases and Tables 53
Viewing the Database on the File System 53
Best Practices When Creating Databases and Tables 54
Using the SHOW Command 55
SHOW DATABASES 55
SHOW TABLES 56
SHOW COLUMNS 56
SHOW INDEX 57
SHOW TABLE STATUS 57
SHOW CREATE TABLE 58
ALTER TABLE Statement 58
Changing a table name 59
Adding columns 59
Dropping columns 60
Adding indexes 60
Dropping indexes 60
Changing column definitions 61
Session 6—Inserting, Updating, and Deleting MySQL Data 63
The INSERT Statement 63
The Basic WHERE Clause 65

The UPDATE Statement 67
The REPLACE Statement 67
The DELETE Statement 68
Creating a Web Form for Inserting, Updating, and Deleting Data 68
Session 7–Getting Data from MySQL, Part I: The Basic SELECT 75
The Basic SELECT 75
Applying the WHERE Clause 76
Grouping portions of the WHERE Clause 77
Using IN/NOT IN 77
Using LIKE 78
Using ORDER BY 79
Using LIMIT 80
Using SELECT DISTINCT 80
Session 8–Getting Data from MySQL, Part II: Using SELECT
with Multiple Tables 83
The Equi-Join 84
Using INNER JOIN Syntax 85
The OUTER JOIN 86
Subselects 87
Unions 89
Self Joins 91
Session 9–Basic Functions in MySQL 95
Function Basics 95
Arguments 95
Aliases 96
GROUP BY and Aggregate Functions 97
count() 97
sum() 98
avg() 98
min() and max() 99
HAVING 99
Mathmatical Operations 99
Trigonometric functions 100
Rounding functions 101
Session 10–Date Functions in MySQL 105
Inserting Dates 105
Selecting and Formatting Dates 106
Simple date formatting functions 107
Using date_format() 109
Calculating Date Ranges 111

Part III—Saturday Afternoon 116
Session 11–Other MySQL Functions 117
Using Flow Control Functions 117
Using ifnull() 118
Using if() 119

Using Cryptographic Functions 119
   password() and md5() 120
   encode() and decode() 120
Using String Functions 121
   ucase() and lcase() 121
   left() and right() 121
   concat() 122
   ltrim()/rtrim()/trim() 123
System Information Functions 123
Other Important MySQL Functions 124
   Using last_insert_id() 124
   Using rand() 125

Session 12–Beyond LIKE: Using Regular Expressions and FULLTEXT Indexes 127
Using Regular Expressions 127
   Regular expression basics 128
   Special characters 128
   Character classes 129
   Expressing "Not" 131
   Multiple occurrences 132
   Grouping characters 132
Using FULLTEXT Indexing 133
   Creating FULLTEXT indexes 133
   Running natural language searches 133
   Using Boolean searches 134

Session 13–Transactions with MyISAM and BDB Tables 137
Understanding Potential Dangers 137
   The problem 137
   The usual solution: Transactions 138
Understanding the ACID Properties 138
Working with MyISAM Tables 139
   Applying table locks 139
   Using locks in applications 140
Working with BDB Tables 142
   Creating BDB tables 142
   Applying transactions 142
   Rewriting code using transactions 143
Configuring BDB Tables 144

Session 14–Using Gemini and InnoDB Tables 147
Understanding Row-Level Locking 147
Using Gemini Tables 148
   Share lock 149
   Exclusive lock 150
   Working with Gemini locks 151
Using InnoDB Tables 152
   Understanding the InnoDB transactional model 153
   Working with InnoDB locks 154

Session 15–Working with MySQL and PHP 157
  Installing PHP with MySQL Support 157
    Installing PHP and Apache on Linux/Unix 158
    Installing PHP on Mac OS X 159
  Installation on Windows 160
  Testing Your Installation 161
  Using PHP's MySQL Functions 162
    Connecting to the server and choosing a database 162
    Sending and viewing queries 162
    Other helpful MySQL functions 164
      mysql_error() *165*
      mysql_affected_rows() *165*
      mysql_insert_id() *165*
    Putting these functions to work 165
Session 16–MySQL and PHP: Best Practices 169
  Cleaning User Data 169
    Escaping string 169
    Removing unwanted HTML 172
  Handling Queries 172
  Establishing a Connection 174
    Creating a connection function 174
    Working with atypical configurations 175
  Organizing your PHP Code 176

Part IV— Saturday Evening **182**
Session 17–Using MySQL with Perl 183
  Installing Perl with MySQL Support 183
    Installing Perl on Linux, Unix, and Mac OS X 184
    Compiling and installing Perl 185
    Installing DBD::mysql — the mysql drivers for DBI 186
    Installing for Windows 187
  Testing Your Installation 187
  Turning Your Perl Script into a CGI Script 188
  Some of DBI's Methods for Sending and Retrieving Data 190
    Retrieving data 191
    Retrieving a scalar or array with selectrow_array() 191
    Protecting yourself from tainted variables with quote() 191
    Retrieving a two-dimensional array of rows with selectall_arrayref() 192
    Selecting data with selectall_hashref() 192
    Inserting data with do() 193
  Pulling It All Together 194
Session 18–MySQL and Perl: Best Practices 195
  Handling User Data 195
  Removing Unwanted HTML 196
  Handling Errors 196

Optimizing Your Queries for the Web 197
Other Ways to Use Perl with Apache and MySQL 198
   A brief introduction to HTML::Mason 199
   Using Mason's autohandlers 202

Session 19–Optimizing MySQL Queries 207
Logging Slow Queries 207
Looking at Indexes 208
Applying and Testing Indexes 209
   Creating multi-column indexes 209
   Using indexes on joins 212
Other Ways to Use Indexes 215

Session 20–Securing MySQL, Part I: The GRANT Tables 217
Understanding the GRANT Tables 217
   Understanding the user table 219
   Understanding the db table 220
   Understanding tables_priv and columns_priv 220
Using the GRANT and REVOKE Statements 221
   Using GRANT 222
   REVOKE 224
   Viewing GRANTS 225
   Reloading GRANTS 225
Logging In from Clients 225

SUNDAY...228

Part V—Sunday Morning 230
Session 21–Securing MySQL, Part II: Your Unix Environment 231
Shutting Down Your MySQL Server 232
Assigning Permissions 233
   Creating users and groups on Unix/Linux 233
   Creating users and groups on Mac OS X 233
   Changing ownership of MySQL files and directories 235
Restarting Applications 236
Examining Your Unix/Linux Environment 236
   Is your system up-to-date? 237
   Are you enforcing good password policies? 237
   Are unnecessary processes running? 237
   Are your TCP Wrappers configured? 238
   Is your firewall watching out for MySQL ? 238

Session 22–Advanced Configuration Options 241
Understanding the my.cnf File 241
   my.cnf locations 242
   my.cnf sections 243
Configuring the MySQL Daemon 243
Configuring the MySQL Command-Line Client 248
Creating Useful Configuration Files 250

Session 23—MySQL Client Applications 253
  Using mysqladmin 253
    Basic administrative commands 254
    Status information commands 254
      mysqladmin ping *254*
      mysqladmin version *255*
      mysqladmin status *255*
      mysqladmin processlist *256*
      mysqladmin kill *257*
    Flush commands 257
      mysqladmin flush-hosts *257*
      mysqladmin flush-logs *257*
      mysqladmin flush-privileges *257*
      mysqladmin flush-tables *258*
  Using mysqlshow 258
  Putting the Clients to Work 259
Session 24—Backing Up and Exporting MySQL Data 263
  Using mysqldump 263
  Using SELECT INTO OUTFILE 267
  Using BACKUP TABLE 268
  Copying Database Files 269
  Using the Binary Log 269
  Instituting Good Backup Practices 271
Session 25—Transferring and Importing Data into MySQL 273
  Using LOAD DATA INFILE 273
  Using mysqlimport 275
  Transferring Applications Data to MySQL 276
    Moving from Excel to MySQL 276
    Moving from Access to MySQL 276
  Importing Apache Log Files 278
Session 26—Replication 283
  Understanding Replication 283
  Setting Up Replication 285
    Setting up the master 285
    Setting up the slave 286
  Replication Commands 289

Part VI—Sunday Afternoon **296**
Session 27—Diagnosing and Repairing Table Problems 297
  Using SQL Commands for Checking and Reparing Tables 297
    Using the CHECK TABLE command 297
    Using REPAIR TABLE 299
    Using ANALYZE TABLE 299
    Using OPTIMIZE TABLE 299

Using Utility Programs for Checking and Repairing Tables 299
    Using mysqlcheck 300
    Using myisamchk 301
Session 28–MySQL GUI Clients **305**
  phpMyAdmin 305
  mysqlFront 308
  MysqlGUI 309
  Using MySQL with ODBC 310
  Using MacSQL 312
Session 29–Optimizing MySQL **315**
  Creating a Cache 316
  Un-Normalizing Data 318
  Examining Your Configuration 320
  Upgrading Hardware 322
  Packing Tables 322
Session 30–Answering Remaining Questions **325**
  RTFM 325
  Using Files Included with the MySQL Installation 326
    Using --help 326
    Using man pages 327
  Mailing Lists 328
    MySQL general mailing list 328
    Win32 mailing list 329
    Other MySQL mailing lists 330
  Web Sites 330
    O'Reilly's ONLamp.com 330
    Developer Shed 330
    PHPBuilder 330
    Perl.com 330
    weberdev.com 330
  Buying Support 330
Appendix A–Answers to the Part Reviews **333**
Appendix B–What's on the CD-ROM? **339**
Index **341**
End-User License Agreement **360**
CD-ROM Installation Instructions **362**

MySQL™ Weekend Crash Course™

☑ **Friday**

☐ Saturday

☐ Sunday

Part I — Friday Evening

Session 1
Why MySQL?

Session 2
MySQL Installation and Post-Installation Review

Session 3
Creating Databases: Governing Principles

Session 4
Creating Databases in MySQL

P A R T

I

Friday Evening

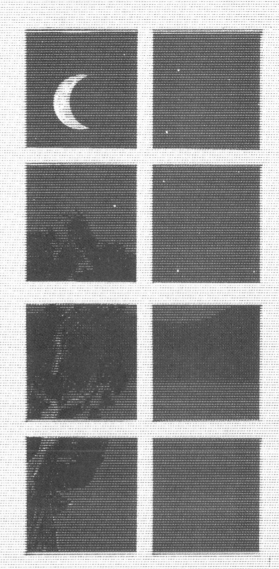

Session 1

Why MySQL?

Session 2

*MySQL Installation and
Post-Installation Review*

Session 3

Creating Databases: Governing Principles

Session 4

Creating Databases in MySQL

SESSION

Why MySQL?

Session Checklist

✔ SQL servers in the development process
✔ MySQL versus the competition

**30 Min.
To Go**

o use MySQL effectively, you need to learn the syntax of a new language and grow
comfortable with a new set of tools. However, before learning the specifics, you should
understand the class of products to which MySQL belongs: database servers. Some of
the early sessions of this book describe many of the theories that govern the majority of
database servers. For starters, you should understand where database servers (also known as
SQL Servers or *Relational Database Management Systems* [RDBMS]) fit into the application
development process.

SQL Servers in the Development Process

When it comes time to develop an application, chances are you're going to need more than
one tool. Whether your application is going to be viewed over the Web in a browser, in a
Microsoft Windows environment, or in the MacOS, there's a good chance that multiple
development packages will be needed to complete the application.

Developing Web applications

If you're interested in using MySQL, you're probably planning on building a dynamic Web
site. MySQL can be used in other environments, but it is used most frequently for the Web.
Creating a dynamic Web site takes at least three distinct pieces of software: the SQL server,

the programming/scripting language, and the Web server. An SQL server (in your case MySQL) is a vital piece of the process, but other pieces are equally necessary to get applications up and running. Figure 1-1 gives a diagram of the tools typically used in Web development.

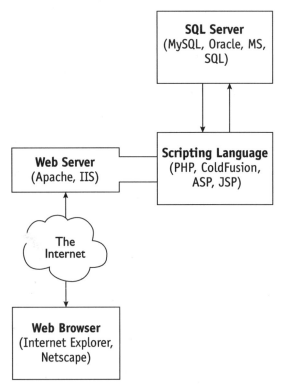

Figure 1-1   *Tools in the Web development process*

In Figure 1-1, you can see the three distinct pieces (the SQL server, the programming/ scripting language, and the Web server). Each has its own responsibilities.

The SQL server

Before describing the responsibilities assigned to the SQL server, you should know what SQL stands for: Structured Query Language. SQL is a standard implemented by many companies in many products. In the course of your career, you may have come across products like Microsoft's Access, FoxPro, and SQL Server 7. These are all implementations of the Structured Query Language. Companies like Oracle, Sybase, Informix, and IBM all make billions of dollars making products that implement this standard. You'll spend a good portion of this book learning the specifics of SQL, but for the sake of this session, all you need to know is what an SQL server's role is in the development process.

What an SQL server can do

An SQL server essentially has two jobs: to store data efficiently and to retrieve that data quickly. The SQL server is where your data — your valuable, crucial, business-dependent data — will live. You have the ability to insert, delete, and alter this information in any way you see fit.

Additionally, and perhaps most importantly, you can *query* this data — pull information out of the SQL server — in about any way you can imagine.

Further, an SQL server can provide statistical information on the data you have stored. If the idea of getting statistical information on your data is a bit vague right now, don't worry. It will become clear as you progress with this weekend-long course. For now, think of this simple example: In MySQL you've stored names and addresses of everyone affiliated with your business. If a time comes when you want to know exactly how many of these people live in a specific state or region of the country, your SQL server is able to quickly and easily return this information.

What an SQL server cannot do

Figure 1-1 illustrates that an SQL server does not interact directly with the Internet or with browsers. In Web-based applications, there are two related but distinct pieces of software that compliment the SQL server: the Web server and the middleware.

When you come down to it, the Web server has a pretty simple job. It is supposed to sit on the Internet and listen for requests made for a specific IP address or domain name. When you type an address into your browser, the Web server responds directly to your request. An SQL server cannot respond to requests that are sent via HTTP (the Hypertext Transfer Protocol), which is the language spoken by browsers and Web servers.

The two most popular Web servers are Microsoft's Internet Information Server (IIS) and the Apache Web server. You can use either Web server when creating dynamic Web sites with MySQL. However, chances are that if you are using MySQL, you're using the Apache Web server. Both of these products are open source and are frequently paired in Web applications. (I talk more about open source later in this session.)

As you can see in Figure 1-1, piece of software sits between the Web server and the SQL server, which is the scripting language, also known as *middleware*. The whole point in creating dynamic Web applications is so your Web site can react differently to different users. For example, the user should be able to add information to the site. The user should also have the ability to view information based on his or her particular needs.

Being dynamic requires your site to act differently based on different pieces of information, whether that information is coming from the user or the database. Here's a quick example:

- A viewer of your online real estate listing wishes to see only houses under $200,000 that are within a certain ZIP code. Based on this information supplied by the user, your Web pages show only the listings that fit these criteria.

In cases such as this, middleware is essential. In this example, the user enters information into form elements on an HTML page and submits the form. Figure 1-2 shows what this Web page may look like.

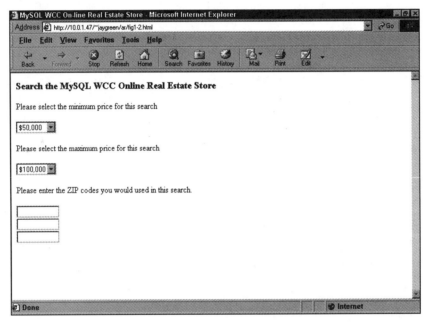

Figure 1-2   *HTML page that gathers user preferences*

The Web server receives the information sent by the browser, which includes the form information. That information needs to be molded into a form that the database server can respond to. Eventually, you need to make a request from the SQL server, but it must be in the format the SQL server is expecting.

This is where your middleware comes in. It can look at the incoming information and perform programmatic tasks on it as necessary. For example, if the user failed to enter location information, such as a ZIP code, the middleware you are using tests for the existence of at least one ZIP. If there isn't a ZIP, the middleware may present the form again with an added message alerting the user of his or her failure to complete the data. (See Figure 1-3 for an example of what this page may look like.)

Similarly, even if the user did fill out all of the form data, there is still a chance that no listing meets the user's criteria. In this case, you want to alert the user and offer him or her a chance to broaden the search parameters (additional ZIPs, higher price range, and so on). (See Figure 1-4 for an example of what this page may look like.)

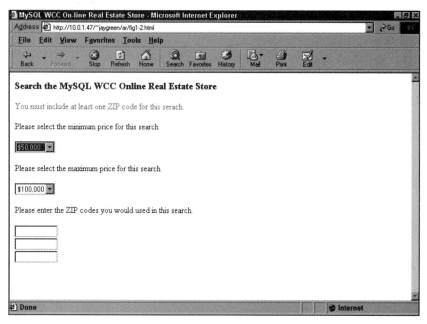

Figure 1-3 *HTML page requesting additional user data*

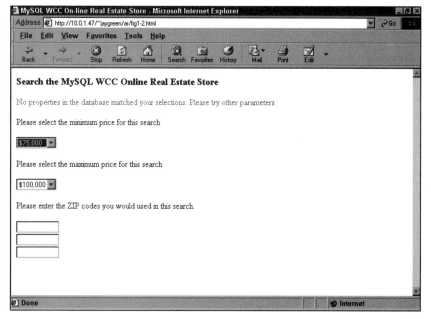

Figure 1-4 *HTML page requesting different parameters*

If the user fills out all of the information correctly and there are matching listings, those listings should be sent to the user's browser. (See Figure 1-5 for an example of what this page may look like.)

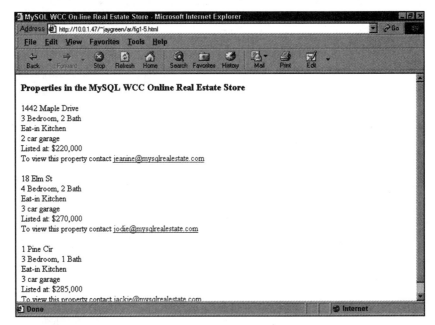

Figure 1-5 *HTML page presenting property listings*

Listing 1-1 shows how the middleware for a page that displays listings may work.

Listing 1-1 *Sample logic for middleware application*

```
if there are no ZIPs or Prices in the HTML forms
    re-display HTML page and notify user of missing data
    then quit the script
    (Figure 1-3)

else if all information has been provided
    request listing from the SQL server, using information
        supplied by user
```

```
        if the SQL server indicates there are no matching results
            tell user about the lack of results and re-display form
            (Figure 1-4)

        else if there are results returned by the SQL server
            while there are listings
                print listing information
                (Figure 1-5)
    end if
```

This listing should make the point clear: All the decision logic is done in your middleware. If you have any familiarity with any type of programming, the listing should seem familiar. There are if branches and loops (the building blocks of programming.

You are going to be imbedding your database requests in middleware. The SQL server responds only to requests that come from the middleware.

There are many types of middleware available for Web applications. ColdFusion and Microsoft's ASP are two common choices. However, the most common companions to MySQL are PHP and Perl. Sessions 15 and 16 discuss using PHP with MySQL, and Sessions 17 and 18 discuss using Perl with MySQL.

**20 Min.
To Go**

Developing desktop applications

If you are coming to MySQL from a background in Microsoft Access, Paradox, or FileMaker Pro, you may feel that the architecture shown in Figure 1-1 and discussed in the previous pages differs substantially from how you're accustomed to working. After all, you probably think that Access, Paradox, FileMaker, or FoxPro require only one software package to get the job done.

Actually, this is not the case. These applications are packaged in a way that makes it seem that only one piece of software is at work. In all of these packages, a core database engine that is quite separate from the tools is used to build forms and tables for the users of the application. In the case of Access and Paradox, the default database server is known as the Jet engine. In fact, the Jet engine can be reached in many different ways: through Paradox or Access, from a development environment like Visual Basic or Delphi, or over the Web. You just have to let the Web server know where to find the Jet engine for that database.

With Access, you have the option of using something other than the Jet engine. In fact, you can configure a Windows machine so that MySQL serves and stores the information that is viewable through Access forms and Windows. Session 23 shows how you can connect MySQL to Microsoft Access.

Figure 1-6 shows how database servers fit into any applications development process. Notice that a single database server can offer data to many different clients simultaneously.

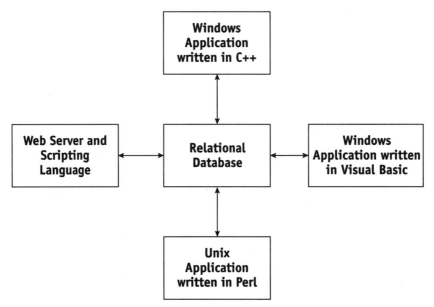

Figure 1-6 *Database servers in desktop applications development environment*

MySQL versus the Competition

You have many choices when it comes to RDBMSs. From Access to Oracle, there are products of many shapes and sizes that can fit your needs.

Before you commit to MySQL, you should know where it excels and where its competitors provide superior alternatives. In order to understand some of the specific advantages and deficiencies of MySQL, you need to understand some of the concepts covered later in this book. For now, I keep this information at a fairly general level.

The advantages of MySQL

Here are some of MySQL's finer points. Each of the attributes discussed below can be used to describe other products, but put together, these features make MySQL an interesting and unique piece of software.

**10 Min.
To Go**

It's fast

MySQL is undeniably quick. It is a true multi-threaded database server that excels at retrieving information. MySQL was originally designed for the purpose of querying information at an amazingly fast pace.

This design introduced some disadvantages that made MySQL a poor choice for some people. A database is used for two basic actions: inserting/modifying data and *querying* (requesting information) from existing data. The creators of MySQL opted for an architecture that sacrificed some speed in the insert/modifying process to gain speed during queries. So if you were developing a database application in 1999 and you foresaw your application dealing with a lot of inserting and modifying of data, MySQL would have been a poor choice. However, MySQL now offers many configuration options that give you the choice of extreme speed in queries at times when heavy inserts are not expected, or you can opt for options that work better while inserting/modifying data.

For a time, the major criticism of MySQL was that it did not support *transactions*. **If at this point you don't know what a transaction is, don't worry — they are explained in detail later in the book. If you do know what a transaction is, you'll be happy to know that MySQL supports this feature.**

Just how fast is MySQL compared to the competition? It's very, very difficult to say. Benchmarking of database servers is very tricky business. The only real way to gauge comparative speed is to do a straight-up comparison with another product using the same hardware and the same code. So without giving numbers, which are easily disputable, I'll say what is generally believed: MySQL is fast, and you'll just have to believe that.

It's relatively easy to use

If you work in a Fortune 1000 business, there's an excellent chance that at many places in your organization, some developers are using a recent version of Oracle. You can be sure that the person in charge of the database went through extensive training and/or went to school to learn how to properly maintain this large and very complex database system.

MySQL doesn't offer much of the power of Oracle, but if you don't need all of the features Oracle offers (and most don't), you'll find it far, far easier to get your database and related applications up and running with MySQL. In fact, I believe that this book and the online manual may be all that you need to be a very competent user and administrator of MySQL.

It's widely used

MySQL is growing in popularity. If you're looking to develop a MySQL-powered Web site, you'll have little difficulty finding an ISP that supports MySQL. Additionally, when you run into problems, you will be able to go to one of the many MySQL support forums to get expert troubleshooting advice.

It's open source

MySQL is an open-source product released under the GPL (GNU Public License). At this point, many independent developers work on the code without any monetary compensation because they get great satisfaction from their efforts. In addition, at least two companies (MySQL AB and NuSphere) offer commercial support for MySQL.

With open-source software, the base code is available to any who wants to see and alter it. So if you happen to be a sophisticated C programmer, you are welcome to add your own enhancements.

If you go the open-source route with MySQL, you will find many products that complement your MySQL database server. If you remember back to Figure 1-1, a Web server and scripting language are used to create dynamic sites. In the open-source space, Apache is a well-known and well-respected Web server. As far as scripting languages go, Perl and PHP are two very popular open-source languages that are often used with MySQL.

When combined, these open-source developer tools make for a powerful development environment. This is especially true of Web-based applications.

The disadvantages of MySQL

Are you starting a bank — you know, a Savings & Loan? Or are you trying to create a site with the functionality of, say, Schwab.com? If so, MySQL is the wrong tool. MySQL does not implement features found in many other products. (If you are familiar with RDBMSs, these other products include triggers, stored procedures, and views).

For now, I think it's useful to think of MySQL's missing features in this way: If you are developing a database that will have many different front ends (maybe one written for the Web, one written in Visual Basic or C, and another for Unix), then MySQL isn't a great choice. In situations like these, when your database must react to many different environments, the database administrator needs more control over the data than MySQL offers. In a case like this, you should look at some of the competitive products like Oracle, Sybase, or in the open-source space, PostgreSQL.

Done!

REVIEW

This session introduced you to the category of products known as database servers. It showed how database servers fit into the applications development process for both Web-based and non-Web-based applications. The session then reviewed MySQL's strengths and weaknesses and gave examples of where MySQL is an appropriate choice and where it is a less-than-ideal alternative.

QUIZ YOURSELF

1. In addition to database servers, what two products are needed to create Web-based applications? (See "Developing Web applications.")
2. Which piece of development software would be responsible for alerting a user that a database contained no relevant information? (See "What an SQL server cannot do.")
3. Name three reasons for selecting MySQL. (See "The advantages of MySQL.")
4. In what sort of environment is MySQL a poor choice? (See "The disadvantages of MySQL.")
5. Name three open-source products that are typically used with MySQL in delivering Web-based applications. (See "It's open source.")

MySQL Installation and Post-Installation Review

Session Checklist

✔ Linux installation

✔ Windows installation

✔ Unix/MacOS X installation

✔ Source installation

✔ Making it easy with NuSphere

✔ Post-installation review

✔ Configuring Unix/Linux to initiate MySQL at startup

**30 Min.
To Go**

Now that you understand the role of MySQL in the development process, as described in Session 1, you can expect the installation process to supply several tools. Most notably, there will be a server engine, which runs as a daemon on Unix/Linux systems (including MacOS X) or as an executable file (.exe) on Windows machines. In addition, a MySQL installation supplies many client tools and libraries that allow interaction with the server engine. After all, the programs you write in C, Perl, or PHP need some way to get information in and out of the server.

There are many ways to install MySQL, and most of the more popular methods are covered here. Many programmers chose to develop their MySQL-related applications on a Windows box and then deploy the application on a more stable and robust machine running some Unix or Linux variant. If you are using an ISP that supports MySQL, chances are that the ISP is running some form of Unix or Linux. For this reason, understanding the Unix or Linux installation is important, even if you have no plan on running the operating system yourself. Chances are you will end up using the Unix version at some time or another.

You can find links to all sorts of installation files on the Web site accompanying this book (www.mysqlwcc.com). I created this Web site because MySQL is a rapidly developing piece of software, and if I was to include installation files on the CD, you'd be practically guaranteed that the installing software was out of date.

If you are installing on a Windows or Linux box, save yourself some time and hassle by using the NuSphere installation, linked to from the www.mysqlwcc.com Web site. This process quickly and painlessly installs MySQL, PHP, Apache, and Perl. More details on the NuSphere install are included in the section "Make Your Life Easy with the NuSphere Install."

Linux Installation

If you've been a Linux user for any period of time, chances are you're accustomed to installing software from the source files by compiling the packages yourself which is, of course, an option for MySQL on Linux. You can download the source and run scripts that compile and install the software. However, neither I nor the makers of MySQL recommend this course of action. The makers of MySQL have created binaries that have been tested and tuned for optimal performance. Unless you have some very particular needs that require you to compile the source yourself, try to get by with the pre-compiled binaries. (I cover compiling from source in the "Installing on Unix/MacOS X" section later in this session.)

There are two methods of installing pre-compiled binaries: *tarballs* (which are groups of files compressed into a single archive (like a zip file) or RPM (Red Hat Package Manager) files. Unless you're a big fan of RPMs, I recommend using the tarballs for your Linux install.

Installing from tarballs

You can find a link to the tarball installation on the www.mysqlwcc.com Web site. Or you can get a copy from www.mysql.com/downloads. The exact page of the download depends on what the most current version of MySQL is when you're reading this book. Look for links to the tarball distribution, and then download the file to a convenient place on your hard drive. The file will be in a format like mysql-max-4.01-pc-linux-gnu-i686.tar.gz.

In your Linux shell, switch to the root user (using the su command) and then enter the following commands:

```
shell> cp /path/to/mysqlversion.tar.gz /usr/local
shell> groupadd mysql
shell> useradd -g mysql mysql
shell> cd /usr/local
shell> gunzip mysql-version.tar.gz
shell> tar xvf mysql-version.tar
shell> ln -s mysql-VERSION-OS mysql
shell> cd mysql
shell> scripts/mysql_install_db
shell> chown -R root  /usr/local/mysql
```

```
shell> chown -R mysql /usr/local/mysql/data
shell> chgrp -R mysql /usr/local/mysql
shell> chown -R root /usr/local/mysql/bin
```

And that's it. You should have everything you need to start using MySQL. You can skip to the "Post-Installation Review" section later in this session to see exactly what has been installed.

Installing from RPMs

The Red Hat Package Manager (RPM) is a preferred method for installation and upkeep of software for some who work with Linux. It is not my favorite because I sometimes find it difficult to keep track of where RPM puts the files included with a software installation. But if this is the way you like to go, that's fine. I cover the location of most of the files in "Post-Installation Review" section later in this chapter. You can find links to the RPM install at www.mysqlwcc.com or from the www.mysql.com/download site. Follow the links for the RPM files and download it to your local hard disk.

Then all you need to do is switch to the root user (using the su command) and run the following command:

```
shell> rpm -I mysql-version-number.rpm
```

This installs and starts the MySQL daemon. If you are updating a previous RPM version of MySQL (perhaps installed with the default installation), run the following:

```
shell> rpm -U mysql-version-number.rpm
```

**20 Min.
To Go**

Installing on Windows

On Windows, the basic install is nothing more than a point and click. All you need to do is get the most recent .zip file from the www.mysqlwcc.com or www.mysql.com/download site. The file will be in the form mysql-version.zip. After you download the file, you need to unzip it with some sort of Zip utility. The most common Zip utility is WinZip, which you can get from www.winzip.com.

When you have unzipped the file, all you have to do is double-click the setup.exe file. You are then guided through a standard Windows install. You have the option of selecting a destination for the install (the default is c:\mysql) and of a typical, compact, or custom install type. Just choose typical; actually, very little difference exists between the install types.

At this point, you should have MySQL and related documentation in c:\mysql\. You can skip to the "Post-Installation Review" section of this session to see what has been installed.

Installing on Unix/MacOS X

On most Unix systems, you are able to use the same method as shown for the Linux tarball installation. If you are using FreeBSD, Solaris, IRIX, or any of the other popular Unix variants, you will be able to get an appropriate tarball from www.mysql.com/downloads. Check the README file that comes with your specific tarball and read through the installation instructions. The instructions are very similar to those given for Linux tarballs, but there may be slight variations for different Unix versions.

At the time of this writing, no binary for MacOS X (Darwin) was available from mysql.com. However, pre-compiled binaries can be found at various places on the Internet. I recommend going to www.versiontracker.com and searching for **mysql.** They always have the most recent version available. They use a great installer, which installs MySQL with little fuss.

Installing from Source

If you are familiar with open-source products that run on Unix systems, you will likely be accustomed to installing software from the source code. This process requires that you download a copy of the source code (from www.mysqlwcc.com or www.mysqlcom/downloads) to your local drive and then compiling the source code. Almost all Unix and Linux variants ship with a compiler; however, if you are using MacOS X, you need to install the developer tools in order to get access to a compiler.

If you want to cut to the chase, on most Unix systems you can install MySQL from the source files by downloading the package and running the following commands:

```
tar xzf myql-4.xx.tar.gz
cd mysql-4.xx/
./configure --prefix=/usr/local/mysql
make
su
make install
bin/mysql_install_dbs
```

And on MacOS X, using the following:

```
tar xzf myql-4.xx.tar.gz
cd mysql-4.xx/
./configure --mandir=/usr/share/man/ --prefix=/usr/local/mysql
make
sudo make install
cd /usr/local/mysql
bin/mysql_install_dbs
```

The first step in the source installation process is to copy the file containing the source from www.mysqlwcc.com or mysql.com site to your local drive. The file will be named something like mysql-4.01.tar.gz. This is a compressed tar achieve, and in order to use it, you must uncompress it by using the following command:

```
shell> tar xzf mysql-x.xx.xx.tar.gz
```

This creates a new directory with a name that is analogous to the version of MySQL you are using. Next, you need to run the configure command. There are dozens of configurable options for MySQL that can be set by providing flags after the configure command. (You can view all the installation options by running ./configure @hyhelp). Most of these options are easier to understand when you have learned more about MySQL. If you find that you need an option that is discussed later in this book, you may need to re-run your installation and specify different options in the `configure` command.

For most installations, you don't need to set any of these flags and can simply run `./configure` without setting any flags. However, I recommend using the `@hyprefix` flag, thereby putting all the installed files in `/usr/local/mysql` folder. For an example of how to use configuration options, look at the following `./configure` command. It specifies that all the MySQL applications and files be placed in `/usr/local/mysql` directory after installation.

```
./configure --prefix=/usr/local/mysql
```

After the configuration stage, run `make`. Following the `make` process, which can take over 15 minutes depending on the speed of your system, switch to a root user (using the `su` command) and entering the root user's password. Then, as the root user, type **make install.** On MacOS X, where there is no root user, type **sudo make install.** (You will need to supply an administrative password in order for `sudo` to work.)

To finish the installation, move to the directory into which you installed MySQL and run the `bin/mysql_install_dbs` script.

```
shell> cd /usr/local/mysql
shell> bin/mysql_install_db
```

Make Your Life Easy with the NuSphere Install

MySQL is an open-source product. In fact, it is released under the GNU Public License (GPL), which ensures that all code related to MySQL is freely available. Despite this license, at least two companies have formed to support this database server. One is MySQL AB, a European company that was co-founded by Michael ("Monty") Windenius. Mr. Windenius wrote most of the early code for MySQL, and he still leads the development of the project. MySQL AB creates the tarballs and RPMs discussed earlier.

Another company, called NuSphere, began contributing to MySQL in 2000. NuSphere's programmers come from working on the Progress database and have contributed significant enhancements to MySQL. Their contributions are discussed later in the book.

For many, NuSphere's work is most readily appreciated during the install process. NuSphere has several products that add various applications and enhancements to MySQL. Its product line changes frequently, so check the NuSphere site for the most recent list. All the products take advantage of the same install process. For the NuSphere install, all you need to do is download the file from www.mysqlwcc.com onto a machine running Microsoft Windows (98, NT, 2000) or Red Hat Linux. Unzip the file, double-click on the setup.exe file, and the process starts automatically. Essentially, all you need to do is click the Install button, and the program installs MySQL and Apache compiled with PHP, mod_perl, and mod_ssl.

Figure 2-1 shows what you can expect from the NuSphere install on Windows. Note that the Linux version is essentially identical.

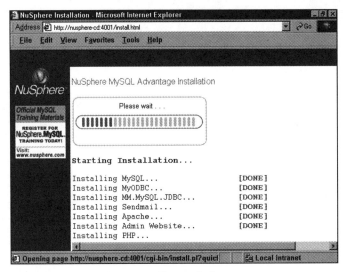

Figure 2-1   *NuSphere install on Windows*

Post-Installation Review

Now it's time to take a look at what you have actually installed. No matter what operating system or method of installation you have installed, you will have the same files and programs available on your system.

At this point, your MySQL is very, very insecure. You don't want to leave a machine in this state live on the Internet. Later in this book you go through steps to ensure that your MySQL installation is reasonably secure. If you haven't taken steps to ensure your installation is safe, make sure your MySQL is off the Internet at a safe distance from hackers.

Scripts and applications

Start out by looking at the scripts and applications now on your system. If you installed from a tarball, the files will be in /usr/local/mysql; if you compiled from source without specifying a prefix, the scripts and applications will be in /usr/local/bin, and if you used RPMs, look in /usr/bin. On Windows, open up a DOS window and look in the \bin\ directory within your MySQL installation (probably c:\mysql\ or c:\Program Files\ Nusphere\mysql).

In addition to the applications discussed in the sections that immediately follow, you will learn about several very important applications in the /bindirectory, in later sessions, including mysqladmin, mysqldump, and mysqlimport.

Starting the MySQL server

There are many important files here that are covered later in the book. The most important to start with are mysqld and mysqld_safe (or mysqld.exe on Windows) is the daemon or server engine. Before you can do anything with MySQL, you need to start the server. To start the server, do not use mysqld; use mysqld_safe instead. To start the server, run the following command from the /bin directory (for DOS, omit the dot and slash):

```
./ mysqld_safe &
```

If you installed on Windows, you'll find an item in the Start menu that starts the MySQL server daemon.

You then see an indication that the server engine has started. Note that if you don't use the ampersand at the end of the command, the shell will not be useable until the server engine is stopped. Chances are, you're not going to want to stop the server engine.

Interacting with the server

At this point your server has been started, but that alone doesn't get you too much. As mentioned in Session 1, any number of applications will be able to interact with the server, but for the most basic work, you need a very simple client that allows you interact with the server. This is the MySQL command-line client, and it can be found in the /bin directory. At this point, you can start the client by typing **mysql** at the shell or DOS prompt. You will see something like this:

```
shell> ./mysql
Welcome to the MySQL monitor.  Commands end with ; or \g.
Your MySQL connection id is 1 to server version: 3.23.39

Type 'help;' or '\h' for help. Type '\c' to clear the buffer.

mysql>
```

The command-line client allows you to send arbitrary SQL commands to the server engine. You learn a lot more about SQL in the coming sessions, but to get a quick idea of what you can do in his application, type **show databases;** at the prompt and hit the return key. You should see something like this:

```
mysql> show databases;
+----------+
| Database |
+----------+
| mysql    |
| test     |
+----------+
2 rows in set (0.01 sec)

mysql>
```

This is a very simple query that shows you the database currently available to the server. At this point, type **exit** at the prompt to exit the command line client and return to your shell or DOS prompt.

Databases and files

MySQL stores each separate database as a folder on the file system. For most, this directory will be in the var/ directory (something like /usr/local/mysql/var). If you're using an RPM install, check /var/lib/mysql.

To find the location of the database directory on your system, log in to the MySQL command-line client and type the following:

```
mysql> SHOW VARIABLES LIKE 'datadir';
+----------------+-----------------------+
| Variable_name  | Value                 |
+----------------+-----------------------+
| datadir        | /usr/local/mysql/var/ |

+----------------+-----------------------+
```

Within this directory you will see a series of folders (each folder represents a database. Now you should see folders named mysql and test. As you add additional databases, additional folders will be added in this location. Enter the mysql/ folder and get a list of the files (use the dir command on Windows; below I've used the Unix ls command):

```
shell> ls
columns_priv.MYD    db.frm      host.MYI          user.MYD
columns_priv.MYI    func.MYD    host.frm          user.MYI
columns_priv.frm    func.MYI    tables_priv.MYD   user.frm
db.MYD              func.frm    tables_priv.MYI
db.MYI             host.MYD    tables_priv.frm
```

These files contain all the needed information for the tables within this database. I discuss each of these files in more detail later. For now, it's enough to know that the .frm files contain table descriptions, the .MYI files contain indexes, and the .MYD files contain table data.

Libraries

Other applications like PHP and MySQL are going to need to connect to the server engine; to connect, they are going to need libraries that allow them to interact. In the course of your application development, you won't be using the libraries directly; however, you should still know where they are. When configuring PHP or Perl, you'll need to know the libraries' locations. For most, they will be located in /usr/local/mysql/lib/mysql.

Configuring Unix/Linux to Initiate MySQL at Startup

If you are using a Unix or Linux system, odds are it would save you some time and effort if MySQL started automatically upon booting the machine and stopped automatically when the system is shut down. If you used an RPM install, all the necessary changes have been made to your configuration files, and MySQL is automatically available when you start your system. However, if you installed from the source files or used the tarballs, you need to make some configuration tweaks to automate this process.

Start by locating the mysql.server script, which is in either the /usr/local/mysql/ support-files/ directory, if you installed MySQL from the binaries, or in the directory into which you uncompressed the source files, if you decided to compile from the source code. When you've located the script, switch to the system's root user (using su) and copy mysql. server to /etc/init.d. Then make the file executable. The following two commands work:

```
shell> cp /usr/local/mysql/support_files/mysql.server /etc/init.d
shell> chmod +x /etc/init.d/mysql.server
```

Now you need to create symbolic links between this file and files in the rc.X directories that will start and shut down the MySQL server. The commands look like this:

```
shell> ln -s /etc/init.d/mysql.server /etc/rc3.d/S99mysql
shell> ln -s /etc/init.d/mysql.server /etc/rc0.d/S01mysql
```

Done!

REVIEW

This session showed you several methods for installing MySQL. You've seen that MySQL is available on many platforms and has a variety of installation options on these systems, which can be indicated with flags in the configure command. You've also learned about the purpose of some of the most important files, applications, and directories created by the MySQL installation. You know how to start the server and interact with the server through the MySQL command-line client.

QUIZ YOURSELF

1. Name two methods for installing MySQL on Linux. (See "Linux Installation.")
2. What configuration flag on Unix will ensure that all MySQL files will be installed in /usr/local/mysql? (See "Installing from Source.")
3. What command starts the MySQL server daemon? (See "Starting the MySQL server.")
4. What application allows you to run arbitrary commands against the server? (See "Interacting with the server.")
5. How does MySQL organize databases on the file system? (See "Databases and files.")

Creating Databases: Governing Principles

Session Checklist

✔ The reason we don't use the file system for data storage

✔ Using tables

✔ Problems with a basic table

✔ Fixing problems through normalization

✔ Relationships

✔ Understanding null, indexes, and referential integrity

At this point, you should have a version of MySQL installed on your computer. Before you start working with this software, you need to understand exactly why relational databases are so useful. In the first couple of sessions, I mentioned that relational databases are designed to store, query, and sort information in an extremely efficient way. Before you put any data in any RDBMS, including MySQL, you need a firm understanding of how these products work.

**30 Min.
To Go**

This session introduces relational database design, which is a complex and important topic. If you're going to be spending a lot of time around relational databases, I recommend seeking out sources beyond this book. For starters, check out Michael J. Hernandez's *Database Design for Mere Mortals: A Hands-On Guide to Relational Database Design* (published by Addison-Wesley).

Why We Don't Use the File System for Data Storage

Many ways exist to go about storing data for your applications. Programming languages have their own internal data structures (arrays, objects, scalar variables, and so on) that are useful for a variety of tasks. No matter what operating system you're using, you can always store information in a file somewhere in the file system and read the contents of that file into your applications.

Depending on the type of application you are writing, storing data in files may be fine. On Windows, many applications have .ini files that define specific parameters for an application. When the program is first executed, the contents of the .ini file are read into the program and the parameters are set. On Unix systems, most applications have some sort of .conf file that works in a similar way.

Files like these are read by applications infrequently and are written to rarely — for good reason. The file system is not designed to efficiently handle rapid and constant changes to a single file. In something like a Web application, where you'd expect multiple users to be accessing the data simultaneously, some real problems could exist. Every time anyone attempted to add, delete, or edit information in a file, you'd have to make sure the file was not in use by another user. You'd have to apply very sophisticated locking mechanisms to make sure all user data remain in an appropriate state, meaning that one user's changes don't unnecessarily overwrite another's.

A RDBMS will largely take care of this balancing act for you. You need to understand and apply concepts like transactions and locking (which are covered later in the book) to make sure your data is sound, but for the most part, these issues are handled easily by the RDBMS.

Working with Tables

MySQL and all other relational databases store data in tables. Conceptually, these tables are no different from the tables you may create in a word processor or work with in a spreadsheet. You can assume that the tables are pretty much immune from the versioning problems you'd encounter with files on the file system — that one application or various applications can interact with the database and be reasonably secure that inserts, updates, and deletes to the tables will not inappropriately overwrite each other.

For the majority of this book, I use a single example to demonstrate how concepts and commands apply to MySQL. The example database stores data for an online shopping cart that will sell its wares. I'm a writer and editor, and this application should help me sell my products — books, articles, and the like. Table 3-1 is an example of what a single table that stores an order at my online shopping care may look like. (Note that this table has many problems that will be fixed through the course of this session.)

Table 3-1 *Sample Data for Online Shopping Cart*

buyer_name	buyer_addr	buyer_zip	item	Item_price	second_item	second_item_price	total
John Doe	1313 Mockingbird Ln	11234	MySQL Weekend Crash Course	19.99	Open Source Rules, a Paper	19.99	38.98
Alan Smith	3456 Sterling Pl	11215	MySQL/ PHP Database Apps	39.99	Open Source Rules: A paper	19.99	58.98
John Doe	1313 Mockingbird Ln	11234	PHP for the Web: A Paper	19.99			19.99

Problems with a Basic Table

Of course, in my real application I'd need far more data than I have in Table 3-1. But there's no point in dealing with all of that data now. There are too many problems (or as we say in the database world, *anomalies* (to solve.

Update anomaly

Imagine what would happen if John Doe were to come back to the shopping cart after he'd moved. His address information is stored in more than one row in the table because he's placed two different orders at different times. When it comes time to update his address, you'd have to make sure the changes are made in all the appropriate rows. This may not sound like a big deal, but keep in mind that tables commonly have tens or hundreds of thousands of rows. In a real-world application, you may not have two rows with information on John Doe; there may be one hundred or more.

One of the goals of relational data structures is to ensure that an update to a single row of a table doesn't risk corrupting data in any other row. If the address in row number 1 were updated and the address in row 3 was not, you would have conflicting data for John Doe (two different addresses). If this situation exists, when an update to a single row of a table leads to conflicting data, you have what is called an *update anomaly* in your table.

How would you solve this problem? By creating another table. If you had another table that stored only information on the customers, John Doe's information would appear in only row in one table. Take a look at Figure 3-1 for an illustration of how this would work.

Customers Table

buyer_id	buyer_name	buyer_addr	buyer_zip
1	Jon Doe	1313 Mockingbird Ln	11234
2	Alan Smith	3456 Sterling Pl	11215

Orders Table

buyer_id	item	item_price	second_item	second_item_price	total
1	MySQL Weekend Crash Course	19.99	Open Source Rules: A Paper	19.99	38.98
2	MySQL/PHP Database Apps	39.99	Open Source Rules: A Paper	19.99	58.98
1	PHP for the Web: A Paper	19.99			19.99

Figure 3-1   *Data divided into two tables*

In Figure 3-1, you can tell what order belongs to which customer by looking at the buyer_id column. If the buyer_id column in the Orders table is 1, you can trace that back to the buyer_id column in the Customers table and see that buyer_id 1 is, in fact, John Doe. With this configuration of data, John Doe's information exists in only one row of one table. So when his address changes, only one row in one table is affected, thereby eliminating the update anomaly.

Note that the addition of the buyer_id columns to the tables in Figure 3-1 creates a relationship between these tables. You can see how these tables work together in what is so appropriately called a *relational* database.

Delete anomaly

What would happen if John Doe decides to cancel his order in the third row of Table 3-1, thereby removing this row from the table? This would be a big problem because the table would also loose information on a product ("PHP for the Web: A Paper").

If I lost this information in my database, I'd have no chance of selling this paper to another potential customer because it would no longer be in the database. I solve this problem by putting information on products in its own table.

Any time a deletion of a row of a table removes data that you intended to keep around, your table contains a *delete anomaly*.

Insert anomaly

A similar situation exists in Table 3-1 for inserts. If I wanted to add another paper or book to my list of products, I'd have to wait to for an order that included the product to get the information in the database. As you can imagine, this would be an unworkable situation. This kind of problem is known as an *insert anomaly*. Breaking the products into its own table eliminates this anomaly.

Fixing Anomalies through Normalization

**20 Min.
To Go**

The goal is to come up with a data structure that is free of anomalies. In database design, the process that rids your data of anomalies is known as *normalization*. Before you can normalize your data, you must first take a thorough inventory of the exact data you need to keep. Be sure to account for all the data you need now plus the data you may need in the future. Take some sample data and put the data into table structures.

It's helpful to think of your data as groups of logical objects. For example, for my shopping cart, I have information related to products (books, whitepapers, and so on); therefore, I have a Products object. I also have information for each order (items in the order, prices, taxes, and so on), thus, I have an Orders object. The same goes for Users. Figure 3-2 shows what these tables look like with some sample data. Note that these tables are full of anomalies, but you have to start somewhere.

Products

p_name	p_type	p_cost	p_length	p_image_name	p_image_location	p_image_height	p_image_width
MySQL WCC	Book	25.00	420	wcc_cover.jpg	images/	230	125
PHP For the Web	Whitepaper	15.00	25	php_web.jpg	images/	220	125

Orders

o_item1	o_item1_cost	o_item_2	o_item_2_cost	o_goes_to	o_total
MySQL WCC	25.00	PHP for the Web	15.00	John Doe	40.00

Users

u_fname	u_lname	u_address_home	u_address_work	u_phone_home	u_fax
John	Doe	1233 Foo St	1425 Bar Ave	212 555 4444	212 555 8888

Figure 3-2 *Shopping cart data broken into tables*

During the process of normalization, you put your data in what are know as *normal forms*. You can think of a normal form as a formal stage in the process of removing anomalies from your data. There are certain specific criteria that must be met before data can be considered to be in any of the normal forms. In the following pages, I put the data for my shopping cart into 1st, 2nd, and 3rd normal forms, thereby fixing just about all of the anomalies.

1st normal form

To get the data into 1st normal form, data need to be in a table structure and must meet the following criteria:

- Each column must contain an "atomic" value. That means that there will be only one value per cell. No arrays or any other manner of representing more than one value will exist in any cell.
- Each column must have a unique name.
- The table must have a set of values that uniquely identifies the row. This is known as the *primary key* of the table
- No two rows can be identical.
- No repeating groups of data are allowed.

Each of the points in the above list is critical. For example, if you find yourself with a cell that contains a series of values (perhaps a comma-delimited list of values) your data are not in a reasonable format and you must rethink your data structure. I don't have that problem in Figure 3-2, but I do have some other problems.

For starters, the Users table does not have a unique value that identifies each row. It is quite possible that another John Doe is out there, and that could lead to confusion. So in this case I'm going to add a column to this table that stores nothing but a unique value for each row. This could be anything that you know cannot possibly be repeated, say a Social Security number or a URL. In MySQL you can create a column with an auto_increment attribute. When this is done, MySQL automatically inserts a unique number for each row. The first row gets the value of 1, the second 2, and so on. Note that a primary key can span more than one column. For example, in the Products table, you may say that a product is identified by its name and type.

There are also repeating groups of data in Figure 3-2. If you look at the Orders table, you see separate columns for items within an order (o_item_1, o_item_2). This kind of structure won't scale well. Imagine how difficult it would be to maintain this table if you wanted to allow users to purchase ten items in an order. The Orders table would have dozens of columns (o_item_1, -o_item_2 . . . o_item_10).

In Figure 3-3, I've put the data into 1st normal form. I've added primary keys and separated repeating groups of data into their own tables. I've also created relationships between the new tables and the old ones. For example, notice that the information for items within an order has been separated into its own table. I've added a column called order_id to the Items table. This column maintains a relationship with the order_id column of the Orders table. The order_id column in the Items table is known as a *foreign key*. A foreign key establishes a relationship with the primary key of another table (in this case, the order_id column in the Orders table). In Figure 3-3, you can look at the data and know that item_id 1 and item_id 2 belong to order_id 1. And order_id belongs to user 10 (John Doe.

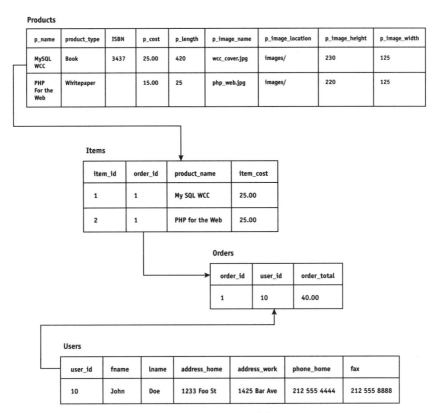

Products

p_name	product_type	ISBN	p_cost	p_length	p_image_name	p_image_location	p_image_height	p_image_width
MySQL WCC	Book	3437	25.00	420	wcc_cover.jpg	images/	230	125
PHP For the Web	Whitepaper		15.00	25	php_web.jpg	images/	220	125

Items

item_id	order_id	product_name	item_cost
1	1	My SQL WCC	25.00
2	1	PHP for the Web	25.00

Orders

order_id	user_id	order_total
1	10	40.00

Users

user_id	fname	lname	address_home	address_work	phone_home	fax
10	John	Doe	1233 Foo St	1425 Bar Ave	212 555 4444	212 555 8888

Figure 3-3   *Shopping cart data in 1st normal form*

2nd normal form

To get data into 2nd normal form, you need to look at your data in terms of *dependencies*. A dependency is pretty much what you would think. A dependent column is one that is inexorably linked to the primary key of the table. To get data into 2nd normal form, you need to remove data from a table that is only partially dependent on a multi-column primary key.

In Figure 3-2, the Products table has a multi-column primary key (product_name and product_type). I've used this structure in the event that I had a product that was available in two media (maybe as both a book and a PDF. Using this structure, the data are not in 2nd normal form because the description column has nothing to do with the type (book or whitepaper). Rather, the description is solely dependent on the title (product_name). So to get these columns into 2nd normal form, I'd have to create a table that stores a product's name and description and have another that stored the product's type and cost.

3rd normal form

Finally, to get your data into 3rd normal form, you need to be on the lookout for *transitive dependencies*. You have a transitive dependency if you have a situation where a column is not dependent on the primary key, but rather, is dependent on another column that is in turn dependent on the primary key. Consider, for example, the p_image_height column in the Products table in Figure 3-3. The height of an image really has nothing to do with the name or format of the product. Therefore, the information on images should be broken out into its own table.

When I finish removing the transitive dependencies and making sure the data is in 3rd normal form, I end up with the tables in Figure 3-4.

Take some time to look at the data carefully. If you are new to databases, it may take some time to understand how these tables are coming together. If you don't understand it immediately, that's okay. This is a tough topic, and it's likely things will make a lot more sense after you've read some of the later sessions. And remember, if you're new to database design, you should take some time to study the topic when you are done with this book.

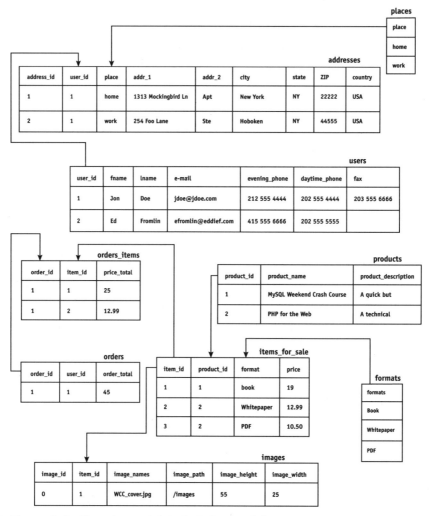

Figure 3-4 *Shopping cart data in 3rd normal form*

Relationships

In addition to the tables, the lines in Figure 3-4 indicate that there are relationships between these tables. There are three different types of relationships on view in the figure.

One-to-many

One-to-many is the most common type of relationship you'll find between tables. Any time one item in a table can relate to many items in another table, a one-to-many relationship exists. You can find many examples of one-to-many relationships in Figure 3-4. Each order for the orders table contains many items; thus, the orders table has a one-to-many relationship with the orders_items table. Similarly, users can have more than one address, so there is a one-to-many relationship between the users table and the addresses table.

One-to-one

Keeping with the rules of normalization, in Figure 3-4, I separated the information for images into a separate table. This makes sense because images really are objects onto themselves. If all the columns in the images table were kept in the items_for_sale table, there would be some transitive dependencies. The image_height column would not be directly dependent on the primary key of the items_for_sale table. Thus, there would be a transitive dependency, and the data would not be in 3rd normal form.

However, there's only one image for every row in the items_for_sale table. These tables have a one-to-one relationship (one item_for_sale has one image).

Many-to-many

There are cases where many items in one table relate to many items in another table. You can see this situation when examining the way the products, formats and items_for_sale tables relate to one another. A product can come in many formats (book, whitepaper, and so on), and a format can be used for many products (MySQL WCC, PHP For the Web, and so on).

To create a relationship that shows where these chunks of information meet, you need another table. In Figure 3-4, you can see that both formats (from the formats table) and the product_id (from the products table) have one-to-many relationships with the items–for–sale table. Each row in the items–for–sale table represents a point where the data in these tables intersect. Each time they intersect, I have something I can sell in my shopping cart.

Other Important Database Concepts

The following sections present come concepts you'll need to be aware of as you start working with relational databases.

Null

The concept of null is extremely important in relational databases. If you remember any algebra, you may recall that a *null* set contains no values. In an RDBMS, null has the same meaning. A field in a table that is null contains no value whatsoever. It is not an empty string, and it is not zero.

 I introduce the concept of null values here because it's important you be aware that null values exist. In the next session, you see how null values affect your table structures. Then, in Session 5, you see how null affects queries.

Indexes

Put simply, an index allows the SQL server to look through a column or group of columns with great speed. When you create tables in MySQL, you have to decide when it is preferable to have an index. This is a complex decision that is discussed initially in Session 4, then in much greater detail in Session 18.

For now it is enough to know that an index saves time by storing the contents of a column of groups of columns in an optimized data structure. An index is also more likely to reside in RAM rather than on the hard disk. Therefore, when an index is available, MySQL fetches information at a very high rate of speed. Using an index is much faster than reading directly from the table.

Referential integrity

In the previous figures, you saw some circumstances where there were relationships between tables. Primary keys and the related foreign keys maintain these relationships. Many database servers have the ability to enforce relationships. For example, say I wanted to add an item to the items_for_sale table (in Figure 3-4) that was in a format not listed in the formats table (maybe a Flash-based tutorial. If referential integrity were enforced, the database server would alert me that I was trying to insert something in the formats column of the items_for_sale table that was not available in the formats column of the formats table.

Referential Integrity enables RDBMSs to execute *cascading deletes.* Imagine that I wanted to get out of the business of selling whitepapers and that I decided to remove them from the formats table. If referential integrity were in place and I indicated that I wanted to go through with cascading deletes, the database server would go to the tables that maintained a foreign key to the formats table and delete all the appropriate rows. So if I removed Whitepaper from the formats table, all rows in the items_for_sale table with a format of Whitepaper would also be deleted.

As of this writing, MySQL has limited support for referential integrity. As you see in the next session, in limited circumstances you can enforce foreign key constraints in MySQL. (Foreign key constraints are explained in the next session.)

Done!

REVIEW

This session introduced many concepts critical to database design. You learned that relational databases store data in tables. To ensure that tables have as little redundant data as is possible, relational databases use multiple tables, and relationships are created between these tables. Primary keys and foreign keys maintain the relationships. You also saw the three types of relationships that can exist between tables: one-to-one, one-to-many, and many-to-many. The session concluded by defining, null, indexes, and referential integrity.

QUIZ YOURSELF

1. If a change in a table leads to conflicting data for a single item, what anomaly exists in the table? (See "Problems with a Basic Table.")
2. A column or group of columns that uniquely identify a row are know as what? (See "1st normal form.")
3. A column that maintains a relationship to another table's primary key is known as what? (See "1st normal form.")
4. True or false: a null value can be compared to another null value (null=null)? (See "Null.")
5. What two features enable an index to search through a column with the maximum speed. (See "Indexes.")

Creating Databases in MySQL

Session Checklist

✔ The CREATE DATABASE statement

✔ The CREATE TABLE command

✔ Loading the sample database

MySQL has two distinct parts; one is called the Data Definition Language, or DDL. You can use DDL to create and alter databases and tables. In this session, you learn to use the commands that make up DDL: CREATE DATABASE, CREATE TABLE, and ALTER TABLE. The other portion of MySQL is known as the Data Manipulation Language, or DML. You learn the commands that make up the DML (SELECT, UPDATE, INSERT, DELETE, and REPLACE) in the following sessions.

DDL, like any other language you're likely to encounter in the programming world, has its own peculiar syntax. In the course of your programming life, you may be able to largely avoid the syntax of DDL by using graphical clients to create and alter databases and tables. There are several programs available on the Web that can help you create databases and tables — and some are discussed later in this book. As useful as these programs are, you need to understand the specifics of DDL in MySQL if you want to be a skilled user of the database server.

**30 Min.
To Go**

CREATE DATABASE Statement

Before you can create the tables needed for a database, you first have to create a new database. The syntax for the command that creates a database is

```
CREATE DATABASE database_name
```

To create a database for your MySQL server, start the MySQL command-line client by going to the /bin directory of your MySQL installation and typing **./mysql -u root** on Unix or Linux; eliminate the **./** if you are working in the DOS prompt on a Windows machine. You should see something like this:

```
shell> ./mysql -u root
Welcome to the MySQL monitor.  Commands end with ; or \g.
Your MySQL connection id is 1 to server version: 3.23.39

Type 'help;' or '\h' for help. Type '\c' to clear the buffer.

mysql>
```

Note that if you are getting an error when starting this application, make sure you have started the MySQL daemon with mysqld_safe.

The flag used above (-u root**) identifies you as the root user of MySQL This gives you the privileges to do anything you want with any database available to your MySQL installation. You learn more about assigning users in MySQL in Session 20.**

To create the database that will store the tables for my online store, I use the following command:

```
mysql> CREATE DATABASE store;
Query OK, 1 row affected (0.06 sec)
```

To let MySQL know that I want to work with the newly created database, I use the USE command:

```
mysql> USE store;
Database changed
```

The USE command associates a specific thread with a specific database. Until you execute a USE statement, MySQL won't know which database you wish to work with.

CREATE TABLE Command

The basic syntax of the CREATE TABLE command is reasonably easy. Here's the basic syntax:

```
CREATE TABLE table_name (
    col_name_1 column_type column_attribute,
    col_name_2 column_type col_attribute,
    primary key(col_name_1),
    index(col_name_2)
) TYPE=table_type
```

The table name can be about any string. Avoid using spaces or any words that you typically use in programming or SQL. For a list of words that are reserved for use by MySQL, see http://mysql.com/documentation/mysql/bychapter/manual_reference.html#Reserved_word. The same restrictions apply to column names.

Column types are addressed in the following section. As for column attributes, there are two available for each column:

- null | not null
- default

The null|not null attribute tells MySQL whether or not to allow null values in this column. If you want to make sure a column contains values in each row, use not null. The default attribute signifies a value that will be inserted into a row if no value for that column is identified. So a CREATE statement that creates a single column that doesn't allow null values and has a default value of zero looks like this:

```
CREATE TABLE my_table (
    my_column int not null default 0
) type=MYISAM;
```

There is one other attribute that can be applied, the auto_increment feature you learned about in Session 3. In cases where you want to have a unique numeric primary key, auto_increment is very helpful. The following command creates a single table with two columns; the first column is an auto_increment primary key. All the syntax in this statement is explained through the course of this session.

```
mysql> CREATE TABLE test_2(
    -> col_id int not null auto_increment primary key,
    -> first_name char(200) not null
    -> );
```

Column types

MySQL comes with a range of column types. Several are similar but have subtle, yet important, differences. Give this section a read and choose carefully when deciding on column types for your tables.

Text column types

MySQL has eight column types suitable for storing text strings:

char

Usage: char (length)

The char column type has a maximum length of 255 characters. This is a fixed-length column type, meaning that when a value is inserted that has fewer characters than the maximum length of the column, the field is right-padded with spaces. So if a column has been defined as char(10) and you want to store the value *happy,* MySQL actually stores *happy* and then five spaces. The spaces are removed from the result when the value is retrieved from the table.

varchar

Usage: varchar (length)

Using char or varchar

For the most part, there is little practical difference between char and varchar. Which ones you decide to use depends on which requires more space, the trailing spaces in a char column or the single character in varchar. If your field stores something like last names, you'll probably want to allow 25 characters, just to be safe. If you were to use the char column type and someone had the last name Smith, your column would contain 20 trailing spaces. There's no need for it; you're much better off using varchar and allowing MySQL to track the size of the column. However, when you want to store passwords of 5 to 7 characters, it would be a waste to use varchar to track the size of the column. Every time a varchar field is updated, MySQL has to check the length of the field and change the character that stores the field length. You'd be better off using char(7).

This is nearly identical to char and is used in many of the same places. It also has a maximum length of 255. The difference is that varchar is a variable-length column type. The values are not padded with spaces. Instead, MySQL adds one character to each varchar field, which stores the length of the field. MySQL removes spaces from the end of strings in varchar fields.

If you define a column as varchar **with a column length of less than four, MySQL automatically changes the column to the** char **type.**

tinytext

Usage: tinytext

This is the first of the four binary (or blob) text character types. All of these types (tinytext, text, mediumtext, and largetext) are variable column types, similar to varchar. They differ only in the size of string they can contain. The tinytext type has a maximum length of 255; so, in fact, it serves the same purpose as varchar(255). An index can be created for an entire tinytext column.

text

Usage: text

The text type has a maximum length of 65,535 characters. Indexes can normally be created on the first 255 characters of a text column. You can use a FULLTEXT index for text columns. More on FULLTEXT in Session 12.

mediumtext

Usage: mediumtext

The mediumtext type has a maximum length of 16,777,215 characters. Indexes can be created on the first 255 characters of a mediumtext column. You can use a FULLTEXT index for mediumtext columns.

longtext

Usage: longtext

The longtext type has a maximum length of 4,294,967,295 characters. Indexes can be created on the first 255 characters of a mediumtext column. However, this column currently is not very useful, as MySQL allows string of only 16 million bytes.

enum

Usage: enum ('value1', 'value2', 'value3' . . .)

With enum, you can limit the potential values of a column to those you specify. It allows for 65,535 values, though it's difficult to see a situation where you'd want to use this column with more than a few potential values. This type would be of use when, for example, you want to allow only values of "yes" or "no." The CREATE statement that makes use of enum looks like this:

```
create table my_table (
    id int auto_increment primary key,
    answer enum ('yes', 'no') default 'no'
);
```

set

Usage: set ('value1', 'value2', 'value3' . . .)

This column type defines a superset of values and allows for zero or more values from the list you specify to be included in a field.

I do not recommend using this column type. Having multiple values in a field violates 1st normal form, and that's not good.

Numeric column types

20 Min. To Go

MySQL has seven column types suitable for storing numeric values. Note that the following are synonyms: int and integer; double, double precision, and real; and decimal and numeric.

For all numeric types, the maximum display size is 255. For most numeric types, you have the option to *zerofill* a column — to left-pad it with zeros. For example, if you have an int column that has a display size of 10 and you insert a value of 25 into this column, MySQL stores and displays 0000000025. The numeric column types may also be defined as signed or unsigned. Signed, meaning that the column accepts both positive and negative values, is the default definition.

int/integer

Usage: int(display size) [unsigned] [zerofill]

If unsigned, this column type can store integers from 0 to 4,294,967,295. If signed, the range is from –2,147,483,648 to 2,147,483,647. int is often used with auto_increment to define the primary key of a table.

```
create table my_table (
    table_id int unsigned auto_increment primary key,
    next_column text
);
```

Note that I've used an `unsigned` column because an `auto_increment` column has no need for negative values.

tinyint

Usage: tinyint(display size) [unsigned] [zerofill]

If `unsigned`, `tinyint` stores integers between 0 and 255. If `signed`, the range is from –128 to 127.

mediumint

Usage: mediumint(display size) [unsigned] [zerofill]

If `unsigned`, `mediumint` stores integers between –8,388,608 and 8,388,607. If `signed`, the range is from 0 to 1677215.

bigint

Usage: bigint(display size) [unsigned] [zerofill]

If `unsigned`, `bigint` stores integers between –9,223,372,036,854,775,808 to 9,223,372,036,854,775,807. If `signed`, the range is from 0 to 18,446,744,073,709,551,615.

Float

Float has two usages.

Usage: float(precision) [zerofill]

In this usage, `float` stores a floating-point number and cannot be unsigned. The precision attribute can be <=24 for a single-precision floating-point number and between 25 and 53 for a double-precision floating-point number. Starting in MySQL 3.23, this is a true floating-point value. In earlier MySQL versions, `float(precision)` always has two decimals.

Usage: FLOAT[(M,D)] [zerofill]

This is a small (single-precision) floating-point number and cannot be unsigned. Allowable values are –3.402823466E+38 to –1.175494351E-38, zero, and 1.175494351E-38 to 3.402823466E+38. M is the display width and D is the number of decimals. `float` without an argument or with an argument of <= 24 stands for a single-precision floating-point number.

double/double precision/real

Usage: double[(M,D)] [zerofill]

This is a double-precision floating-point number and cannot be unsigned. Allowable values are –1.7976931348623157E+308 to –2.2250738585072014E-308, zero, and 2.2250738585072014E-308 to 1.7976931348623157E+308. M is the display width and D is the number of decimals.

decimal

Usage: decimal[(M[,D])] [zerofill]

Numbers in a `decimal` column are stored as characters. Each number is stored as a string, with one character for each digit of the value. If D is 0, values have no decimal point. The maximum range of `decimal` values is the same as for `double`. If M is left out, it's set to 10.

Date and time types

MySQL has five column types suitable for storing dates and times.

date

Usage: date

The date column type stores values in the format YYYY-MM-DD. It allows values between 1000-01-01 and 9999-12-31.

datetime

Usage: datetime

The `datetime` type stores values in the format: YYYY-MM-DD HH:MM:SS. It allows values between 1000-01-01 00:00:00 and 9999-12-31 23:59:59.

timestamp

Usage: timestamp(size)

This is a handy column type that automatically records the time of the most recent change to a row, whether it is an insert or an update. `size` can be defined as any number between 2 and 14. Table 4-1 shows the values stored with each column size. The default value is 14.

Table 4-1 *timestamp Formats*

Size	Format
2	YY
4	YYMM
6	YYMMDD
8	YYYYMMDD
10	YYMMDDHHMM
12	YYMMDDHHMMSS
14	YYYYMMDDHHMMSS

time

Usage: time

Stores time in HH:MM:SS format and has a value range from −838:59:59 to 838:59:59. The reason for the large values is that the time column type can be used to store the result of mathematical equations involving times.

year

Usage: year[(2|4)]

In these post-Y2K days, it's hard to imagine that you'd want to store your years in two-digit format, but you can. In two-digit format, allowable dates are between 1970 and 2069. The digits 70 to 99 are prepended with 19 and 01 to 69 are prepended with 20.

Four-digit year format allows values from 1901 to 2155.

10 Min. To Go

Table types

MySQL offers several table types: ISAM, MyISAM, BDB, Heap, InnoDB, and Gemini. ISAM is an older table type and is not recommended for new applications. The default table type is MyISAM. The syntax for declaring a table type is

```
create table table_name(
    col_name column attribute
)type=table_type;
```

MyISAM tables are extremely fast and very stable. Heap tables are actually memory-resident hash tables. They are not stored in any physical location and therefore disappear in the case of a crash or power outage. But because of their nature, they are blazingly fast. You should use these only for temporary tables.

The MyISAM, BDB, InnoDB, and Gemini tables have some very different features, and the table that you choose largely depends on the needs of your application. I discuss the different table types in detail in later sessions. For now, you can assume that all tables are using the default MyISAM table type.

Creating indexes

Starting in version 3.23.6, MySQL can create an index on any column with a maximum of 16 columns for any table. The basic syntax is

```
index index_name (indexed_column)
```

Although the index name is optional, always name your indexes. The naming becomes very important should you want to delete or change your index using the ALTER statement.

Another way to create an index is to declare a column as a primary key. Note that any auto_increment column must be indexed, and you'll probably want to declare it as your primary key. In the following table, the id_col column is indexed.

```
create table my_table (
    id_col int unsigned auto_increment primary key,
    another_col text
);
```

The primary key can also be declared like other indexes after the column definitions.

```
create table my_table (
    id_col int unsigned auto_increment,
    another_col text,
    primary key(id_col)
);
```

Indexes can span more than one row. If two rows are used in concert in searching, you can create an index to cover the two with this statement:

```
create table mytable(
    id_col int unsigned not null,
    another_col char(200) not null,
    index dual_col_index(id_col, another_col)
);
```

This index is used for searches on id_col and another_col. These indexes work in a left-to-right fashion. So this index will be used for searches that are exclusively on id_col. However, it will not be used for searches on another_col.

Finally, indexes can be created on only part of a column. Starting in MySQL version 3.23, tinytext, text, mediumtext, and longtext columns, can be indexed on the initial 255 characters. For char and varchar columns, indexes can be created for the initial portion of a column. Here the syntax is

```
index index_name (column_name(column_length))
```

For example:

```
create table my_table(
    char_column char (255) not null,
    text_column text not null,
    index index_on_char (char_column(20)),
    index index_on_text (text_column(200))
);
```

An index can also assure that unique values exist in every row in a table by using the unique constraint. Uniqueness is also enforced in columns declared as primary keys.

```
create table my_table(
    char_column char (255) not null,
    text_column text not null,
    unique index_on_char (char_column)
);
```

Applying the proper indexes ensures that your applications run with peak efficiency. Session 19 describes how you can be sure you are using indexes properly with your queries.

Creating foreign key constraints

In Session 3, I talked briefly about referential integrity. When a database system enforces referential integrity, you can be a bit more confident that your database will not contain bogus data. For example, take another look at Figure 3-4. Notice the one-to-many relationship between the `format` table and the `items_for_sale` table. You would never want to see a value in the `formats` column in the `items_for_sale` table (which is a foreign key) that wasn't in the `format` table itself. In certain circumstances, you can force MySQL to check that a value you are attempting to insert into a foreign key exists as a key in another table in the database.

At the time of this writing, the InnoDB table is the only MySQL table type that supports foreign key constrains. Using the example of the relationship between the `format` and `items_for_sale` tables, you can create a table that stores the names of the available formats, like so:

```
mysql> CREATE TABLE formats(format_name char(50) not null primary key)
    > type=innodb;
```

Then you can create the `items_for_sale` table. In this table, you need to let MySQL know that the `format_name` column is actually a foreign key and should look to the `format` table to check for valid values. This is done using the `FOREIGN KEY` and `REFERENCES` keywords, as shown below:

```
mysql> CREATE TABLE items_for_sale (
    -> item_id int not null primary key,
    -> product_id int not null,
    -> format_name char(50) not null,
    -> price decimal(6,2),
    -> index index_on_format_name(format_name),
    -> FOREIGN_KEY (format_name) REFERENCES formats(format_name)
    -> )type=innodb;
```

After the keywords `FOREIGN KEY`, the column in this table that is a foreign key is listed. Then you must use the keyword `REFERENCES`, followed by the table and column the foreign key should look to for valid values. In the above example, the foreign key looks to the `format_name` column of the `format` table.

You learn more about InnoDB tables in Session 14.

Loading the Sample Database

On the CD accompanying this book, you find a file (`/book/session4/tables_1.sql`) that contains a series of MySQL statements for creating a database and the tables I normalized in Session 2. The document also contains some sample data. You can go to your favorite text editor (vi, emacs, Homesite, Notepad, BBedit, and so on) and take a look at this document.

The next thing you need to do is load the database, tables, and data into MySQL. If you are running the MySQL command-line client, exit it at this time (by typing **exit**). Then run the following command from the MySQL /bin directory (on Linux/Unix you may need to prepend the statement with a ./)

```
mysql -u root < /path/to/tables_1.sql
```

On most Windows machines, the full command is likely:

```
mysql -u root < d:\\book\db\\tables_1.sql
```

The less than sign (<) tells the MySQL application to read this file, thereby executing each SQL statement in the file.

Done!

REVIEW

In this session, you learned how to create databases and tables in MySQL. You learned the various column types MySQL offers for strings, numbers, and dates. You saw that MySQL offers several different table types and learned the proper syntax for creating indexes. In addition, you saw how to apply foreign key constraints with InnoDB tables.

QUIZ YOURSELF

1. What command would create a database named your_db? (See "CREATE DATABASE Statement.")
2. What three attributes can be applied to columns in MySQL? (See "CREATE TABLE Command.")
3. If you have a column storing last names, which is a better column type, char or varchar? (See "Using char or varchar.")
4. What column type automatically stores the date and time of the most recent update to a row? (See "Date and time types.")
5. What table type supports foreign key constraints? (See "Creating foreign key constraints.")

PART

I

Friday Evening Part Review

1. Name at least three clients that can interact with the MySQL server engine.
2. Name one advantage MySQL has over a database like Oracle. Then name one advantage Oracle has over MySQL.
3. Name the two companies contributing to MySQL development, along with their Web sites.
4. What products other than MySQL does the NuSphere installer install?
5. What are the three methods of installing MySQL on a Unix system?
6. What file should be used to start the MySQL server daemon?
7. When starting the daemon on Unix, you can include a character at the end of the startup command that will return the shell to your control after the daemon starts. What character is this?
8. What folder on your system holds the files containing MySQL tables and indexes?
9. What directory on your system holds the MySQL client libraries?
10. The process of removing anomalies from tables is known as what?
11. In a normalized table, each table must have a value that uniquely identifies a row. What is the term used to describe that unique value?
12. What term is used to describe columns that maintain relationships to the primary keys of other tables?
13. What conditions must be met for a table to be in 1st Normal Form?
14. What is the only MySQL table type that supports foreign key constraints?
15. What three types of relationships can exist between tables?
16. What term describes an absence of value?
17. Which two attributes can be declared for any column type?
18. What is the only MySQL column type designed to store non-atomic values (arrays)?
19. What column type automatically stores the time of the most recent insert or update to a row?
20. What types of MySQL tables are only resident in memory (that is, they are never written to disk)?

☑ Friday

☑ **Saturday**

☐ Sunday

Part II — Saturday Morning

Session 5
Viewing and Altering Databases and Tables

Session 6
Inserting, Updating, and Deleting MySQL Data

Session 7
Getting Data from MySQL, Part I: The Basic SELECT

Session 8
Getting Data from MySQL, Part II: Using SELECT with Multiple Tables

Session 9
Basic Functions in MySQL

Session 10
Date Functions in MySQL

Part III — Saturday Afternoon

Session 11
Other MySQL Functions

Session 12
Beyond LIKE: Using Regular Expressions and FULLTEXT Indexes

Session 13
Transactions with MyISAM and BDB Tables

Session 14
Using Gemini and InnoDB Tables

Session 15
Working with MySQL and PHP

Session 16
MySQL and PHP: Best Practices

Part IV — Saturday Evening

Session 17
Using MySQL with Perl

Session 18
MySQL and Perl: Best Practices

Session 19
Optimizing MySQL Queries

Session 20
Securing MySQL, Part I: The GRANT Tables

PART

II

Saturday Morning

Session 5

Viewing and Altering Databases and Tables

Session 6

Inserting, Updating, and Deleting MySQL Data

Session 7

Getting Data from MySQL, Part I: The Basic SELECT

Session 8

Getting Data from MySQL, Part II: Using SELECT with Multiple Tables

Session 9

Basic Functions in MySQL

Session 10

Date Functions in MySQL

Viewing and Altering Databases and Tables

Session Checklist

✔ Viewing the database on the file system

✔ Best practices for creating databases and tables

✔ Using the SHOW command

✔ Using the ALTER command

**30 Min.
To Go**

I n Session 4, you learned a good portion of the Data Definition Language. In this session, you get the remaining portion of the DDL: the ALTER statements. In addition, you find out how to get information about your database and tables from MySQL by using the SHOW commands.

Viewing the Database on the File System

If you followed the instructions at the end of Session 2 and received no error messages, you should have added a database to your MySQL server. In Session 2, I noted that each database is stored as a directory in the file system. If you look in the directory that stores your databases (probably in the /var directory within your MySQL installation) you should now see an additional folder with the name store. Enter this directory and list the files to see a series of files, each with a name analogous to a table you created.

```
[localhost:mysql/var/store] jay% ls -Fla
total 320
drwx------  26 jay   wheel    840 Sep  7 12:37 ./
drwx------  19 jay   wheel    602 Sep  7 12:37 ../
-rw-rw----   1 jay   wheel    120 Sep  7 13:25 addresses.MYD
-rw-rw----   1 jay   wheel   2048 Sep  7 13:25 addresses.MYI
```

```
-rw-rw----  1 jay  wheel  8780 Sep  7 12:37 addresses.frm
-rw-rw----  1 jay  wheel    72 Sep  7 12:51 formats.MYD
-rw-rw----  1 jay  wheel  2048 Sep  7 12:51 formats.MYI
-rw-rw----  1 jay  wheel  8560 Sep  7 12:37 formats.frm
-rw-rw----  1 jay  wheel   104 Sep  7 13:25 items_for_sale.MYD
-rw-rw----  1 jay  wheel  2048 Sep  7 13:25 items_for_sale.MYI
-rw-rw----  1 jay  wheel  8650 Sep  7 12:37 items_for_sale.frm
-rw-rw----  1 jay  wheel    42 Sep  7 13:25 order_items.MYD
-rw-rw----  1 jay  wheel  1024 Sep  7 13:25 order_items.MYI
-rw-rw----  1 jay  wheel  8618 Sep  7 12:37 order_items.frm
-rw-rw----  1 jay  wheel    21 Sep  7 13:25 orders.MYD
-rw-rw----  1 jay  wheel  2048 Sep  7 13:25 orders.MYI
-rw-rw----  1 jay  wheel  8630 Sep  7 12:37 orders.frm
-rw-rw----  1 jay  wheel    52 Sep  7 12:53 places.MYD
-rw-rw----  1 jay  wheel  2048 Sep  7 12:53 places.MYI
-rw-rw----  1 jay  wheel  8556 Sep  7 12:37 places.frm
-rw-rw----  1 jay  wheel   200 Sep  7 12:55 products.MYD
-rw-rw----  1 jay  wheel  2048 Sep  7 12:56 products.MYI
-rw-rw----  1 jay  wheel  8660 Sep  7 12:37 products.frm
-rw-rw----  1 jay  wheel   128 Sep  7 12:54 users.MYD
-rw-rw----  1 jay  wheel  2048 Sep  7 12:55 users.MYI
-rw-rw----  1 jay  wheel  8732 Sep  7 12:37 users.frm
```

Keep the relationship between databases and tables to directories and files in mind because it has some important consequences. For starters, you need to be careful about deleting, moving, or renaming files and directories. You'll want to make sure that you grant only the necessary permissions to these files and directories to prevent accidental or malicious loss of data. (I cover permissions and other security issues in Session 21.)

 Keep in mind that MySQL's different table types create different file names. BDB, Gemini, and InnoDB create different types of files with different extensions to store tables and indexes. You learn more about these tables in Sessions 13 and 14.

The file system also affects the case-sensitivity of your databases and tables. If you use an operating system that has a case-sensitive file system (Linux, Unix), you need to make sure that all table and database names in your SQL statements are of the proper case. On non-case-sensitive file systems, you have a little more flexibility. For example, the following two SQL statements work equally well on MacOS X and Windows.

```
SELECT * FROM STore;

SELECT * FROM store;
```

Best Practices When Creating Databases and Tables

When designing databases and tables in the future, devise a series of standards before you commit anything to the database. Have naming conventions for databases, tables, and columns. For example, you may choose to have initial caps for your database or table names (for example, Store, Orders) or internal capitalization for complex table or column names (for example, itemsForSale, imageName).

I prefer to keep everything (databases names, table names, column names, index names (in lowercase letters with underscores separating logical portions of the names (for example, image_name). I like this method because it leaves me less to think about. No matter what I'm accessing, I know it has the same convention as everything else.

However, your own background or aesthetic sensibilities may lead you to take a different approach. That's fine. The important thing is to establish a naming convention and stick to it. When writing applications, you do not want to be spending time trying to remember whether a column name does or does not contain capital letters or underscores.

Using the SHOW Command

20 Min.
To Go

There are a series of commands in MySQL that enable you examine the databases on your system. Keep these commands in mind, because they come in handy at times.

SHOW DATABASES

When you start your MySQL command line client (using mysql -u root from the /bin directory), you are connected to the MySQL server but are initially given no indication as to what is available to the server.

```
shell> ./mysql -u root;
Welcome to the MySQL monitor.  Commands end with ; or \g.
Your MySQL connection id is 73 to server version: 3.23.39

Type 'help;' or '\h' for help. Type '\c' to clear the buffer.

mysql>
```

That prompt is nice but not especially helpful. Your initial interest is probably in seeing what databases are available. You can get a list of databases by issuing the SHOW DATABASES command:

```
mysql> SHOW DATABASES;
+-----------+
| Database  |
+-----------+
| mysql     |
| store     |
| test      |
+-----------+
3 rows in set (0.14 sec)
```

You created the store database with the commands specified at the end of Session 4. The MySQL installation includes the other two databases (mysql and test) automatically. I cover the mysql database in great detail in Session 20.

If you want to work with any of these databases in the command-line client, issue the USE command. The syntax of this command is very simple: USE `database_name`.

```
mysql> USE store;
Database changed
mysql>
```

SHOW TABLES

After you are connected to a specific database, you can view the tables that make up the database by running the SHOW TABLES command.

```
mysql> SHOW TABLES;
+-----------------+
| Tables_in_store |
+-----------------+
| addresses       |
| formats         |
| items_for_sale  |
| order_items     |
| orders          |
| places          |
| products        |
| users           |
+-----------------+
8 rows in set (0.01 sec)
mysql>
```

SHOW COLUMNS

Now that you have a list of available tables, you can get specific information on the columns within the tables. The syntax of the command is SHOW COLUMNS FROM `table_name`. Note that there are two synonyms to SHOW COLUMNS: SHOW FIELDS (SHOW FIELDS FROM `table_name`) and DESCRIBE (DESCRIBE `table_name`).

```
mysql> SHOW COLUMNS FROM users;
+------------+-------------+------+-----+---------+----------------+
| Field      | Type        | Null | Key | Default | Extra          |
+------------+-------------+------+-----+---------+----------------+
| user_id    | int(11)     |      | PRI | NULL    | auto_increment |
| fname      | varchar(25) |      |     |         |                |
| lname      | varchar(40) |      |     |         |                |
| email      | varchar(60) | YES  |     | NULL    |                |
| home_phone | varchar(14) | YES  |     | NULL    |                |
| work_phone | varchar(14) | YES  |     | NULL    |                |
| fax        | varchar(14) | YES  |     | NULL    |                |
+------------+-------------+------+-----+---------+----------------+
7 rows in set (0.12 sec)

mysql>
```

The preceding query lists most of what you need to know about this table. The first column (Field) lists the column name; Type (logically enough) shows the column type; Null indicates whether or not null values are permitted in the column; Key shows if and what type of index was created for the column; Default shows the default value if one was indicated in the CREATE statement; and Extra gives some added information (in the case of user_id, you know it is an auto_increment column).

SHOW INDEX

There will be times when you need to examine the indexes on your tables. You can get a lot of information from the SHOW INDEX command. The following command lists all indexes on the addresses table:

```
mysql> SHOW INDEX from addresses \G
*************************** 1. row ***************************
        Table: addresses
   Non_unique: 0
     Key_name: PRIMARY
 Seq_in_index: 1
  Column_name: address_id
    Collation: A
  Cardinality: 7
     Sub_part: NULL
       Packed: NULL
      Comment:
1 row in set (0.13 sec)
```

Notice that in the above command I used \G to terminate the command. This let MySQL know that the data listed is in the format you see above, rather than in the tabular format you've seen so far. This kind of layout, where you have the column name, a colon, and then the value, is convenient when there are more rows in a query result than can comfortably fit in a table.

I revisit both the SHOW INDEX and SHOW COLUMNS commands in Session 19. There you see how proper indexing can speed queries.

SHOW TABLE STATUS

If you want to get more detailed information on each table, you can run the SHOW TABLE STATUS command. This command shows you the number of rows in each table, the time the table was created, and quite a few other interesting other tidbits. You can get the information on all tables in a database at once by simply running SHOW TABLE STATUS, or you can get the information on a specific table by using a command like the following:

```
mysql> show table status like 'addresses' \G
*************************** 1. row ***************************
          Name: addresses
          Type: MyISAM
    Row_format: Dynamic
```

```
           Rows: 7
  Avg_row_length: 58
     Data_length: 412
 Max_data_length: 4294967295
    Index_length: 2048
       Data_free: 0
  Auto_increment: 8
     Create_time: 2001-10-25 15:32:08
     Update_time: 2001-10-27 08:51:44
      Check_time: 2001-11-27 09:45:46
   Create_options:
         Comment:
1 row in set (0.01 sec)
```

SHOW CREATE TABLE

In a moment you'll see how to change table definitions by running the ALTER command. Before running ALTER, you may want to know exactly what statement was used to create the table in the first place. You can get this information using the SHOW CREATE TABLE command. The following command returns the create statement for the addresses table:

```
mysql> SHOW CREATE TABLE addresses \G
*************************** 1. row ***************************
       Table: addresses
Create Table: CREATE TABLE `addresses` (
  `address_id` int(11) NOT NULL auto_increment,
  `user_id` int(11) default NULL,
  `place` varchar(25) NOT NULL default '',
  `addr_1` varchar(255) NOT NULL default '',
  `addr_2` varchar(255) default NULL,
  `city` varchar(50) NOT NULL default '',
  `state` char(2) NOT NULL default '',
  `ZIP` varchar(5) NOT NULL default '',
  `country` varchar(5) default NULL,
  PRIMARY KEY  (`address_id`)
) TYPE=MyISAM
1 row in set (0.00 sec)
```

**10 Min.
To Go**

ALTER TABLE Statement

If you're not happy with the form of your table, you can modify it with the ALTER TABLE statement. Specifically, this statement allows you to rename tables, columns, and indexes; add or drop columns and indexes; and redefine the definitions of columns and indexes. It also lets you change tables from one type to another (from MyISAM to InnoDB, for example). This statement always starts with ALTER TABLE table_name. The rest of the command depends on the action needed, as described below.

Changing a table name

The syntax for changing a table name is as follows:

```
ALTER TABLE table_name RENAME new_table_name
```

So to rename the users table to users_old, I would use the following command:

```
mysql> ALTER TABLE users RENAME users_old;
Query OK, 0 rows affected (2.24 sec)
```

> **If you have MySQL version 3.23.27 or higher, you can make use of the
> RENAME statement. The basic syntax is**
>
> ```
> RENAME table_name TO new_table_name
> ```

Adding columns

When adding a column, include all column definitions expected in the CREATE statement (column name, type, null|not null, default value, and so on). The basic syntax is

```
ALTER TABLE table_name ADD COLUMN column_name column attributes
```

For example, to add a column to the users table that stores a cell phone number, I could run the following command:

```
mysql> ALTER TABLE users ADD COLUMN cell_phone varchar(14) not null;
Query OK, 2 rows affected (0.61 sec)
Records: 2  Duplicates: 0  Warnings: 0
```

In MySQL you can also specify the location of a column (that is, where in the listing of columns it should appear (first, last, or before or after a specific column).

Add the word FIRST to the end of your ALTER statement to place your inserted column as the first column in the table; use the word AFTER to place the column following a column that already exists, as shown in the following examples. So if I wanted to put the cell_phone column first in my users table, I would use the following command:

```
mysql> ALTER TABLE users ADD COLUMN cell_phone varchar(14) not null FIRST;
```

If I wanted to place the cell_phone column between the home_phone and work_phone columns, I would use the following:

```
mysql> ALTER TABLE users ADD COLUMN cell_phone varchar(14) not null AFTER home_phone;
```

> **Don't spend a lot of time worrying about the order of your columns within a
> table. One of the tenets of database design holds that column order is arbi-
> trary. Any time the order of columns retrieved from the database is impor-
> tant, you need so specify the column order in your queries.**

Dropping columns

To drop a column, you need only the following:

```
ALTER TABLE table_name DROP COLUMN column_name
```

So, to drop the cell_phone column, use

```
mysql> ALTER TABLE users DROP COLUMN cell_phone;
```

Adding indexes

You can add indexes using the index, unique, and primary key commands in the same way they are used in the CREATE statement.

```
ALTER TABLE my_table ADD INDEX index_name (column_name1, column_name2,
...)
ALTER TABLE my_table ADD UNIQUE index_name(column_name)
ALTER TABLE my_table ADD PRIMARY KEY(my_column)
```

For example, if I wanted to add an index on the email column of the users table the following would do the trick:

```
mysql> ALTER TABLE users ADD INDEX index_on_email (email);
Query OK, 2 rows affected (0.52 sec)
Records: 2  Duplicates: 0  Warnings: 0
```

Dropping indexes

Making your indexes go away is easy enough with the DROP command.

```
ALTER TABLE table_name DROP INDEX index_name
```

To drop the index on the email column, use

```
mysql> ALTER TABLE users DROP INDEX index_on_email;
Query OK, 2 rows affected (0.45 sec)
Records: 2  Duplicates: 0  Warnings: 0
```

 If in your CREATE **or** ALTER **statement you fail to give your index a name, you can find that name by running the** SHOW INDEX **command (for example,** SHOW INDEX FROM table_name**). Left to its own devices, MySQL gives the index the same name as the column it is indexing.**

Changing column definitions

It is possible to change a column's name or attributes with either the CHANGE or MODIFY commands. To change a column's name, you must also redefine the column's attributes. The following will work:

```
ALTER TABLE table_name CHANGE original_column_name new_column_name int not null
```

But this will not:

```
ALTER TABLE table_name CHANGE my_col2 my_col3;
```

If you wish to change only the column's attributes, you can use the CHANGE command and make the new column name the same as the old column name. For example, to change the lname column from a varchar(25) column to a char(25) column, you can use the following:

```
mysql> ALTER TABLE users CHANGE lname lname char(25);
```

Or, you may prefer the MODIFY command:

```
mysql> ALTER TABLE users MODIFY lname char(25);
```

When altering a table, try to get all of your changes into a single ALTER statement and separate the different portions by commas. It's better practice than, for example, deleting an index in one statement and creating a new one in another statement. For example, the following statement would run a single ALTER command on the users table that modifies the column type of lname and adds an index on the email column:

```
mysql> ALTER TABLE users
    -> MODIFY lname char(25),
    -> ADD INDEX index_on_email(email);
```

Done!

REVIEW

In this session, you saw how to view and modify MySQL databases and tables. First, you saw the directories and files MySQL made after running the CREATE statements in Session 4. You learned the importance of defining and sticking to a naming convention. Then you saw how the SHOW command can be used to view databases, tables, and specifics on columns within a table. Finally, you saw how the ALTER command can be used to play with your column definitions. You can add, delete, or modify columns and indexes in any way you see fit.

Quiz Yourself

1. What determines whether your table and database names are case-sensitive? (See "Viewing the Database on the File System.")

2. What command would give you a listing of the columns in the my_data table along with the table's important attributes? (See "SHOW COLUMNS.")

3. What command would add a column named phone to a table named my_data? (See "Adding columns.")

4. What command would you use to change the column definition from date to time-stamp for a column named last_updated? (See "Changing column definitions.")

5. Give the exact syntax for the command that would drop a column name fname from a table named your_users. (See "Dropping columns.")

Inserting, Updating, and Deleting MySQL Data

Session Checklist

✔ The INSERT statement

✔ The basic WHERE clause

✔ The UPDATE statement

✔ The REPLACE statement

✔ The DELETE statement

✔ Creating a Web form for inserting, updating, and deleting data

**30 Min.
To Go**

Now that you have a database and tables within your database, you need a method for putting rows of data into the tables. Further, you need a way to edit records after they have been inserted into the tables and to remove records that are unnecessary.

The INSERT Statement

You can insert data into a MySQL table by using the SQL INSERT command. The basic syntax of the command is as follows:

```
INSERT INTO table_name (col1, col2, col3, ...) VALUES(val1, val2, val3,
...);
```

Note that strings must be surrounded by single quotes (') and numeric values should not be surrounded by quotes. So a basic insert into the formats table, which has a single column named formats of the type char(35), would be

```
mysql> INSERT INTO formats(formats) VALUES('Web Article');
```

You can also use double quotes (") to delimit strings, but the majority use single quotes with SQL syntax, so you should go that route as well.

MySQL has added an enhancement to the SQL syntax that enables you to insert multiple rows at once. All you need to do is provide multiple sets of values separated by commas. To insert two columns into the `formats` table, the following would work:

```
INSERT INTO formats(formats) VALUES('Web Article'), ('Magazine Article')
```

If there are columns in the table for which you do not wish to include data, do not put those columns in the column list. For example, in the `items_for_sale` table, the `item_id` column is an `auto_increment` column. Therefore, when inserting data, I'm better off letting MySQL take care of the value for that column. When I insert a row of data for this table, the command will look something like this:

```
mysql> INSERT INTO items_for_sale
    -> (product_id, format, price)
    -> VALUES(1,'Book', 49.95);
```

There is still one potential difficulty when it comes to inserting data. What if the string you need to insert into a column contains a single quote? For example, a string may contain a contraction, like the word *don't*. If you didn't take some precautions, an INSERT statement may look something like this:

```
INSERT INTO my_table(string_col) VALUES('I don't think so');
```

This would cause an error. MySQL sees the single quote in *don't* as the end of the string and therefore doesn't know what to do with the remaining characters. You can insert single quotes into a table, but you need to *escape* the single quote character. When you escape a character, you're telling MySQL to treat the character literally, not as part of the command syntax. This can be done with either a backslash (\) or an additional single quote('). The previous command would work with the changes made in the following two statements:

```
INSERT INTO my_table(foo) VALUES('I don\'t think so');
INSERT INTO my_table(foo) VALUES('I don''t think so')
```

 In your MySQL-driven applications, you have to make sure that you escape the necessary characters. You should have some sort of utility function that makes sure that anything you attempt to insert into MySQL is in the proper format. Later in this book, you see how to create such a function in both PHP and Perl.

If you wish to insert a backslash into a MySQL, it will need to be escaped with a preceding backslash (\\). For example, if you needed to include a DOS file path, you'd have to escape each of the backslashes:

```
INSERT INTO my_table (file_path) VALUES('c:\\my\\path\\to\\file');
```

The Basic WHERE Clause

In addition to the INSERT statement, there are several other major SQL statements you will work with on a regular basis. All of these statements (UPDATE, REPLACE, DELETE, and SELECT) make use of a WHERE clause. The WHERE clause specifies which rows in a table are subject to the actions of the statement. For example, an UPDATE query, as you will soon see, edits rows in a table. The WHERE clause allows you to identify which rows should be changed by the UPDATE query.

The WHERE clause contains a set of conditions that narrow down the rows you want to work with. Frequently, you identify a row by its primary key. So, for example, to address the first row of the orders table, in which order_id is the primary key, I'd use the following WHERE clause in my SQL statement:

```
WHERE order_id = 1
```

There's a lot more to the WHERE clause, as you will see in Sessions 7 and 8 as you learn about the SELECT statement.

The equal sign is just one of the operators you can use in your WHERE clause; Table 6-1 lists others.

Table 6-1 *MySQL Comparison Operators*

Operator	Meaning	Example
=	equal	WHERE col_1 = 1
>	greater than	WHERE col_1 > 10
>=	greater than or equal	WHERE col_1 >= 10
<	less than	WHERE col_1 < 10
<=	less than or equal	WHERE col_1 <= 10
!=	not equal	WHERE col_1 != 'yes'
IS NULL	indicates that a field contains a value	WHERE col_1 IS NULL
IS NOT NULL	indicates that a field contains no value	WHERE col_1 IS NOT NULL
BETWEEN	indicates a range, and can work with numeric values, dates or strings (using alphabetic order)	WHERE col_1 BETWEEN 1 and 10; WHERE col_1 BETWEEN 'a' and 'm' (note that 1, 10, a, and m will be included in the respective results.

Working with null

As mentioned in previous sessions, null values require special attention. Null values cannot be used in any way in any comparison to any other values, including other null values. For example, imagine null values were permitted in the state field of the addresses table, and the table looked something like this:

fname	lname	addr_1	state	zip
Jay	Greenspan	63 21st st	NY	11211
Waldo	Rickman	33 3rd ave	TX	33242
Jerry	Zahn	111 18th	NULL	44444

If you ran the following query, you'd get the one row you expected, the one for me, Jay Greenspan:

```
mysql> SELECT * FROM addresses WHERE state='NY';
```

However, you may be surprised by the results from the following query, which retrieves all rows where the state is something other than NY.

```
mysql> SELECT * FROM addresses WHERE state!='NY';
```

The query returns only the second row of this table. The third row, where state is null, is left out of the query result because null cannot be compared, in either the affirmative or the negative with any other value. In fact, null values cannot even be compared to other null values.

Table 6-1 shows that in WHERE clauses you must use the phrases IS NULL and IS NOT NULL any time null values can affect the output of a query. So using the preceding table, if you wanted to return all rows where state is not equal to NY and rows where state is null, you have to construct your query in the following manner:

```
mysql> SELECT * FROM addresses WHERE state!='NY' and state IS NULL;
```

Keep this in mind, as you'll be dealing with null values again during the discussion of OUTER JOINs in Session 8.

In addition, in the WHERE clause, you can indicate multiple conditions by using the keywords AND and OR in your statement. For example, the following WHERE clause would be directed at two rows in the orders table:

```
WHERE order_id = 1 AND order_id = 5
```

If I wanted to work with the items from the items_for_sale table that cost more than $100 or are less than $20, the following WHERE clause would do the trick:

```
WHERE price > 100 or price < 20
```

But if you wanted to find all of the items that cost between $20 and $100, you could use the following:

```
WHERE price between 20 and 100
```

The UPDATE Statement

**20 Min.
To Go**

The UPDATE statement edits a row or multiple rows in a table. The basic syntax is

```
UPDATE table_name SET col_1=val_1,col2=val2, ... WHERE ...
```

For a simple example, if I wanted to change the price of item_id 1 from the items_for_sale table, I could run the following query:

```
mysql> UPDATE items_for_sale SET price=19.95 WHERE item_id=1;
```

You can change as many or as few columns as you wish, just add additional col_name=value pairs in the SET clause. The rules for delimiting strings and escaping characters are the same as those for the INSERT statement.

You can update more than one row at a time. If you wanted to make sure that every item in your cart was at least $20, you could update all rows where the price column has a value less than 20.

```
mysql> UPDATE items_for_sale SET price=20.00 WHERE price < 20;
```

The REPLACE Statement

You won't find MySQL's REPLACE statement in other database systems, and it is not part of the SQL standard. However, it is convenient in places. The REPLACE statement works with a row where you know what the primary key should be. When you run the REPLACE statement, MySQL searches for a row with the primary key indicated in statement. If a row with the indicated primary key exists, that row is updated. If not, a new row is inserted. The basic syntax is

```
REPLACE INTO table_name (col_1, col_2, ...) VALUES(val_1, val_2, ...)
```

For an example of where REPLACE would be helpful, imagine you had a table with two columns: email and full_name with email as the primary key. If I wanted to write a script that gave a user the opportunity to insert and edit this information, I'd have some sort of form where the user could enter the data. Then, when the user submits the form, the script would have to go through some decision logic. Without REPLACE, the logic would be something like this:

```
examine form data
check with database to see if a row with the submitted primary key (email) already exists
if the email already exists in the table
    run UPDATE statement
else
    run INSERT statement
```

But because MySQL has the REPLACE statement, you could loose all of this logic and just run the REPLACE. For example:

```
REPLACE INTO users (email, full_name) VALUES ('john@doe.com', 'John Doe');
```

The DELETE Statement

The DELETE statement removes a row or multiple rows from a table. The syntax is

```
DELETE FROM table_name WHERE ...
```

To remove the row from items_for_sale where item_id is 1, run the following command.

```
DELETE FROM items_for_sale WHERE item_id = 1
```

Be careful when working with DELETE. The rows you remove are not recoverable, except from backup.

Creating a Web Form for Inserting, Updating, and Deleting Data

10 Min. To Go

You could try to insert and edit all of your data using the MySQL command-line client, but that would be amazingly tedious. You and the users of your application are much better off writing an application that allows you to manipulate data in a database or tables.

To show how the statements you've learned in this session can work together, I've created a very simple Web application that enables someone to insert, update, and delete data from the users table. I've written the application in the PHP programming language, and it can be served by any Web server that is PHP-aware and has access to a MySQL server with the store database loaded. If you've used the NuSphere installation or otherwise have a PHP installation you may want to copy the file (book/session6/session6.php) to your Web server and see it in action. But even if you are unable to run the file at this time, you should look at this page to get a basic idea of what needs to be done. You can see the entire script in Listing 6-1. If you're new to PHP, you may want to look at Listing 6-2, which shows the logic of the application in pseudo-code.

Listing 6-1   *Code for simple PHP application that manipulates a MySQL table*

```php
<?php

//make db connection and select database.
$conn = mysql_connect("localhost", "root", "");
$db = mysql_select_db("store");

//if only a user_id is available @hy should be just after a
//name is selected but no action (update or delete) has been chosen
if(!empty($user_id) && empty($submit)) {
```

```php
        $result = mysql_query("SELECT fname, lname, email, home_phone,
                                    work_phone, fax
                            FROM users
                            WHERE user_id = $user_id");
    list($fname, $lname, $email, $home_phone, $work_phone, $fax)=
    mysql_fetch_array($result);
    //print_r($row);
}
//if the submit button has been pressed and a user_id exists, we
//know this is an update to an existing row, therefore we need an UPDATE
//query.
elseif(!empty($user_id) && $submit=="update"){
        $sql = "UPDATE users SET
                        fname = '$fname',
                        lname='$lname',
                        email='$email',
                        home_phone='$home_phone',
                        work_phone='$work_phone',
                        fax='$fax'
                WHERE user_id=$user_id";
        mysql_query($sql);
    header("Location: session6.php?user_id=$user_id");

}


//if user_id is empty and the update button has been hit, this is a
//new entry
elseif(empty($user_id) && $submit=="update"){
    $sql = "INSERT INTO users
            (fname, lname, email, home_phone, work_phone, fax)
            VALUES
            ('$fname', '$lname', '$email', '$home_phone', '$work_phone',
'$fax')
        ";
    mysql_query($sql);
    header("Location: session6.php");
}


//if there is a user_id and the delete button has been pressed
//delete that entry from the database
elseif(!empty($user_id) && $submit=="delete"){
    $sql = "DELETE FROM users WHERE user_id = $user_id";
    mysql_query($sql);
    header("Location: session6.php");

}


echo "For a blank entry form, click <a href=\"session6.php\">here</a>";
echo "<br>";
echo "<br>";
```

Continued

Listing 6-1

Continued

```php
//print list of everyone in users table.
$result = mysql_query("SELECT * from users");
while($row=mysql_fetch_array($result)){
    //print_r($row);
    echo "<a href=\"session6.php?user_id=" . $row["user_id"] . "\">";
    echo $row["fname"] . " " . $row["lname"] . "<br>";
    echo "</a>";
}



?>

<table>
<form method="get">
<input type="hidden" name="user_id" value="<?php echo $user_id;?>">
<tr>
<td>first name</td>
<td><input type="text" name="fname" value="<?php echo $fname;?>"></td>
</tr>

<tr>
<td>last name</td>
<td><input type="text" name="lname" value="<?php echo $lname;?>"></td>
</tr>

<tr>
<td>email</td>
<td><input type="text" name="email" value="<?php echo $email;?>"></td>
</tr>

<tr>
<td>home phone</td>
<td><input type="text" name="home_phone" value="<?php echo
$home_phone;?>"></td>
</tr>

<tr>
<td>work phone</td>
<td><input type="text" name="work_phone" value="<?php echo
$work_phone;?>"></td>
</tr>

<tr>
<td>fax</td>
<td><input type="text" name="fax" value="<?php echo $fax;?>"></td>
</tr>

<tr>
```

```
<td>
<input type="submit" name="submit" value="update"></button>
</td>

<td>
<input type="submit" name="submit" value="delete"></button>
</td>

</tr>

</form>
</table>

</html>
```

If you're new to Web applications in general or PHP in particular, this page may be difficult to read. At this point, don't worry too much about the specifics as I'll cover PHP in greater detail later in the book. For now, just try to understand how the statements you learned so far can be brought together to create a simple application.

This single page performs a series of actions. The type of action taken depends upon two things: the value of user_id and the value of submit. Because user_id is the primary key of the table, I can learn quite a bit by examining the user_id value in my script. For example, if a value for user_id does not exist when the script is invoked, I can assume that one of two things should be done within the script. One possibility is that a blank form should be presented in the Web page into which someone can enter data for a new user. The other possibility is that someone has entered data into a blank form and that data should be inserted into the database.

The application enables someone to select the user_id value in one of two ways: by clicking on a name in the list of entries at the top of the page or via a hidden form field when the form is submitted. Figure 6-1 shows the portions of the page.

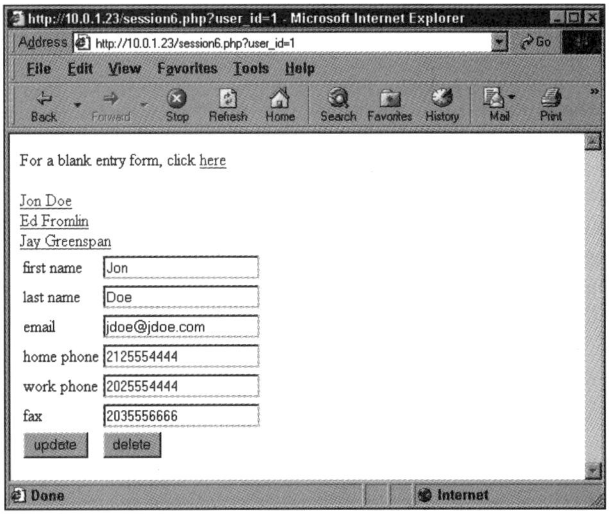

Figure 6-1 *Simple application for manipulating a MySQL table*

The other factor in the decision logic for this script is the value for the submit button. The Web form presents two buttons, one with the value of "update," and the other with a value of "delete." By testing various combinations of submit and user_id, the script can do everything we need.

Listing 6-2 shows the structure of this page in pseudo-code.

Listing 6-2 *Logic of simple application*

```
connect to MySQL and choose database
if user_id has a value and a submit button has not been pressed
    get the values for each column in the row indicated by user_id
    assign these column names to variables in the programming language

else if user_id has a value and the update submit button has been pressed
    run an UPDATE query
    reload page with only user_id

else if user_id does not have a value and update has been pressed
    run an INSERT query
    reload page with no user_id

else if user_id has a value and the delete button has been pressed
    run a DELETE query
end if

print link for a blank form (one without a user_id)
print listing of all entries in the table, with links for user_id
print form. form should include values for each column of a row (for
editing)
if user_id [MW1]is available.
```

Done!

REVIEW

In this session, you have learned about several SQL statements and the basic WHERE clause. You saw the syntax for the INSERT statement and saw how to ensure that strings within an INSERT statement deal properly with single quotes and backslashes. Then you learned how a record is edited with the UPDATE statement and how the WHERE clause specifies which rows are affected by the statement. You also saw the syntax for the REPLACE and DELETE statements. The session ended by putting most of these statements to work in a simple Web-based application where you saw how decision logic can determine which action is taken within a script.

QUIZ YOURSELF

1. Strings must be surrounded by what characters in INSERT, UPDATE, and RELACE statements? (See "The INSERT Statement.")

2. What is the name of the process by which MySQL is told to treat a character (such as a single quote) literally? (See "The INSERT Statement.")

3. What two keywords enable an SQL statement to specify a variety of conditions in a WHERE clause? (See "The Basic WHERE Clause.")

4. The REPLACE statement is a combination of what two SQL statements? (See "The REPLACE Statement.")

5. What symbols are used to say "is not equal to" in a WHERE clause. (See Table 6-1, "MySQL Comparison Operators.")

Getting Data from MySQL, Part I: The Basic SELECT

Session Checklist

✔ The basic SELECT

✔ Applying the WHERE clause

✔ Using LIKE

✔ Using ORDER BY

✔ Using LIMIT

✔ Using SELECT DISTINCT

**30 Min.
To Go**

The SELECT statement retrieves data from the tables in your database. In this session, you learn the basics of the SQL SELECT statement and how you can best work with SELECT in MySQL. SELECT queries can get very complex, and by the time you finish this book, you will understand advanced techniques for manipulating data.

The Basic SELECT

The best way to understand what you can do with SELECT is to see it in action. For the examples in most of this session, I run SELECT queries against the addresses table in the store database. The basic syntax of the SELECT query is

```
SELECT col_1, col_2, col3... FROM table_name WHERE ...
```

In place of column names, you can use an asterisk (), which means "grab all columns." To get a look at all the data in the addresses table, you can run SELECT * FROM addresses. Listing 7-1 shows the results of this query from the command-line client.

Listing 7-1 *SELECT * FROM addresses*

```
mysql> SELECT * FROM addresses;
+------------+---------+-------+------------------+--------+---------------+-------+----
---+
| address_id | user_id | place | addr_1           | addr_2 | city          | state | ZIP
|
+------------+---------+-------+------------------+--------+---------------+-------+----
---+
|          1 |       1 | home  | 1313 Mockingbirdn | Apt 2  | New York      | NY    |
22222 |
|          2 |       1 | work  | 254 Foo Lane     | Ste 2  | Hoboken       | NY    |
44555 |
|          3 |       2 | home  | 17 Maple Rd      | NULL   | Setauket      | CA    |
11733 |
|          4 |       2 | work  | 2020 Wall St     | Ste 25 | New York      | NY    |
11144 |
|          5 |       3 | home  | 1845 Fair Oaks   | Apt 6  | San Francisco | CA    |
92147 |
|          6 |       4 | home  | 30445 Haines St  | Apt 8G | San Francisco | CA    |
92149 |
|          7 |       5 | home  | 8 Oak Rd         | NULL   | Atlanta       | GA    |
14119 |
+------------+---------+-------+------------------+--------+---------------+-------+----
---+
7 rows in set (0.01 sec)
```

Note that there is actually one more column (country) in the addresses table. It was eliminated in Listing 7-1 because it couldn't fit on the published page.

If I want to retrieve only a few columns from the table, I can put the names of the columns in the SELECT statements. For example:

```
mysql> SELECT city, state, ZIP FROM addresses;
+---------------+-------+-------+
| city          | state | ZIP   |
+---------------+-------+-------+
| New York      | NY    | 22222 |
| Hoboken       | NY    | 44555 |
| Setauket      | CA    | 11733 |
| New York      | NY    | 11144 |
| San Francisco | CA    | 92147 |
| San Francisco | CA    | 92149 |
| Atlanta       | GA    | 14119 |
+---------------+-------+-------+
7 rows in set (0.85 sec)
```

Applying the WHERE Clause

For the most part, when you are running UPDATE and DELETE queries, the WHERE clauses are pretty simple. Chances are, your edits and deletions run against a narrowly defined set of rows. In the SELECT statement, however, you can expect lengthy WHERE clauses with lots of

ANDs and ORs. You also use some additional syntax that is unlikely to come up in UPDATE or DELETE queries.

Grouping portions of the WHERE clause

At times in your queries, you'll need to group sets of conditions. For example, consider how you would retrieve all rows from addresses where state is NY and ZIP is 11733. And in the same query you want rows where state is CA and ZIP is 92147. You can write the query like this:

```
SELECT * FROM addresses WHERE state='NY' and ZIP='44555' or state='CA' and ZIP='92147';
```

But this is difficult to read. It is much easier to look at if the portions are grouped. With MySQL and all other relational databases, you group portions of WHERE clauses with parentheses:

```
SELECT * FROM addresses WHERE (state='NY' and ZIP='44555') or (state='CA' and ZIP='92147');
```

In the above example, grouping is not strictly necessary, but there are circumstances where grouping offers the only way to properly write a query. For example:

```
SELECT *
FROM ADDRESSES
WHERE (state='NY' and place='home' or place='work') or
      (state='CA' and place='work')
```

This query cannot be written correctly without parentheses. As your WHERE clauses get long and complex, you'll need to make sure you are grouping properly. It's all too easy to misplace a set of parentheses and find a query returning unexpected results.

It's also important to be aware of MySQL's order of precedence when not using parentheses. MySQL first looks at uses of OR then at uses of AND. This can have an impact on the output of a query. For example, this WHERE clause:

```
where state='NY' or state='NV' and ZIP='44555' or state='CA'
```

is actually executed as

```
where (state='NY') or (state='CA' and ZIP='44555') or (state='CA')
```

In other databases this might not be the case. If AND came before OR in the order of precedence, the query would be executed in the following manner:

```
where (state='NY' or state='NV') and (ZIP='44555' or state='CA')
```

As you can see, there is a big difference.

Using IN/NOT IN

If you want to get a listing of all the home addresses in a New England state, you may run a query like this:

```
SELECT place, addr_1, addr_2, city, state, ZIP
FROM addresses WHERE place='home'
    and (state='NY' or state='NH' or state='VT' or state='ME')
```

But the query would get very lengthy if there were, say, a dozen states that needed to be included in the results. A better choice is to use the IN predicate. Using IN, I can rewrite the preceding query like so:

```
SELECT place, addr_1, addr_2, city, state, ZIP
FROM addresses WHERE place='home'
    and state IN ('NY', 'NH', 'VT', 'ME')
```

The IN predicate is often used with subqueries. You learn about subqueries, and their availability in MySQL, in Session 8.

You can alter the preceding query to get a list of all address that are not in New England by changing IN to NOT IN:

```
SELECT place, addr_1, addr_2, city, state, ZIP
FROM addresses WHERE place='home'
    and state NOT IN ('NY', 'NH', 'VT', 'ME')
```

Using LIKE

20 Min. To Go

Imagine that a shopper comes to my online store and is interested in seeing all the products I have available with "MySQL" in the title. You can't conduct this kind of search using the operators you've seen so far (=, <, >, >=, and so on). For this kind of search, you need to use the LIKE predicate and wildcard characters.

There are two wildcard characters for the SQL LIKE predicate: the percentage sign (%) and the underscore (_). The percentage sign means "match zero or more characters" and the underscore means "match a single character." To retrieve rows from the products table where the product_name title starts with "MySQL," use the following:

```
SELECT * FROM products WHERE product_name LIKE 'MySQL%'
```

To alter this query to get all rows where "MySQL" is anywhere in the title, use

```
SELECT * FROM products WHERE product_name LIKE '%MySQL%'
```

The underscore matches only a single character and is useful in limited situations. For example, say there was a user in your users table for whom you needed information. You wrote yourself a note with the user's name but you can't quite read your handwriting. You're pretty sure that the user's first name starts with a "J" and has four letters — something like "John" or "Jack." Your LIKE predicate needs a "J" and three single-character wildcards (underscores):

```
SELECT * FROM users WHERE fname LIKE 'J___'
```

If you want to search for either a percentage sign or an underscore within a LIKE clause, you must escape those characters with backslashes. For example, the following searches for an occurrence of an underscore anywhere in a column:

```
SELECT product_description FROM products WHERE product_description LIKE
'%\_%'
```

In this query, the percentage signs are wildcards, but the underscore is a literal underscore.

Using ORDER BY

You may have noticed that in Listing 7-1, the rows are listed with the address_id column in ascending order. But in fact, you cannot be sure that any query will retrieve rows in any particular order unless the order is specified in the query. Use the ORDER BY clause for this purpose. ORDER BY uses the following syntax:

```
SELECT col_1, col_2, ... WHERE ... ORDER BY col_1 ASC, col_2 DESC
```

ASC and DESC indicate, respectively, whether the rows should be retrieved in ascending or descending order. If an ORDER BY clause omits ASC or DESC, ASC is assumed. To retrieve columns from the addresses table so that they are ordered by their ZIP code in descending order, you can do the following:

```
mysql> SELECT user_id, addr_1, state, ZIP FROM addresses ORDER BY ZIP
DESC;
+---------+--------------------+-------+-------+
| user_id | addr_1             | state | ZIP   |
+---------+--------------------+-------+-------+
|       4 | 30445 Haines St    | CA    | 92149 |
|       3 | 1845 Fair Oaks     | CA    | 92147 |
|       1 | 254 Foo Lane       | NY    | 44555 |
|       1 | 1313 Mockingbird Ln | NY   | 22222 |
|       5 | 8 Oak Rd           | GA    | 14119 |
|       2 | 17 Maple Rd        | CA    | 11733 |
|       2 | 2020 Wall St       | NY    | 11144 |
+---------+--------------------+-------+-------+
7 rows in set (0.01 sec)
```

You can use ORDER BY with more than one column. For example, if I wanted to get names from the users table, chances are I would want them alphabetized by last name, then first name. For example:

```
mysql> SELECT lname, fname FROM users ORDER BY lname ASC, fname ASC;
+-----------+-------+
| lname     | fname |
+-----------+-------+
| Doe       | Jon   |
| Fromlin   | Ed    |
| Greenspan | Jay   |
+-----------+-------+
3 rows in set (0.41 sec)
```

10 Min.
To Go

Using LIMIT

The LIMIT clause is not part of the SQL standard, but you'll be happy that the makers of MySQL included it in their product. It comes in very handy. The LIMIT clause cuts down on the number of results returned by a given query. Imagine, for example, that the online store contains a page that allows shoppers to browse all the products for sale. You don't want to deliver every single item on a single page — it would take forever to download. Instead, deliver maybe ten results at a time. To get the first ten, use the following query:

```
SELECT product_name, product_description
FROM products
ORDER BY product_name
LIMIT 10
```

With LIMIT, you can also determine where in the results you wish to start. For example, the preceding query gave you the first ten results. The next time around, you want to get another ten records, but you'd want to start with the 11th row, so that there is no repetition. The proper query to get rows 11 through 20 is as follows:

```
SELECT product_name, product_description
FROM products
ORDER BY product_name
LIMIT 10, 10
```

You may be wondering why the first number in the LIMIT clause is 10 rather than 11. That's because MySQL considers the first row to be row 0. Therefore, "10" is actually row number 11. And the following clauses are identical:

```
LIMIT 10
LIMIT 0,10
```

Using SELECT DISTINCT

What if you want to find out what states were included in the addresses table? From what you've seen so far, you can try the following:

```
mysql> SELECT state from addresses ORDER BY state;
+-------+
| state |
+-------+
| CA    |
| CA    |
| CA    |
| GA    |
| NY    |
| NY    |
| NY    |
+-------+
7 rows in set (1.09 sec)
```

Using LIMIT to Save Resources

LIMIT can be helpful in your applications when you need to know if any rows in a table are returned by a SELECT query.

For example, before you insert a new record into the users table, you may want to make sure that no records currently in the table have a value in the work_phone column that is identical to the one input by the current user. In this circumstance, you may want to give a specific error message or alert the current user that his information may already be in the database.

You can run a simple query without LIMIT to see if the work_phone already exists in the table and then in your application check to see if any rows were returned. Something like:

```
SELECT work_phone FROM users where work_phone='some number'
```

However, it is possible that the query may return many results. The larger the result set, the more resources that are used by your MySQL server. If you put a LIMIT 1 on the end of the query, you know that only one row will be returned by the query, thereby saving valuable memory and CPU cycles.

If you want to make sure you're using the fewest possible resources, you don't have to put a column name in your SELECT statement. Instead, you can just use the number 1, which in programming circles, is the same as true:

```
SELECT 1 FROM users WHERE work_phone='some number' LIMIT 1
```

But as you can see, there are some repeats in this dataset. For a list of states without any repetition, use SELECT DISTINCT:

```
mysql> SELECT DISTINCT state from addresses ORDER BY state;
+-------+
| state |
+-------+
| CA    |
| GA    |
| NY    |
+-------+
3 rows in set (0.19 sec)\
```

You can run SELECT DISTINCT against multiple columns. The server returns a set of unique row combinations. You can apply WHERE, ORDER BY, and LIMIT clauses to SELECT DISTINCT if need be.

Done!

REVIEW

In this session, you saw some of the many uses of the SQL SELECT statement. You expanded your knowledge of the WHERE clause by seeing how grouping is used for complex criteria. You also saw how LIKE and IN are applied. Then you learned two methods for restricting the results returned from a SELECT: LIMIT and SELECT DISTINCT.

QUIZ YOURSELF

1. What characters are used to group portions of a WHERE clause? (See "Grouping portions of the WHERE clause.")
2. Which character in a LIKE clause represents zero or more characters? (See "Using LIKE.")
3. How would you search for a percentage sign within a LIKE clause? (See "Using LIKE.")
4. What do the two numbers in a LIMIT statement represent? (See "Using LIMIT.")
5. Can WHERE clauses be applied to SELECT DISTINCT? (See "Using SELECT DISTINCT.")

Getting Data from MySQL, Part II: Using SELECT with Multiple Tables

Session Checklist

✔ Equi-joins

✔ Inner joins

✔ Outer joins

✔ Subselects

✔ Unions

✔ Self joins

**30 Min.
To Go**

In Sessions 3 and 4, you saw how relational databases maintain data integrity by breaking data into multiple tables, and in Session 7, you saw the basics of getting data from tables with the SELECT statement. However, you may have noticed that the data you can get from a single table is often inadequate. Take for example, a single row from the addresses table:

```
mysql> SELECT address_id, user_id, addr_1, city, state, ZIP
    -> FROM addresses
    -> WHERE address_id=2;
+------------+---------+--------------+---------+-------+-------+
| address_id | user_id | addr_1       | city    | state | ZIP   |
+------------+---------+--------------+---------+-------+-------+
|          2 |       1 | 254 Foo Lane | Hoboken | NY    | 44555 |
+------------+---------+--------------+---------+-------+-------+
```

Here, user_id is a foreign key that maintains a relationship to the users table. And the information on user_id 1 is in that table:

```
mysql> SELECT user_id, fname, lname, email, home_phone, work_phone
    -> FROM users
    -> WHERE user_id=1;
```

```
+---------+-------+-------+---------------+-------------+-------------+
| user_id | fname | lname | email         | home_phone  | work_phone  |
+---------+-------+-------+---------------+-------------+-------------+
|       1 | Jon   | Doe   | jdoe@jdoe.com | 2125554444  | 2025554444  |
+---------+-------+-------+---------------+-------------+-------------+
```

What's needed is a way to join these two tables together so that all relevant information can be retrieved in a single query.

The Equi-Join

The previous example is fairly typical. You want to join tables based on values that are equal in two tables (in the above case, the user_id field). The technique by which you accomplish this is known as an *equi-join*. You may also see it referred to as a *straight join* or an *inner join*. You indicate which tables in the FROM clause you want to join and on what fields in the WHERE clause. Here's an example that I explain in detail:

```
mysql> SELECT users.user_id, fname, lname, addr_1, city, state, ZIP
    -> FROM users, addresses
    -> WHERE
    -> users.user_id = addresses.user_id and
    -> address_id=2;
+---------+-------+-------+--------------+---------+-------+-------+
| user_id | fname | lname | addr_1       | city    | state | ZIP   |
+---------+-------+-------+--------------+---------+-------+-------+
|       1 | Jon   | Doe   | 254 Foo Lane | Hoboken | NY    | 44555 |
+---------+-------+-------+--------------+---------+-------+-------+
```

First notice the FROM clause. Instead of a single table, the two tables I need to join are listed. Now look at the list of columns. Fields from both tables are included, and MySQL is smart enough to figure out which columns belong to which tables in the FROM clause. The only unusual thing here is that I indicated which table the user_id column belongs to using the format table_name.column_name. I had to do this because a field named user_id exists in both tables. If didn't indicate the table name in the query, MySQL would send an error message stating that the column name was ambiguous.

And finally, look at the WHERE clause. The first portion tells the database engine which columns will be the basis of the join of the two tables in the FROM clause. Once again, I specified both the table name and the column name to avoid any ambiguity.

More than two tables can be joined by an equi-join. In fact, you can join as many tables as you need access to. (MySQL actually cannot join more than 16 tables, but you will rarely, if ever, need to do a join that large.) Say you wanted to get information on a specific order indicated by order_id 1 in the orders table. There is a one-to-many relationship between the orders table and the order_items table, so these tables need to be joined. In addition, to get the name of the user associated with the order, you need to join the users table to the orders table.

```
mysql> SELECT fname, lname, orders.order_id, item_id, price
    -> FROM users, orders, order_items
    -> WHERE users.user_id=orders.user_id and
```

```
    -> orders.order_id=order_items.order_id and
    -> orders.order_id=1;
+-------+-------+----------+---------+-------+
| fname | lname | order_id | item_id | price |
+-------+-------+----------+---------+-------+
| Jon   | Doe   |        1 |       1 | 25.00 |
| Jon   | Doe   |        1 |       2 | 12.99 |
+-------+-------+----------+---------+-------+
```

So now these three tables give much of the information you need. However, item_id is a foreign key to the items_for_sale table. And items_for_sale, in turn, has a foreign key (product_id) to the products table. So, in order to get all the information you may need on a single order, you need to join five tables. The following query does the trick:

```
mysql> SELECT fname, lname, orders.order_id,
    -> order_items.item_id, product_name, format, order_items.price
    -> FROM users, orders, order_items, items_for_sale, products
    -> WHERE users.user_id=orders.user_id and
    -> orders.order_id=order_items.order_id and
    -> order_items.item_id=items_for_sale.item_id and
    -> items_for_sale.product_id=products.product_id and
    -> orders.order_id=1;
+-------+-------+----------+---------+-------------------------+------------+-------+
| fname | lname | order_id | item_id | product_name            | format     | price |
+-------+-------+----------+---------+-------------------------+------------+-------+
| Jon   | Doe   |        1 |       1 | MySQL Weekend Crash Course | book    | 25.00 |
| Jon   | Doe   |        1 |       2 | PHP for the Web         | Whitepaper | 12.99 |
+-------+-------+----------+---------+-------------------------+------------+-------+
```

Using INNER JOIN Syntax

Above I mention that an equi-join is also known as an *inner join*. MySQL, like many other SQL databases, allows you to use a syntax that uses the phrase INNER JOIN. Below, I've rewritten a portion of the previous query using INNER JOIN syntax.

```
mysql> SELECT fname, lname, orders.order_id, item_id, price
    -> FROM users
    -> INNER JOIN orders on users.user_id=orders.user_id
    -> INNER JOIN order_items on orders.order_id=order_items.order_id
    -> where orders.order_id=1;
```

Notice that the column listing remains the same. You must list all columns and give table names whenever there is possible ambiguity. Instead of listing all tables in the FROM clause, put only the primary table in the query, in this case users. Following that, add the phrase INNER JOIN followed by the table name and the keyword on. Finally, give the join condition. The join condition can be anything you'd find in the WHERE clause. In the previous query, the INNER JOIN condition is equality of values in columns in different tables.

Note that when using INNER JOIN syntax, you need to be aware of the order in which you're joining tables in the query. For example, say I wanted to add the product_id column from the items_for_sale table. The items_for_sale table has a relationship with the order_items table but not the orders table. In order for this join to work correctly, I first have to join orders or `order_items`, and only then can I join `order_items` to `items_for_sale`.

```
mysql> SELECT fname, lname, orders.order_id, order_items.item_id,
    -> order_items.price, product_id
    -> FROM users
    -> INNER JOIN orders on users.user_id=orders.user_id
    -> INNER JOIN order_items on orders.order_id=order_items.order_id
    -> INNER JOIN items_for_sale on
order_items.item_id=items_for_sale.item_id
    -> where orders.order_id=1;
```

20 Min.
To Go

The OUTER JOIN

There is a potential problem with the equi-join or inner join. As you've seen, there is a one-to-many relationship between the `users` table and the `addresses` table. That's because one user can have a home and work address. However, it's also possible that no addresses exist for a user. If, for example, a user purchases a whitepaper that can be delivered via e-mail, there's no need for that person to enter a mailing address. This may be a problem when it comes time to get a complete list of users. You may think that the following query will get you all the rows you need.

```
SELECT fname, lname, email, addresses.*
FROM users, addresses
WHERE users.user_id=addresses.user_id
ORDER BY lname, fname;
```

This query gets you a list of everyone in the `users` table with at least one corresponding row in the `addresses` table. But it is possible that some users will not show up in this query because they have no corresponding rows in the `addresses` table. (After all, `users.user_id=addresses.user_id` must test false if there is no address row for that user.) What is needed is a way to say "preserve all of the rows in the `users` table and join when a corresponding row in the `addresses` table is available." This is where the OUTER JOIN (also known as a LEFT OUTER JOIN or LEFT JOIN) comes in. The query in Listing 8-1 solves the problem.

Listing 8-1   *Sample outer join*

```
mysql> SELECT users.user_id, fname, lname, addresses.user_id, address_id, addr_1, addr_2
    -> FROM users
    -> LEFT JOIN addresses
    -> ON users.user_id=addresses.user_id
    -> ORDER BY lname, fname;
```

user_id	fname	lname	user_id	address_id	addr_1	addr_2
1	Jon	Doe	1	1	1313 Mockingbird Ln	Apt 2
1	Jon	Doe	1	2	254 Foo Lane	Ste 2
2	Ed	Fromlin	2	3	17 Maple Rd	NULL
2	Ed	Fromlin	2	4	2020 Wall St	Ste 25

```
|        4 | Jay     | Greenspan |        4 |        6 | 30445 Haines St       | Apt 8G |
|        5 | Elliot  | Krug      |        5 |        7 | 8 Oak Rd              | NULL   |
|        6 | Willy   | Krug      |     NULL |     NULL | NULL                  | NULL   |
+----------+---------+-----------+----------+----------+-----------------------+--------+
```

The last row (user_id 6) would not be listed in a equi-join because the second user_id (from the addresses table does not exist). The query starts with a list of columns that is similar to all the other SELECT statements you have seen. The table in the FROM clause is the table that should be listed in its entirety (that is, the left-most table). The LEFT JOIN clause specifies the table that should be joined onto users when possible. Finally, the ON predicate shows the join condition.

An OUTER JOIN works any time you wish to preserve one table, including circumstances when a table contains a foreign key that is null. You can also left join multiple tables with syntax:

```
SELECT col_1, col_2, ...
FROM table_1
LEFT JOIN table_2 ON table_1.foo=table2.foo
LEFT JOIN table_3 ON table_2.bar=table3.bar
```

Some databases support full outer joins. You'd use a full outer join when you wanted to preserve both tables involved in a join. Imagine you had the following two tables, named orders_1 and orders_2 (Table 8-1 and Table 8-2, respectively).

Table 8-1   *orders_1 table*

user_id	payment_cash
1	25
2	50

Table 8-2   *orders_2 table*

user_id	payment_credit
2	75
3	88

With these two tables, it's likely you'd want to perform a query that preserved both orders_1 and orders_2 and joined the tables on user_id, when there is a user_id in common. But MySQL does not support full outer joins. However, you can mimic full outer join behavior with UNIONS, which are discussed shortly.

Subselects

In Session 7, you saw how the IN and NOT IN predicates can be used to specify multiple values for a single column in a WHERE clause. In the example given in Session 7, I had the advantage of knowing exactly what values I needed within the IN predicate, and I can specify those explicitly. There will be times when you won't be able to key in the potential values. Instead, the list of potential values will be the result of another query.

For a simple example, consider this scenario: You're doing a phone survey and want to call all users who have a home phone in New York. Phone numbers are in the users table and the state is in the addresses table. What you need to do is get a list of user_ids from the addresses table where state equals "NY" and include each of those results into the IN predicate of a WHERE clause. Using subselects, the query would look like this:

```
SELECT * FROM users
WHERE user_id IN(SELECT user_id FROM addresses WHERE state='NY');
```

At the time of this writing, subselects were not available in MySQL. However, they are planned for version 4.1, which is due out in late 2002.

To check what version of MySQL you are running, use the following query:

```
SELECT version();
```

If you are working on a version of MySQL earlier than 4.1, you can work around the absence of subselects by running well-planned table joins. The above example can be rewritten as an equi-join:

```
SELECT users.*
FROM users, addresses
WHERE users.user_id=addresses.user_id and
      state='NY'
```

A slightly different situation occurs when you need to search for the absence of a value. You saw earlier that it's possible for a user to have a phone number in the database but no address. Imagine you were calling people trying to get addresses where none existed — perhaps you're preparing for a large mailing. You'd need to run a query that found all the people who have entries in the users table but do not have entries in the addresses table. In most databases, you can do this with subqueries:

```
SELECT users.*
FROM users
WHERE user_id NOT IN (SELECT user_id FROM addresses)
```

In MySQL versions prior to 4.1, you'd rewrite this as an OUTER JOIN. If you look at Listing 8-1, you see that an OUTER JOIN returns rows when there is no corresponding row in a different table. To restrict the results of the query to only those rows that have no join values, you'd test for NULL values. So the previous query would be rewritten in this way:

```
SELECT users.*, addresses.user_id
FROM users
LEFT JOIN addresses ON users.user_id=addresses.user_id
WHERE addresses.user_id IS NULL
```

Take a look at Listing 8-1 again and you see that with the addition of the WHERE clause, the query returns only a single row — for user_id 6.

Unions

**10 Min.
To Go**

A *union* brings together similar rows from different tables into one result set. The database I have used for all the examples so far doesn't contain tables that are in need of a union. But unions are an important part of SQL, and chances are you will need them eventually, so here's an example.

In the store database, there is a table that lists products:

```
mysql> SELECT * FROM products;
+------------+-------------------------------+----------------------------------------+
| product_id | product_name                  | product_description                    |
+------------+-------------------------------+----------------------------------------+
|          1 | MySQL Weekend Crash Course    | A quick but complete intoduction....   |
|          2 | PHP for the Web               | A technical introduction to a ...guage.|
|          3 | MySQL/PHP Database Applications | A guide to this great opens source    |
+------------+-------------------------------+----------------------------------------+
```

If I had a lot of turnover in my products, it's possible that I'd create a table for products that are no longer being sold. It may have the name products_old and have the same column names and definitions that exist for the products table. To get a full list of all products that I ever sold in a single query, I'd use the keyword UNION to marry two SELECT statements.

```
SELECT product_id, product_name, product_description
FROM products
UNION
SELECT product_id, product_name, product_description
FROM products
```

The columns in both portions must contain the same number of columns and those columns must be of the same type.

MySQL versions before 4.0 do not support unions. The workaround for unions is a bit odd. You create a temporary table and insert the output of the queries you would have unioned into the temporary table, and then you run a SELECT * on the temporary table.

You can easily create a temporary table by using the CREATE TEMPORARY TABLE table_name syntax. Then within the same statement, you can define column definitions and insert data by running a SELECT statement on another table. For example:

```
mysql> CREATE TEMPORARY TABLE product_temp
    -> SELECT product_id, product_name, product_description
    -> FROM products
-> WHERE product_id=1;
```

The result of this operation is

```
+-------------+-------------------------+-----------------------------------------
-+
| product_id | product_name            | product_description
|
+-------------+-------------------------+-----------------------------------------
-+
|           1 | MySQL Weekend Crash Course | A quick but complete introduction to ...
|
+-------------+-------------------------+-----------------------------------------
-+
```

Now that this temporary table exists, you can insert the results of the second query into this table by combining an INSERT and a SELECT:

```
mysql> INSERT INTO product_temp(product_id, product_name,
product_description)
    ->SELECT product_id, product_name, product_description
    ->FROM product_old where product_id>1
```

This gives you a complete result set, against which you can run SELECT * FROM product_temp.

As I mentioned earlier, unions can be used to mimic the function of full outer joins. For example, take a look at Tables 8-1 and 8-2. If you had these tables in your database, you'd probably want to find a way to join these tables so that you ended up with a query result like this one:

```
+---------+---------------+----------------+-------+
| user_id | payment_cash | payment_credit | total |
+---------+---------------+----------------+-------+
|       1 |            25 |           NULL |    25 |
|       2 |            50 |             75 |   125 |
|       3 |          NULL |             88 |    88 |
+---------+---------------+----------------+-------+
```

As you can see, when the user_ids of the two tables match, the rows are joined on that column, and the two payments are totaled. All rows from both tables where there are no matching user_ids, are maintained and accurate totals are reported. You'd create this result by writing two LEFT JOINs. Here's the first:

```
mysql> SELECT orders_1.user_id, payment_cash, payment_credit,
    -> (payment_cash + ifnull(payment_credit,0)) as total
    -> FROM orders_1
    -> LEFT JOIN orders_2 on orders_1.user_id=orders_2.user_id;
+---------+---------------+----------------+-------+
|user_id | payment_cash | payment_credit | total |
+---------+---------------+----------------+-------+
|       1 |            25 |           NULL |    25 |
|       2 |            50 |             75 |   125 |
+---------+---------------+----------------+-------+
```

This query preserves all rows in orders_1 and joins rows from orders_2 when there are matching values for the user_id columns. Notice how I had to go about totaling the values of payment_cash and payment_credit. I had to use the ifnull() function, which I discuss in great detail in Session 11. In this case, the ifnull() function returns the value of payment_credit if the value of that column is not null. If the value is null, the function returns a value of 0. I need to do this because databases cannot use null values in arithmetic operations. In the above example, if I were trying to add 25 to NULL, the result would be NULL.

In addition to the rows returned by the above query, I'd want to include rows from orders_2 that had no matching rows in orders_1. I accomplish this with a LEFT JOIN that omits rows where payment_cash IS NULL. Notice that in the following query I omit the arithmetic function. It's unnecessary because all of the rows that needed the two columns added were included in the first query.

```
mysql> SELECT orders_2.user_id, payment_cash, payment_credit,
    -> payment_credit as total
    -> FROM orders_2
    -> LEFT JOIN orders_1 on orders_2.user_d=orders_1.user_id
    -> WHERE payment_cash IS NULL;
+---------+--------------+----------------+-------+
|user_id  | payment_cash | payment_credit | total |
+---------+--------------+----------------+-------+
|      3  |         NULL |             88 |    88 |
+---------+--------------+----------------+-------+
```

You'd put these two queries together with a UNION.

```
SELECT orders_1.user_id, payment_cash, payment_credit,
(payment_cash + ifnull(payment_credit,0)) as total
FROM orders_1
LEFT JOIN orders_2 on orders_1.user_id=orders_2.user_id
UNION
SELECT orders_2.user_id, payment_cash, payment_credit, payment_credit as
total
FROM orders_2
LEFT JOIN orders_1 on orders_2.user_id=orders_1.user_id
WHERE payment_cash IS NULL;
```

If you find yourself in a situation where you want to replicate a table's definition (column names and types) without keeping any of the data from that table, you can use a CREATE TABLE and a SELECT statement together. For example:

```
CREATE TABLE prod_temp
SELECT * from products WHERE 0=1
```

Obviously, 1 will never be equal to 0, so no rows will be copied into this new table.

Self Joins

As strange as it may sound, there are times when you will need to join a table onto a copy of itself. Normally, you'll perform this operation while you are looking for duplicates. For an example of how this applies to our store database, take a look at a few rows of data from the order_items table:

```
mysql> SELECT * FROM order_items;
+---------------+----------+---------+-------+----------------+
| order_items_id | order_id | item_id | price | last_update    |
+---------------+----------+---------+-------+----------------+
|             1 |        1 |       1 | 25.00 | 20010920143305 |
|             2 |        1 |       2 | 12.99 | 20010920143305 |
|             3 |        2 |       2 | 14.99 | 20010921105145 |
|             4 |        2 |       3 | 25.99 | 20010921105737 |
|             5 |        2 |       2 | 14.99 | 20010921110308 |
+---------------+----------+---------+-------+----------------+
```

Say you wanted to get a listing of all order_ids where a single item was repeated — that is, the shopper bought more than one copy of the item. To do this, you'd need to find rows where order_id and item_id are identical. In the above data, rows 3 and 6 show that order_id 2 contains two copies of item_id 2.

To start with, in the FROM clause of your query, you need to create copies of tables by using aliasies. To create an alias, all you have to do is give the table name and follow it with an alias. Then in your column list and WHERE clause, refer to the alias name. Here's what may first occur to you:

```
SELECT t1.*
FROM order_items as t1, order_items as t2
WHERE t1.item_id = t2.item_id
```

But this returns far too many rows.

```
+---------------+----------+---------+-------+----------------+
| order_items_id | order_id | item_id | price | last_update    |
+---------------+----------+---------+-------+----------------+
|             1 |        1 |       1 | 25.00 | 20010920143305 |
|             2 |        1 |       2 | 12.99 | 20010920143305 |
|             3 |        2 |       2 | 14.99 | 20010921105145 |
|             5 |        2 |       2 | 14.99 | 20010921110308 |
|             2 |        1 |       2 | 12.99 | 20010920143305 |
|             3 |        2 |       2 | 14.99 | 20010921105145 |
|             5 |        2 |       2 | 14.99 | 20010921110308 |
|             4 |        2 |       3 | 25.99 | 20010921105737 |
|             2 |        1 |       2 | 12.99 | 20010920143305 |
|             3 |        2 |       2 | 14.99 | 20010921105145 |
|             5 |        2 |       2 | 14.99 | 20010921110308 |
+---------------+----------+---------+-------+----------------+
```

```
SELECT t1.*
FROM order_items t1, order_items t2
WHERE t1.item_id = t2.item_id and
t1.order_id != t2.order_id
```

If you try running this query, you'll see that you still get far too many rows in the result.

```
+----------------+----------+---------+-------+----------------+
| order_items_id | order_id | item_id | price | last_update    |
+----------------+----------+---------+-------+----------------+
|              3 |        2 |       2 | 14.99 | 20010921105145 |
|              5 |        2 |       2 | 14.99 | 20010921110308 |
|              2 |        1 |       2 | 12.99 | 20010920143305 |
|              2 |        1 |       2 | 12.99 | 20010920143305 |
+----------------+----------+---------+-------+----------------+
```

Rows with identical order_items_ids can still match themselves. To make sure each row is included only once in the result, you can make use of the auto_increment primary key, order_items_id. If you specify that the order_items_id from one alias must be less than that from the other alias, you eliminate the possibility that a row will match itself:

```
mysql> SELECT t1.*
    -> FROM order_items t1, order_items t2
    -> WHERE t1.item_id = t2.item_id and
    -> t1.order_id != t2.order_id and
    -> t1.order_items_id < t2.order_items_id;
+----------------+----------+---------+-------+----------------+
| order_items_id | order_id | item_id | price | last_update    |
+----------------+----------+---------+-------+----------------+
|              2 |        1 |       2 | 12.99 | 20010920143305 |
|              2 |        1 |       2 | 12.99 | 20010920143305 |
+----------------+----------+---------+-------+----------------+
2 rows in set (0.00 sec)
```

Done!

REVIEW

In this session, you learned several ways of applying queries to multiple tables. You saw how the equi-join can be used to merge tables on a primary key–foreign key relationship, giving complete information in a single query. You saw how equi-joins can be applied to two, three, or more tables. Following that, you saw how to deal with null values in joins, by using outer joins. You saw how unions marry similar columns from different tables in a single query and how to work around the absence of unions in some versions of MySQL. You learned the usefulness of subqueries and how to work around the absence of subqueries in versions prior to 4.1. Finally, you saw how to work with self joins.

QUIZ YOURSELF

1. Name two synonyms for the equi-join. (See "The Equi-Join.")
2. Sometimes you must indicate table names in the column field list. Why? (See "The Equi-Join.")
3. In a left join, what portion of the query specifies the join condition? (See "The OUTER JOIN.")
4. What statements are used in place of unions in MySQL versions prior to 4.0? (See "Unions.")
5. In what situation do you normally use self joins? (See "Self Joins.")

Basic Functions in MySQL

Session Checklist

✔ Covering the basics of functions

✔ GROUP BY and aggregate functions

✔ Mathematical operations

**30 Min.
To Go**

Much of the time, the data you put into and select from MySQL will be fine. You won't need to manipulate that data in any way. However, there are times when you will need to process some values. When you need to process data, you use *functions*. (Functions take one or more values, process them in a known way, and return a modified value.)

Function Basics

If you've worked with any programming or scripting language, you know what functions do. If you haven't, MySQL functions are easy enough to pick up.

Arguments

Functions in MySQL are usually surrounded by parentheses. Within the parentheses are one or more *arguments*. An argument is a distinct value, and commas separate arguments within functions. There can be no space between the function name and the opening parenthesis.

Here are two quick examples of functions, wherein you can see an example of an argument. The ucase() function, which converts a string to all uppercase letters, takes a single argument. For example:

```
mysql> SELECT ucase('my Book');
+------------------+
| ucase('my Book') |
+------------------+
| MY BOOK          |
+------------------+
```

In this case, the function operated on a string provided in the query ('my Book'). But functions can also work on values from tables. For example, in the query below, ucase() operates on a column value.

```
mysql> SELECT ucase(product_name) FROM products WHERE product_id=1;
+----------------------------+
| ucase(product_name)        |
+----------------------------+
| MYSQL WEEKEND CRASH COURSE |
+----------------------------+
```

Some functions have two, three, or an arbitrary number of arguments. left(), for example, takes two arguments and returns the left-most characters in a string. The first argument is the string you wish to manipulate; the second specifies the number of characters you wish to return. For example:

```
mysql> SELECT left('I Love the MySQL Database', 10);
+---------------------------------------+
| left('I Love the MySQL Database', 10) |
+---------------------------------------+
| I Love the                            |
+---------------------------------------+
```

Aliases

You saw an example of an alias in Session 8 while reading about self joins. There an alias (an alternate name) was applied to a table name. Aliases are frequently applied to functions as well. All you have to do is use the keyword AS and identify an alias name, and then, in other portions of your query and in the result, you can refer to the alias name instead of the function. For example:

```
mysql> SELECT ucase(product_name) as CapLetters FROM products
    -> WHERE product_id=1;
+----------------------------+
| CapLetters                 |
+----------------------------+
| MYSQL WEEKEND CRASH COURSE |
+----------------------------+
```

When working with applications, a column named CapLetters is far easier to work with than ucase(product_name).

**20 Min.
To Go**

GROUP BY and Aggregate Functions

The SQL standard contains a set of *aggregate functions* that are extremely useful and frequently used. An aggregate function, as you will see, in some way analyzes a group of rows. Aggregate functions work with the GROUP BY clause. When you use GROUP BY, MySQL knows to work with rows that contain identical column values.

This should be clear as you look at the following examples. First, take a look at this basic query on the addresses table.

```
mysql> SELECT addr_1, city, state, ZIP FROM addresses ORDER BY state;
+---------------------+----------------+-------+-------+
| addr_1              | city           | state | ZIP   |
+---------------------+----------------+-------+-------+
| 17 Maple Rd         | Setauket       | CA    | 11733 |
| 1845 Fair Oaks      | San Francisco  | CA    | 92147 |
| 30445 Haines St     | San Francisco  | CA    | 92149 |
| 8 Oak Rd            | Atlanta        | GA    | 14119 |
| 1313 Mockingbird Ln | New York       | NY    | 22222 |
| 254 Foo Lane        | Hoboken        | NY    | 44555 |
| 2020 Wall St        | New York       | NY    | 11144 |
+---------------------+----------------+-------+-------+
```

count()

If I were doing some analyses on these rows, I may want to know how many addresses I had from each state. I would need to group this data by the state column. Once grouped, I can use aggregate functions to get statistical information on these groups (a group with CA as a value, a group with NY as a value, and so on). For starters, I can use the count() function, which counts all the rows in a given group.

```
mysql> SELECT state, count(state) AS 'number from state'
    -> FROM addresses
    -> GROUP BY state;
+-------+------------------+
| state | number from state |
+-------+------------------+
| CA    |                3 |
| GA    |                1 |
| NY    |                3 |
+-------+------------------+
```

Developers often use the count() **function to determine the number of rows in a table. For example,** SELECT count(*) from users **returns the number or rows in the** users **table. I've heard people express concerns that counting all rows may be a very slow process, particularly for large tables, but this is not the case. This is an optimized query in MySQL, and the result can be retrieved almost instantaneously.**

When you use count with a column name, for example count(state) as the single argument, MySQL counts the number of rows with non-null values. However, if you use count(*), MySQL returns the total number of rows in the result set.

Keep in mind that you can group by more than one column.

In addition to count(), MySQL performs several other aggregate functions: sum(),avg(), min(), and max().

sum()

The sum() function adds up the values in the column given as an argument to the function.

I may want to know the total spent by each user — not for each order, but the total for every order for a user_id. So I'd run a query on the orders table:

```
mysql> SELECT user_id, sum(order_total) as 'Total per User'
    -> FROM orders
    -> GROUP BY user_id;
+---------+----------------+
| user_id | Total per User |
+---------+----------------+
|       1 |          45.00 |
|       3 |          19.95 |
+---------+----------------+
2 rows in set (0.24 sec)
```

You can use GROUP BY to get specific information from a table while joining to another table. To add the first name and last name of the user to the previous query, use

```
SELECT orders.user_id, fname, lname, sum(order_total) as 'Total per User'
FROM users, orders
WHERE users.user_id=orders.user_id
GROUP BY orders.user_id
```

avg()

The avg() function returns the average from a group. If I wanted to find the average price for items of each format (that is, the average price of books, the average price for whitepapers, and so on), I can run the following:

```
mysql> SELECT format, avg(price) AS 'Format Average'
    -> FROM items_for_sale
    -> GROUP BY format
    -> ;
+------------+----------------+
| format     | Format Average |
+------------+----------------+
| book       |      26.816667 |
| Whitepaper |      12.990000 |
+------------+----------------+

2 rows in set (0.46 sec)
```

min() and max()

The min() and max() functions retrieve, respectively, the minimum and maximum values form a grouped column set. For example to get the highest, lowest, and average price for items of a particular format, you can use this query on the items_for_sale table:

```
SELECT format, avg(price) AS 'Format Average',
    min(price) as Minimum, max(price) as Maximum
FROM items_for_sale
GROUP BY format
```

HAVING

The HAVING predicate restricts the rows displayed by a GROUP BY. This is not the same as the WHERE clause. The WHERE clause actually restricts the rows used in the GROUP BY. The HAVING clause only prevents their display.

If you want to get the average price of books that cost more than $20, you need to specify the condition using a WHERE clause, thereby eliminating books less than $20 in the grouping:

```
SELECT avg(price)
FROM items_for_sale
WHERE format='book' and
price > 20
```

However, if I want to display formats where the average is greater than $20, I need to use the HAVING predicate. I want all rows to be grouped so I get proper averages, but I want to display only the groupings that meet a specific condition:

```
SELECT format, avg(price) as Average FROM items_for_sale
GROUP BY format
HAVING Average > 20
```

Note that you cannot use the results of an aggregate function in a WHERE clause.

Mathematical Operations

**10 Min.
To Go**

In addition to the aggregate functions, you often need to perform mathematical operations on column values. For example, say I decide that I want to offer a 10 percent discount on all my products. I can retrieve the full price of items from the database, and then alter this price in whatever programming language I'm using. In PHP, I may do the following:

```
$result=mysql_query("SELECT item_id, price FROM items_for_sale");
$row=mysql_fetch_array($result);
$discounted_price=$row["price"]*.9;
echo "New great price is: $discounted_price;
```

However, you can also perform all sorts of calculations within a query. I may be better off getting the discount in a query. Something like:

```
mysql> SELECT item_id, price, price * .9 as discount_price
    -> FROM items_for_sale
    -> WHERE item_id < 4;
+---------+-------+----------------+
| item_id | price | discount_price |
+---------+-------+----------------+
|       1 | 19.95 |          17.95 |
|       2 | 12.99 |          11.69 |
|       3 | 49.95 |          44.96 |
+---------+-------+----------------+
```

There's nothing especially interesting about the mathematical operators in MySQL. The typical operators (+, -, /, *) stand for the typical operations (addition, subtraction, division, and multiplication). You can use parentheses to determine order of operations.

```
mysql> SELECT 4 * 10 + 12;
+------------+
| 4 * 10 + 12 |
+------------+
|         52 |
+------------+
```

```
mysql> SELECT 4 * (10 + 12);
+--------------+
| 4 * (10 + 12) |
+--------------+
|           88 |
+--------------+
```

Notice how parentheses in the second query determine that 10 + 12 is conducted before the multiplication by 4.

In addition to simple mathematical operators, MySQL has many functions that perform more advanced math, including trigonometric and rounding functions.

Trigonometric functions

I don't have the need for trigonometry in my shopping cart, but if I needed to find the cosine of something, MySQL can assist me. Table 9-1 lists these functions, all of which take a single argument of a floating-point (decimal) numeric quantity:

Table 9-1 *MySQL's Trigonometric Functions*

Function	Meaning
cos()	cosine
sin()	sine
tan()	tangent
acos()	arc cosine

Function	Meaning
asin()	arc sine
atan()	arc tangent
cot()	cotangent

Here's an example of a trigonometric function:

```
mysql> SELECT cos(100.00);
+-------------+
| cos(100.00) |
+-------------+
|    0.862319 |
+-------------+
```

Rounding functions

MySQL offers many options to round numeric values, which can be useful in a variety of ways. For example, as you saw earlier, I can use the aggregate function avg() to get the average amount paid per order. All I'd have to do is average all rows in the order_items table:

```
mysql> SELECT avg(price) as 'Average Order' FROM order_items;
+---------------+
| Average Order |
+---------------+
|     18.792000 |
+---------------+
```

But when I'm examining this information, I may want this rounded off to the nearest dollar or nearest cent. I can use the round() function. round() takes two arguments: The first is the value to be operated upon; the second is the number of decimal places in the result. To round to the nearest dollar, use the following query:

```
mysql> SELECT round(avg(price),0)  as 'Average Order' FROM order_items;
+---------------+
| Average Order |
+---------------+
|            19 |
+---------------+
```

To round to the nearest cent, use

```
mysql> SELECT round(avg(price),2) as 'Average Order' FROM order_items;
+---------------+
| Average Order |
+---------------+
|         18.79 |
+---------------+
```

Note that the MySQL round( ) function rounds 5 down. The following query may return a result that is not what you expected.

```
mysql> select round(6.5);
+------------+
| round(6.5) |
+------------+
|          6 |
+------------+
1 row in set (0.46 sec)
```

In an example on this page, you saw how functions can be nested. If you look at the function round(avg(price),2), **you see that the first argument of the round function is another function. This is perfectly acceptable and quite common. You see other examples of nested function in the next couple of sessions.**

In addition to round( ), MySQL offers the floor( ), ceiling( ), and truncate( ) functions. The floor( ) function returns an integer closest to but less than the value of the single argument. For example:

```
mysql> select floor(6.9);
+------------+
| floor(6.9) |
+------------+
|          6 |
+------------+
1 row in set (0.00 sec)
```

You can also use this function with columns.

```
mysql> SELECT floor(avg(price))  as 'Average Order' FROM order_items;
+---------------+
| Average Order |
+---------------+
|            18 |
+---------------+
```

The ceiling( ) function returns the integer closest to but greater than the argument value.

```
mysql> select ceiling(6.1);
+--------------+
| ceiling(6.1) |
+--------------+
|            7 |
+--------------+
1 row in set (0.15 sec)
```

You can also use this function with columns.

```
mysql> SELECT ceiling(avg(price))  as 'Average Order' FROM order_items;
+---------------+
| Average Order |
+---------------+
|            19 |
+---------------+
```

The truncate() function, instead of rounding, removes decimal places in the result. It takes two arguments: The first is the value to be operated upon; the second is the number of decimal places you want in the result. For example:

```
mysql> SELECT truncate(1.45378, 2), truncate(1.45638,4);
+----------------------+---------------------+
| truncate(1.45378, 2) | truncate(1.45638,4) |
+----------------------+---------------------+
|                 1.45 |              1.4563 |
+----------------------+---------------------+
```

> **There are many other mathematical functions in MySQL — more than I can document here. At some point in the not too distant future, after you finish this book, you should go to the MySQL complete function list at www.mysql. com/doc/functions.html and bookmark the site. Then, when you have the time, browse through the functions just to see what's available.**

REVIEW

In this session, you got started with MySQL functions. The session started by defining arguments and aliases. It then moved on to the GROUP BY clause and showed how GROUP BY, when used with aggregate functions, can return powerful statistical information from databases. You saw how to use the HAVING predicate and how it differs from the WHERE clause. Following aggregate functions, you got a look at MySQL's ability to perform mathematical operations. Basic math operators and order of precedence were explained. Then trigonometric and rounding functions were reviewed.

Done!

QUIZ YOURSELF

1. What keyword lets MySQL know it should use an alias? (See "Aliases.")
2. True or False. You can use GROUP BY with more than one column? (See "GROUP BY and Aggregate Functions.")
3. How does the HAVING predicate differ from the WHERE clause? (See "HAVING.")
4. What characters are used to determine order of precedence in mathematical operations? (See "Mathematical Operations.")
5. What function eliminates decimal places from a result? (See "Rounding functions.")

SESSION

10

Date Functions in MySQL

Session Checklist

✔ Inserting dates

✔ Selecting and formatting dates

✔ Calculating date ranges

**30 Min.
To Go**

D ates play an important role in database applications. As you use MySQL, you will
undoubtedly find that you need to store dates and times for many reasons. You may
need to store items like appointments or delivery dates. Even if you have no time-
sensitive columns in your database, it's often a good idea to record the date and time of
your latest change to a row by using the timestamp column type.

Inserting Dates

MySQL provides some flexibility when dealing with date formats. For all date/time column
types, you can insert dates as either strings or integers without worrying that MySQL will
generate errors when executing the INSERT statement. For example, consider the following
simple table:

```
mysql> create table dates_test (
    -> the_date date
    -> );
Query OK, 0 rows affected (0.50 sec)
```

**Session 4 covers TIMESTAMP and all other date/time column types. You may
want to review these column types before continuing.**

MySQL internally stores the date column type using the following format: YYYY-MM-DD. But when executing statements that insert data into the table created above, any of the following INSERT statements work:

```
INSERT into dates_test (the_date) VALUES (20010425);
INSERT into dates_test (the_date) VALUES ('20010425');
INSERT into dates_test (the_date) VALUES ('2001-04-25');
INSERT into dates_test (the_date) VALUES ('01-04-25');
```

Notice that the first INSERT statement treats the value as an integer whereas the second INSERT statement treats the value as a string. The third and fourth statements are both strings, but the fourth omits the first two numbers in the year (20). Each of these results in the MySQL storing a date in the following format: 2001-04-25.

Although MySQL allows you flexibility in storing date and time column types, use the string variable type when inserting or updating date and time values. Furthermore, you can be assured that MySQL supports INSERT statements using strings in subsequent versions.

Selecting and Formatting Dates

In the store database I have used for examples throughout this book, a table called orders contains essential information about each sale. Within the orders table, I created the time_of_order column, which uses a TIMESTAMP format. As I mentioned in Session 4, the TIMESTAMP column automatically records the time of the most recent change to the row, whether it came by way of an INSERT or UPDATE. Below you can see the first two rows from the orders table.

```
mysql> SELECT * FROM orders WHERE order_id <= 2;
+----------+---------+-------------+------------------+
| order_id | user_id | order_total | time_of_order    |
+----------+---------+-------------+------------------+
|        1 |       1 |       45.00 | 20010922105419   |
|        2 |       3 |       19.95 | 20010922106425   |
+----------+---------+-------------+------------------+
```

In this query, the time_of_order column does supply the needed information, but in this format the time_of_order column is difficult to read. If you retrieve the data in this format, in your application, you'd have no choice but to parse this rather long string so that you can present it in a more readable way. It is far easier to retrieve this column in a more standard and readable way (for example June 4, 2001 09:59 am). You can achieve this by using MySQL's date and time functions. MySQL allows you to use simple date formatting functions or the more powerful date_format() function.

Most of MySQL's date and time functions are covered here. For a complete list of these functions see http://mysql.com/documentation/mysql/ bychapter/manual_Reference.html#Date_and_time_functions.

Simple date formatting functions

Several functions return basic information from a TIMESTAMP or other date/time column. For example, if you need to get the day of the week from the timestamp, you can use the dayname() function.

```
mysql> SELECT order_id, dayname(time_of_order) as 'Order Time'
    -> FROM orders
    -> WHERE order_id <= 2;
+----------+------------+
| order_id | Order Time |
+----------+------------+
|        1 | Saturday   |
|        2 | Saturday   |
+----------+------------+
2 rows in set (0.50 sec)
```

Similarly, if I want to get the name of the month, I can use the monthname() function.

```
mysql> SELECT order_id, monthname(time_of_order) as 'Order Time'
    -> FROM orders
    -> WHERE order_id <= 2;
+----------+------------+
| order_id | Order Time |
+----------+------------+
|        1 | September  |
|        2 | September  |
+----------+------------+
```

Table 10-1 lists MySQL's simple date formatting functions.

Table 10-1 *MySQL's Simple Date/Time Formatting Functions*

Functions Name	Returned Value
dayofweek()	Weekday as an integer. Sunday=1, Monday=2, etc.
weekday()	Weekday as an integer. Monday=0, Tuesday=1, etc.
dayofmonth()	Day of the month, from 1 to 31
dayofyear()	Day of the year, from 1 to 366
month()	Month as an integer, from 1 to 12
dayname()	Name of the weekday
monthname()	Name of the month
quarter()	Quarter of the year as integer. From 1 to 4
week()	Week of the year as integer. From 1 to 53

Continued

Table 10-1 *Continued*

Functions Name	Returned Value
year()	Year as integer
yearweek()	Year and week as integer, in format YYYYWW
hour()	Hour as integer in military time (0 to 23)
minute()	Minute as integer, from 0 to 59
second()	Seconds as integer, from 0-59

Keep in mind that these functions can be used any place in your query, not just in the column list at the start of a SELECT. For example, if you want to find information on sales that took place on a specific day of the week or specific month, you can use one of the functions in Table 10-1 in a WHERE or GROUP BY clause. For example, if you want to find the total number of orders that took place on Wednesdays during September, you can use a query like this:

```
mysql> SELECT count(*) as 'Total Orders' FROM orders
    -> WHERE dayname(time_of_order)='Wednesday' and
    -> monthname(time_of_order)='January';
+--------------+
| Total Orders |
+--------------+
|            2 |
+--------------+
1 row in set (0.00 sec)
```

Or, if you want to do a bit of comparison, you can find out how many orders occurred on each day of the week — that it, how many orders you get on Mondays, Tuesdays, and so on — by using GROUP BY with the dayname() function:

```
mysql> SELECT dayname(time_of_order) as 'Day or Week',
    -> count(order_id) as 'Orders per Day'
    -> FROM orders
    -> GROUP BY dayname(time_of_order);
+-------------+----------------+
| Day or Week | Orders per Day |
+-------------+----------------+
| Monday      |              2 |
| Tuesday     |             23 |
| Wednesday   |             41 |
| Thursday    |             92 |
| Friday      |             76 |
| Saturday    |              8 |
| Sunday      |            132 |
+-------------+----------------+
```

Date functions and the GROUP BY **clause can be used together to analyze your information in all sorts of useful ways. Keep this in mind as you develop your applications.**

Although these functions are useful for obtaining simple pieces of information, they are not great for retrieving dates in complex formats. For example, suppose that you want to retrieve a TIMESTAMP in a format that looks something like this: "Tuesday April 24, 2001." You would have to use several of the above functions and hold them together with the concat() function (which combines — or *concatenates* — two or more strings into one). In addition, you would need to account for spaces in the result so that strings don't just run together. The resulting query, which you can see below, is very ugly.

```
SELECT order_id,
    concat(
        dayname(time_of_order),
        ' ',
        monthname(time_of_order),
        ' ',
        dayofmonth(time_of_order),
        ', ',
        year(time_of_order)
    )
    as 'Order Time'
FROM orders
```

In cases like this, it is far easier to use the date_format()function, which is the subject of the next section.

Using date_format()

The date_format() function can mimic all the formats available to the functions in Table 10-1. The date_format() function takes two arguments. The first argument is the date you wish to have formatted. Most often this is the name of the column that needs formatting. The second argument is the specific format of the date.

Choose the exact format by using the specifiers listed in Table 10-2.

Table 10-2 *Date_Format Specifiers*

Specifier	Meaning
'%M'	Month name ('January'..'December')
'%W'	Weekday name ('Sunday'..'Saturday')
'%D'	Day of the month with English suffix ('1st', '2nd', '3rd', etc.)
'%Y'	Year, numeric, 4 digits
'%y'	Year, numeric, 2 digits

Continued

Table 10-2   *Continued*

Specifier	Meaning
`'%X'`	Year for the week where Sunday is the first day of the week, numeric, 4 digits, used with '%V'
`'%x'`	Year for the week, where Monday is the first day of the week, numeric, 4 digits, used with '%v'
`'%a'`	Abbreviated weekday name ('Sun'.. 'Sat')
`'%d'`	Day of the month, numeric ('00'..'31')
`'%e'`	Day of the month, numeric ('0'..'31')
`'%m'`	Month, numeric ('01'..'12')
`'%c'`	Month, numeric ('1'..'12')
`'%b'`	Abbreviated month name ('Jan'..'Dec')
`'%j'`	Day of year ('001'..'366')
`'%H'`	Hour ('00'..'23')
`'%k'`	Hour ('0'..'23')
`'%h'`	Hour ('01'..'12')
`'%I'`	Hour ('01'..'12')
`'%1'`	Hour ('1'..'12')
`'%i'`	Minutes, numeric ('00'..'59')
`'%r'`	Time, 12-hour ('hh:mm:ss [AP]M')
`'%T'`	Time, 24-hour ('hh:mm:ss')
`'%S'`	Seconds ('00'..'59')
`'%s'`	Seconds ('00'..'59')
`'%p'`	'AM' or 'PM'
`'%w'`	Day of the week ('0'=Sunday..'6'=Saturday)
`'%U'`	Week ('0'..'53'), where Sunday is the first day of the week
`'%u'`	Week ('0'..'53'), where Monday is the first day of the week
`'%V'`	Week ('1'..'53'), where Sunday is the first day of the week. Used with '%X'
`'%v'`	Week ('1'..'53'), where Monday is the first day of the week. Used with '%x'
`'%%'`	A literal '%'

Put spaces between the specificers where necessary, and surround the entire format with single quotes. So to return the date values in a format that give reasonably compete date information, the following statement works very well:

```
mysql> SELECT order_id, date_format(time_of_order, '%W %M %d, %Y')
    -> FROM orders
    -> WHERE order_id <=2;
+----------+----------------------------------------------+
| order_id | date_format(time_of_order, '%W %M %d, %Y')   |
+----------+----------------------------------------------+
|        1 | Saturday September 22, 2001                   |
|        2 | Saturday September 22, 2001                   |
+----------+----------------------------------------------+
```

Notice that table also includes time specifiers that you can add to any output.

There are people who prefer to parse the values of timestamp **and** date **columns in their middleware applications. On the Internet, there are many custom functions that people have written to turn MySQL date formats into a more human-readable form. This is a simple matter of preference. If you'd rather manipulate date values in Perl or PHP, that's fine. I tend to think it's easier to use MySQL's built-in functions. Perl users can take a look at this CPAN module:** http://search.cpan.org/doc/TONKIN/MySQL-DateFormat-1.00/ DateFormat.pm; **and PHP users might look to this offering:** http://search. cpan.org/doc/TONKIN/MySQL-DateFormat-1.00/DateFormat.pm.

Calculating Date Ranges

**10 Min.
To Go**

You will find that calculating date ranges is essential in many tasks. You may want to create a report that calculates your e-commerce site's sales by day or month, or you may want to be able to punch up a Web page that tells you the activity on your site for the past 24 hours.

In MySQL, you can calculate a date by using plus and minus signs and indicating the period (year, hour, month, and so on) you want used in the calculation. The following example returns the date and time 24 hours prior to the query being run. Note that the now() function returns the current date and time:

```
mysql> SELECT now() - INTERVAL 24 hour;
+--------------------------+
| now() - INTERVAL 24 hour |
+--------------------------+
| 2001-04-23 13:00:06      |
+--------------------------+
```

In this code, I have indicated that I want to subtract from the current date/time (with the minus sign), and then I use the keyword INTERVAL to indicate exactly what I want to subtract. I chose the hour option, but there are several other intervals you can choose from. Table 10-3 shows the other intervals you can use in MySQL date calculations, their meanings, and the exact format you need to apply in the calculation.

Table 10-3   *Date_add() Operators*

type	Meaning	Expected* Format
SECOND	Seconds	SECONDS
MINUTE	Minutes	MINUTES
HOUR	Hours	HOURS
DAY	Days	DAYS
MONTH	Months	MONTHS
YEAR	Years	YEARS
MINUTE_SECOND	Minutes and seconds	MINUTES:SECONDS
HOUR_MINUTE	Hours and minutes	HOURS:MINUTES
DAY_HOUR	Days and hours	DAYS HOURS
YEAR_MONTH	Years and months	YEARS-MONTHS
HOUR_SECOND	Hours, minutes,	HOURS:MINUTES:SECONDS
DAY_MINUTE	Days, hours, minutes	DAYS HOURS:MINUTES
DAY_SECOND	Days, hours, minutes, seconds	DAYSHOURS:MINUTES:SECONDS

If from the orders table you wanted the number of sales from the previous day, week, month, and year, you can use the following queries, respectively.

```
#get sales from the previous 24 hours
SELECT count(*) as 'Number of Sales'
FROM orders
WHERE time_of_order > (now() - interval 24 hour);

#get sales from the previous 1 month
SELECT count(*) as 'Number of Sales'
FROM orders
WHERE time_of_order > (now() - interval 1 month);

#get sales from the previous 1 year
SELECT count(*) as 'Number of Sales'
FROM orders
WHERE time_of_order > (now() - interval 1 year);
```

In addition, you can use any of the formats in Table 10-3 to calculate dates based on more detailed criteria. To find the date and time one day, two hours, three minutes, and four seconds from the current moment, use the following:

```
SELECT now() + interval '1:2:3:4' day_second;
```

The result of a date calculation can be formatted using the functions listed in Table 10-1 or with the date_format() function. To use calculations with date_format(), the result of the calculation needs to be the first argument given to the function; the second argument is the format. For example:

```
select date_format(now() + interval '1:2:3:4' day_second, '%W %M %d,
%Y');
```

Using these date range calculations along with the date/time functions and the GROUP BY clause, you can analyze data based on very specific temporal criteria (which should be very helpful if you're ever recruited by Star Fleet Academy).

Done!

REVIEW

In this session, you learned how to format date/time columns and how to calculate date time ranges. You saw how simple date and time information can be retrieved with a single function and how more complex dates can be formatted using the date_format() function and the specifiers in Table 10-2. Now that you know how to work with dates in MySQL, you can start using date functions with the other querying techniques you have learned. For example, consider the power you'll have at your disposal when you use date functions with GROUP BY and aggregate functions. You'll be able to get your hands on all kinds of statistical information based on date ranges.

QUIZ YOURSELF

1. Using the simple date/time functions, how can you query the orders table of the store database so that the time_or_order column returns only the number of the week the row was most recently updated? (See "Simple date formatting functions.")

2. What MySQL function would you use to combine the results of two simple date functions into a single string? (See "Simple date formatting functions.")

3. What combination of date_format() specifiers would create a result with the following format: YYYY-MM-DD HH-MM-SS (am|pm); for example (2001-11-31 09:31:31 am)? (See "Using date_format().")

4. What query would retrieve rows from the items table that were altered 25 days, 8 hours, and 7 minutes prior to the time you ran the query? (See "Calculating Date Ranges.")

5. Write a query that uses date functions and a GROUP BY clause to find out the number of items sold in each month. (See "Simple date formatting functions.")

PART

II

Saturday Morning
Part Review

1. What command lists all tables within a database?
2. What command lists all databases in a MySQL installation?
3. What keyword in an ALTER statement indicates that a new column should be the first column in the table?
4. In what circumstances would you use MODIFY in an ALTER statement??
5. What characters need to be escaped in order to work properly with INSERT statements?
6. REPLACE is a combination of what two SQL statements?
7. What phrase in a WHERE clause would return only rows where a field contains a NULL value?
8. For table types where DROP TABLE doesn't work, how can you delete tables?
9. What LIMIT clause would return only the first five rows in the result of a SELECT?
10. What LIMIT clause would return the next five rows?
11. What clause other then WHERE is useful for finding columns that could be equal to a set of values?
12. What keywords in an ORDER BY statement determine whether the result is returned in ascending or descending order?
13. What punctuation marks allow you to group portions of a WHERE clause?
14. When do you want to use an OUTER JOIN instead of an equi-join?
15. OUTER JOINS are used to replace what SQL operation commonly found in an SQL server but is absent from MySQL?
16. What operation joins two tables with nearly identical columns?
17. What are the values passed to a function known as?
18. What is the difference between WHERE and HAVING when used in a GROUP BY?
19. What function returns the name of the month from a TIMESTAMP column?
20. What date_format() specifier returns the name of the month from a TIMESTAMP column?
21. What date calculation interval works on days, hours, and minutes?

PART

III

Saturday Afternoon

Session 11

Other MySQL Functions

Session 12

Beyond LIKE: Using Regular Expressions and FULLTEXT Indexes

Session 13

Transactions with MyISAM and BDB Tables

Session 14

Using InnoDB and Gemini Tables

Session 15

Working with MySQL and PHP

Session 16

MySQL and PHP: Best Practices

Other MySQL Functions

Session Checklist

✔ Using flow control functions

✔ Using cryptographic functions

✔ Using string functions

✔ System information functions

✔ Other important MySQL functions

**30 Min.
To Go**

This is the third and final session on MySQL functions. The functions you saw in the previous two sessions offer processing power that you'd probably expect from a tool that stores and processes data. If you think about it, it would be kind of silly if a data processing engine didn't offer something like the sum() and count() functions. Even if I didn't cover these functions in the book, you'd probably assume that this could be done, and you'd search the manuals for a way to accomplish the task.

But this session covers at least a few functions that you may not expect. That's not to say the functions in this session aren't useful — they've very useful, in fact.

Using Flow Control Functions

Say I wanted a listing of all users and the states in which they live. As I showed in Session 8, this requires an outer join.

```
mysql> SELECT fname, lname, state
    -> FROM users
    -> LEFT JOIN addresses ON users.user_id=addresses.user_id;
```

```
+--------+-----------+-------+
| fname  | lname     | state |
+--------+-----------+-------+
| Jon    | Doe       | NY    |
| Ed     | Fromlin   | CA    |
| Elliot | Krug      | GA    |
| Jay    | Greenspan | CA    |
| Willy  | Krug      | NULL  |
+--------+-----------+-------+
```

This is fine, but let's say that in an application I want to show the state when a value existed, but write out the word "unknown" when the value is null. I'd have to branch my code like so:

```
run query against mysql
print fname, lname
if state is not null
    print state
if state is null
    print "unknown"
```

There's nothing wrong with writing code like this, but MySQL's flow control functions make it unnecessary.

Using ifnull()

In the previous example, I could use the ifnull() function. ifnull() takes two arguments. The function tests the first argument to see if it is null. If it is not null, the value of the first argument is returned. If it *is* null, the value in the second argument is returned. So I would re-write the previous query like so:

```
mysql> SELECT fname, lname, ifnull(state, 'unknown') as state
    -> FROM users
    -> LEFT JOIN addresses ON users.user_id=addresses.user_id;
+--------+-----------+---------+
| fname  | lname     | state   |
+--------+-----------+---------+
| Jon    | Doe       | NY      |
| Ed     | Fromlin   | NY      |
| Elliot | Krug      | GA      |
| Jay    | Greenspan | CA      |
| Willy  | Krug      | unknown |
+--------+-----------+---------+
```

Notice that I used an alias for the function. If I did not, the third column in the table would have a heading of ifnull(state, 'unknown'). That kind of column name would be very difficult to work with in your applications.

Using if()

The if() function is similar to ifnull() but can test a wider variety of conditions. The if() function takes three arguments. The first argument needs to be a condition. This can be any mathematical or string operator — it can even be a LIKE phrase. The function will return the second argument if the condition is true. It will return the third argument if the condition evaluates as false.

Let's say that I want to offer a 20 percent discount on all books in my items_for_sale table. The basic query that returns all items for sale, including the product name, requires an equi-join and looks like this:

```
mysql> SELECT product_name, format, price
    -> FROM products, items_for_sale
    -> WHERE products.product_id=items_for_sale.product_id;
+----------------------------+------------+-------+
| product_name               | format     | price |
+----------------------------+------------+-------+
| MySQL Weekend Crash Course | book       | 19.95 |
| PHP for the Web            | Whitepaper | 12.99 |
| MySQL Weekend Crash Course | book       | 49.95 |
+----------------------------+------------+-------+
```

To give a 20 percent discount on books, I use the if() function. If the format column equals 'book', I'll give the discount; otherwise, it will be full price.

```
mysql> SELECT product_name, format, if(format='book', price * .8, price) as price
    -> FROM products, items_for_sale
    -> WHERE products.product_id=items_for_sale.product_id;
+----------------------------+------------+-------+
| product_name               | format     | price |
+----------------------------+------------+-------+
| MySQL Weekend Crash Course | book       | 15.96 |
| PHP for the Web            | Whitepaper | 12.99 |
| MySQL Weekend Crash Course | book       | 39.96 |
+----------------------------+------------+-------+
```

When should you use if() and ifnull() in your queries instead of in the programming language that you use to build your application? It's a matter of personal preference. When the circumstances are as simple as the those shown in these examples, you're probably better of saving a few lines of code and doing the work in the query. However, if you have to nest multiple functions within your if() function, you're probably better off doing the work in programming language, where that kind of code is easier to read.

Using Cryptographic Functions

**20 Min.
To Go**

In the users table, it's quite possible that I'd want to store some sensitive information, such as credit card numbers. If this were the case, I'd want to take a lot of security precautions. For starters, I need to make sure that each user has a password to be reasonably sure that the user is who he or she claims to be.

You can simply add a column that stores the password value without any encryption and leave it at that. But there's a big potential problem. If you are using a shared server or shared database, a lot of people may have access to those passwords. Even if the server belongs only to your company, you want to protect passwords from both immoral employees and possible hackers.

password() and md5()

Using a one-way algorithm is the best way to make sure no one can figure out what a password is. A *one-way algorithm* scrambles a string in a way that it can never be descrambled. So even if someone manages to hack into your server, there's no way that person will be able to figure out what the original password is. These algorithms process the same string in the same way every time. There are two one-way algorithm functions that you can use for passwords: password() and md5().

password() creates a 16-character alphanumeric string. For example, when you enter a new user into the users_test table, make sure to run the password string through the password() function:

```
INSERT INTO users_test (fname, lname, email, psswd)
VALUES ('Jay', 'Greenspan', 'jay@trans-city.com', password('jpass1!'));
```

Here's the actual data that was inserted:

```
+--------+-----------+--------------------+------------------+
| fname  | lname     | email              | psswd            |
+--------+-----------+--------------------+------------------+
| Jay    | Greenspan | jay@trans-city.com | 73b3f5c94f1e4dda |
```

In your application, where users log in, make sure that you use the password() function in a SELECT statement that verifies the user. In my application, I'd run a query making sure the e-mail and password combination are correct.

```
SELECT *
FROM users_test
WHERE email='jay@trans-city.com' and
psswd=password('jpass1!');
```

If the query returns a row, the user has passed the test. If not, make the person try again.

MySQL also offers the md5() function. The md5 algorithm upon which this function is based returns a 64-character alphanumeric string. This algorithm is well-known and has been implemented in most common programming languages. Feel free to use md5() in place of password() if you feel there is any advantage.

encode() and decode()

The encode() function takes two arguments, the string you want encrypted and the *salt*. The salt is an arbitrary string that specifies how the initial string will be encrypted. In order to decrypt, you need to specify the same salt. Unlike password() and md5(), encode() does not create a string; it creates a binary object, something more like a digital image than a string. So the value created by encode() must go into a column that supports binary objects, such as text.

The decode() function also takes two arguments: the string to be decoded and the salt. For example, to insert an encoded value, you need a table that can support a binary object, like the psswd column below:

```
CREATE TABLE test_table(
    fname char(25) not null,
    lname char(25) not null,
    psswd text not null
)
```

Then to insert an encrypted value (say, a password), use an INSERT like this:

```
INSERT into test_table (fname, lname, psswd) values ('Jay', 'Greenspan',
encode('mypass', 'mysalt'))
```

Now, to run a query that checks if a value encrypted by these parameters exists in the database, use

```
SELECT fname, lname FROM test_table WHERE decode(psswd,
'mysalt')='mypass';
```

Using String Functions

Most people reading this book will end up writing applications that interact with MySQL in languages with strong text-processing abilities. Perl, PHP, and other languages used to create Web sites were designed to make string manipulation easy. For this reason, I don't imagine you will use MySQL's string manipulation too often. But it's good to know that these functions exist, in case you need them.

There are more string functions in MySQL than I can cover here; check the MySQL manual for a complete list.

ucase() and lcase()

The ucase() and lcase() functions convert strings to all uppercase and lowercase characters, respectively, and take a single argument. For example, if I want to make passwords case-insensitive and have all alphabetic characters evaluated as lowercase, I can use the following in my query:

```
password(lcase('Password String'))
```

left() and right()

The left() and right() functions take two arguments and return either the left-most or right-most characters in a string. The first argument is the string to be operated upon; the second is the number of characters you want returned.

For example, if I were writing an administrative page that lists all items in the `products` table within an HTML table, I may not want the entirety of the `product_description` column printed. The first 25 characters will give me a good enough idea of what I can expect.

```
mysql> SELECT product_name, left(product_description, 25) as description
    -> FROM products;
+-----------------------------------+---------------------------+
| product_name                      | description               |
+-----------------------------------+---------------------------+
| MySQL Weekend Crash Course        | A quick but complete intr |
| PHP for the Web                   | A technical introduction  |
| MySQL/PHP Database Applications   | A guide to this great ope |
+-----------------------------------+---------------------------+
```

concat()

You saw the `concat()` function briefly in the last session. It is quite useful in many occasions. `concat()` takes an arbitrary number of arguments — that is, any number. It concatenates the strings, meaning that it appends one string onto the end of another. For example, in the previous example, I may want to add a set of ellipses onto the end of the 25-character string to make it clear in the output that there is more to that particular field. So I'd concatenate the periods onto the end of the string:

```
mysql> SELECT product_name, concat(left(product_description, 25), '...')
    -> as description
    -> FROM products;
+-----------------------------------+------------------------------+
| product_name                      | description                  |
+-----------------------------------+------------------------------+
| MySQL Weekend Crash Course        | A quick but complete intr... |
| PHP for the Web                   | A technical introduction ... |
| MySQL/PHP Database Applications   | A guide to this great ope... |
+-----------------------------------+------------------------------+
```

There's one technique you can use with `concat()` that is very useful, and a little unexpected. Imagine that you had a series of domains listed in a table in your database. Something like the following:

```
+-----------+
| domains   |
+-----------+
| yahoo.com |
| wired.com |
| mysql.com |
+-----------+
```

These are base domains, and you don't want any of these repeated. If you consider adding another row to this table, you first have to make sure that the new entry isn't part of the same base domain (so you don't want "mail.yahoo.com" or "investing.wired.com"). To protect yourself, before running an INSERT, run a SELECT to make sure there are no problems. To get the right information from this SELECT, add a wildcard character on the beginning of each column value. This is done with concat(). For example:

```
mysql> SELECT * FROM test_table
    -> WHERE 'mail.yahoo.com' LIKE concat('%', domains);
+------------+
| domains    |
+------------+
| yahoo.com  |
+------------+
```

ltrim()/rtrim()/trim()

Sometimes when users enter information via in an application, they inadvertently include spaces either before or after the string they typed. These functions strip spaces. ltrim() and rtrim() each take a single argument and remove spaces from the start and end of a string, respectively.

The trim() function is a bit more involved. If trim() is used with only a single argument, both leading and trailing spaces are removed from the string. It can also be used to remove arbitrary strings from either the start, the end, or both the start and end of a string. It takes the form:

```
trim([BOTH | LEADING | TRAILING] [string_to_strip] FROM string)
```

The string_to_strip portion can be any string you want removed from the data and can be a single character or multiple characters. For example, to remove the letter "x" from the start of a column named my_column, you can use the following:

```
trim(LEADING 'x' FROM my_column)
```

The trim() functions, while useful, probably won't turn up in your applications all that often. You should make sure your data is fit for insertion into your database in your applications before your database ever encounters it.

10 Min.
To Go

System Information Functions

MySQL offers a few functions that can help you keep track of how you are using the database server.

The database() function returns the name of the database that you have chosen to work with when you execute the USE command. It takes no arguments.

```
mysql> select database();
+------------+
| database() |
+------------+
| store      |
+------------+
```

The user() function returns the name used to log in to MySQL. Notice that in the following command both the username and the host name are indicated. You see why this is so important in Session 20.

```
mysql> select user();
+----------------+
| user()         |
+----------------+
| root@localhost |
+----------------+
```

The version() function lets you know which release of MySQL you are working with. This information can be especially helpful if you are working with an ISP or other host and need to know the exact abilities of your version of MySQL.

```
mysql> SELECT version();
+-----------+
| version() |
+-----------+
| 3.23.39   |
+-----------+
```

Other Important MySQL Functions

There are two other functions I want to mention; they're quite important but don't fit easily to any of the categories mentioned previously.

Using last_insert_id()

As you can see throughout the tables in my example database, the auto_increment column is very handy. It gets you a unique value with no fuss at all. However, auto_increments can present a slight problem because the value of the primary key is only known *after* an insert has taken place. So, immediately after inserting data into a row, you won't know what the primary key is.

You can retrieve the most recent auto_increment value by running the last_insert_id() function. You can simply run SELECT last_insert_id(). In PHP, the last_insert_id() has been mapped to a native PHP function, mysql_insert_id(). In the psuedo-code below, you can see how handy this function can be.

```
// page for inserting new and editing existing rows in the user table
if user_id exists and the edit button has been pressed
    run UPDATE query based on the user_id
if user_id does not exist and the edit button has been pressed
    run INSERT query
    get primary key via last_insert_id()
run SELECT query to get row data based on user_id primary key
Display forms with current data
```

You may think that instead of using msyql_insert_id(), you can just use the max() function to get the highest value from a column after an INSERT. This is not the case. MySQL is a multi-threaded database, meaning that several clients can work on the data simultaneously. If two threads run INSERTs nearly simultaneously, it's possible that the value of max() would actually belong to another client. The last_insert_id() is thread-specific, so you can be sure the value you get is the one you're after.

Using rand()

The rand() function returns a random number between 0 and 1. You can supply a single argument (an integer) as a seed value for the random number generator. But it is rarely used for the purpose of generating a random number. This function is most frequently used in the ORDER BY clause when you want the results of a query to be in a randomized order. For example, if you were running a sweepstakes and you wanted to get two random rows from the users table, you can run the following query:

```
SELECT * FROM users ORDER BY rand() LIMIT 2
```

Done!

REVIEW

At this point, you've learned most of what you need to know to deliver applications with MySQL serving data. In this session you saw how to apply many of MySQL's functions. Starting with the flow control functions, you learned how you can cut down on branching in your code by using conditional statements within your SQL statements. Then you saw how cryptographic functions can be used to ensure that key information such as passwords are not more available than they should be. Then you saw some of the string manipulation and system information functions. At the end of the session, you saw how rand() and last_insert_id() offer needed functionality.

QUIZ YOURSELF

1. When using the ifnull() function, what happens when the value for this first argument is not null? (See "Using ifnull().")
2. How is the value returned by encode different from those returned by password() and md5()? (See "Using Cryptographic Functions.")
3. Using trim() write a function that would remove leading and trailing question marks from the string "???mystring???. (See "ltrim()/rtrim()/trim().")
4. The last_insert_id() function maps to what native PHP function? (See " Using last_insert_id().")
5. What clause, when used with rand(), would ensure that only one random row was returned by a query? (See "Using rand().")

SESSION

12

Beyond LIKE: Using Regular Expressions and FULLTEXT Indexes

Session Checklist

✔ Using regular expressions

✔ Using FULLTEXT indexing

**30 Min.
To Go**

So far, you've seen some fairly sophisticated techniques for retrieving and manipulating information from MySQL. You've seen how to use the WHERE clause to restrict the results returned by a SELECT, and you saw how the LIKE predicate can use wildcard characters for more generalized searching. But LIKE and its wildcard characters are limited. However, times may arise when you need more powerful text searching functionality.

If you have a background in Perl, PHP, or even JavaScript, you probably have worked with regular expressions. And if you have, you may want to just skim the first portion of this section to see how to apply regular expression syntax to MySQL. If you haven't, this is as good a time as any to learn this topic. Chances are, you won't be using regular expression too often with MySQL, but you will use them frequently in your applications that interact with MySQL.

In addition to regular expressions, MySQL offers another way to run sophisticated text searches: FULLTEXT indexing. You see how to work with this feature later in this session.

Using Regular Expressions

In my products table, I have a list of all products along with a description. The description can be quite long and may contain some really important information. If I have only 10, 20, or 50 records in the table, I can easily read through the records to see what I have, and if I needed to do programmatic searches, the LIKE clause is usually just fine. But now consider this dilemma: I need to search through the product_description column to find occasions where "MySQL" appears in the description along with "PHP," "Perl," or "Java." I can write a query like this:

```
SELECT * FROM products
WHERE product_description LIKE '%Mysql%PHP%' or
product_description LIKE '%Mysql%Perl%' or
product_description LIKE '%Mysql%Java%'
```

But this is rather inelegant and lengthy. It is much cleaner to express all of my needs in one string. More importantly, LIKE will get me only so far. For example, say I want to return rows where product_description contains "MySQL" and a set of versions in the 3.x family — anything from 3.22.01 to 3.23.41. The LIKE clause and simple wildcards leave no way to address this sort of situation. The best I can do with LIKE is something like '%MySQL 3.%', and this would return more rows than you'd want.

Regular expressions provide a means for very sophisticated pattern matching. As you will see in this session, regular expressions can match about any string you'd want to find.

 If you're used to working with a language like Perl or PHP, you are probably accustomed to not only matching but parsing strings with the help of regular expressions. You won't be parsing string with regular expressions in MySQL or any other database server. Those tasks are best conducted in your applications.

Regular expression basics

You indicate that you want to use regular expressions in MySQL with the REGEXP clause. You use this clause just as you do LIKE, in this manner:

```
SELECT * from products
WHERE product_description REGEXP 'regular_expression_string'
```

First you indicate the string you want to match (above, the product_description field), the keyword REGEXP, and the regular expression string.

You will construct the string using the wildcard characters, character classes, and other methods that you learn later in this session, but the most basic matching elements in regular expressions are literal characters. For example,

```
SELECT * from products
WHERE product_description REGEXP 'MySQL'
```

matches any row where product_description contains a "MySQL" anywhere in the field. The preceding is effectively the same as

```
SELECT * from products
WHERE product_description LIKE '%MySQL%'
```

Note that if I didn't include the first % in the LIKE predicate, the query would match only those rows where "MySQL" are the first characters in the field.

Special characters

**20 Min.
To Go**

There are several characters that have special meaning in regular expressions. A good example is the asterisk (*), which means "zero or more of the previous character." So the regular expression string "ba*ll" matches "ball," "baal," "baaal," "baaaaaaaal," and "bll." Table 12-1 shows all regular expression special characters. Note that to match any of these literally, you must first escape the character with a backslash. So to match an asterisk in a regular expression, use '*'.

Table 12-1   *Regular Expression Special Characters*

Character	Meaning	Example
*	zero or more of preceding character or class	"ba*d" matches "bad," "baad," and "bd"
+	one or more of preceding character or class	"ba+d" matches "bad," "baaad," but not "bd"
?	zero or one of the preceding character or class	"ba?d" matches "bad" and "bd"
. (period)	matches an character	"b.d" matches "bad," "bod," and "b d"
^	matches the start of a string	"^bad" matches "bad" but not "bbad"
$	matches the end of a string	"bad$" matches "bad" but not "bad dog"

One combination of these characters appears quite frequently: .* (a dot followed by an asterisk). The combination means "any number of characters." The following queries are identical:

```
SELECT * FROM products
WHERE product_description LIKE 'MySQL%"

SELECT * FROM products
WHERE product_description REGEXP '^MySQL.*'
```

In the second query, the carat (Shift+6) indicates the start of the string, so if "MySQL" does not occupy the first characters of the product_description field, this expression tests false. Also, note that in the second query, the .* serves little purpose because MySQL would match any field that started with "MySQL" regardless of the characters that came after it. The .* combination would serve a purpose, however, if there were more characters that needed to be matched by the regular expression. You'll see examples of this shortly.

Character classes

Character classes provide a way to indicate a set of characters. In the example I described earlier, where I want to match any version of MySQL from 3.22.01 to 3.23.41, I need to be fairly flexible. After the literal string "MySQL," in spots, I need to match periods and digits. For digits, I need a way of indicating that a character should match any member of a set (that is 0, 1 ,2, 3, 4, 5, 6, 7, 8, and 9). These sets are known as *character classes*.

Character classes go within brackets. You can assign any character to a class. If I wanted to match "Jay" in the fname column where the first letter could be either upper- or lower-case, I'd need a class that contained both case options: '[Jj]ay'.

Another option is to use ranges within character classes. To include all lowercase letters, use the range a-z. For all uppercase letters, A-Z, and for all numeric characters, 0-9. If you want to match all alphanumeric characters, you can put the following within a class:

```
[a-zA-Z0-9]
```

To match "MySQL 3.1" to "MySQL 3.9," I'd use the following regular expression string: "MySQL 3\.[0-9]". Note that the backlash escapes the period, letting the regular expression handler know I'm looking for a literal period, not any single characters. In addition to these ranges, MySQL has several predefined character classes, as listed in Table 12-2.

Table 12-2   *Regular Expression Character Classes*

Class Name	Meaning	Equivalent
alpha	matches all alphabetic characters	[a-zA-Z]
lower	matches any lowercase character	[a-z]
upper	matches any uppercase character	[A-Z]
digit	matches any digit	[0-9]
alnum	matches any alphanumeric characters	[a-zA-Z0-9]
space	matches any white space (blanks, tabs, newlines)	
punct	any punctuation mark	
graph	any printable characters, except space	
print	any printable characters, including space	
cntrl	any non-printable character	

Colons and brackets must first surround these pre-defined class names. So, you'd use something like [:punct:]. The syntax of the pre-defined cases gets quite messy, as these classes themselves must be placed within a class. For example, if you want to match any punctuation mark or the letter "a," you have to use the following:

```
[[:punct:]a]
```

Or, to match only punctuation, use

```
[[:punct:]]
```

10 Min.
To Go

Expressing "Not"

In Table 12-1, you saw that the carat mark (^) means "start of a string." Well, confusingly enough, the carat mark has another meaning as well. If the carat appears in a regular expression's character class, it means "must not include." So the regular expression j[^a]y says "match a literal letter 'j', any character that is not an 'a', and then a literal 'y'; the expression j[^a]y will match "joy" and "jiy" but not "jay."

If you want to match a non-numeric character, you can use either of the following expressions: [^0-9] or [^[:numeric:]].

An Example: Matching an HTML anchor

With the techniques you've learned so far, you can do some fairly sophisticated matching. For example, say you want to return rows where the product_description column of the products table contains an HTML link, something like:

```
<a href="http://www.mysql.com">
```

For starters, I'd want to match the literal string that will start such a tag:

```
<a
```

Because HTML rendering engines (browsers) deal flexibly with white space, I want to be flexible on what goes between the "a" and the "href." I'll allow for one or more space characters:

```
<a[[:space:]]+
```

Now I'll add the literal "href" and the equals sign. However, it's possible that one space will occur on either side of the equals sign. So I need to account for zero or one space characters on either side of the equal sign:

```
<a[[:space:]]+href ?= ?
```

Now you have to match the quote sign just before the URL. This can be either a single quote or a double quote, so those two characters must be put into a character class. The quotes are also optional characters, so I'll need to account for occasions when they exist and when they don't (using the question mark). This gets a little tricky, because if you're running this regular expression in a query, the regular expression string will be enclosed in quotes — either double quotes or single quotes. In the query you will need to let MySQL know that the quote character within the character class does not delimit the regular expression string. It must be treated as a literal and therefore must be escaped. In the following query, I surrounded the entire regular expression with single quotes, so I had to escape the single quote in the character class:

```
SELECT ... REGEXP '<a[[:space:]]+href ?= ?["\']?'
```

Continued

An Example: Matching an HTML anchor   *Continued*

At this point, you match all the alphanumeric characters that fall between the quotes:

```
<a[[:space:]]+href ?= ?["\']?[a-zA-Z0-9]+
```

Now I'll finish the regular expression by matching the closing quote and greater than sign and put the whole thing within a query:

```
SELECT product_description
FROM products
WHERE product_description

REGEXP'<a[[:space:]]+href ?= ?["\']?[a-zA-Z0-9]+["\']?>'
```

Multiple occurrences

In Table 12-1, you saw that the ?, +, and * characters indicate how many times a specific character must occur. Now that you know about character classes, it should be no surprise that these symbols can be applied to classes. To make sure I have a number that was at least one digit in length, I can use [0-9]+.

But while these symbols are helpful, at times more exact matching tools are required. You'll need a way, for example, to match either one or two characters. You do this with curly braces — {}. Within the braces you can include two numbers. The first indicates the minimum number of the previous character or class that should occur. The second indicates the maximum number of the previous character or class that should occur. For example, to match a one- or two-digit number, use [0-9]{1,2}.

In the curly braces, you can omit the second number, which tells the regular expression handler that there is no upper limit. So using [0-9]{1, } is exactly the same as [0-9]+.

With this information, you now have a way of matching all version of MySQL, from versions 3.22.01 to 3.23.41.

```
"MySQL 3\.2[23]\.[0-9]{1,2}"
```

Grouping characters

Now that I have a way to match specific versions of MySQL, I may want to make sure that I return rows that contain either "PHP" or "Perl." If I want to match just "PHP," I can augment the previous expression like so:

```
" MySQL 3\.2[23]\.[0-9]{1,2}.*PHP"
```

However, to match either "Perl" or "PHP," I need to put the groups of characters within parentheses and separate the different groups with the bar character (|). So to match "Perl" or "PHP," I'd use the following:

```
" MySQL 3\.2[23]\.[0-9]{1,2}.*(PHP|Perl)"
```

For more information on regular expressions in MySQL see the online manual: www.mysql.com/doc/R/e/Regexp.html.

Using FULLTEXT Indexing

Starting in version 3.23.23, MySQL offers FULLTEXT indexing, which provides a sophisticated and convenient way to conduct complex text searches in queries. In order to use FULLTEXT indexing, you need to learn some additional syntax for creating and conducting searches.

Creating FULLTEXT indexes

In order to make use of MySQL's FULLTEXT feature, you need to create a special type of index on your tables. This type of index can only be applied to varchar and text column types. In my store database, I may want to apply a FULLTEXT index to the product_description column. To do this, my CREATE TABLE statement would look like this:

```
CREATE TABLE products (
  product_id int(11) NOT NULL auto_increment,
  product_name varchar(75) NOT NULL default '',
  product_description text NOT NULL,
  PRIMARY KEY  (product_id),
  FULLTEXT(product_description)
) TYPE=MyISAM;
```

Or to change the existing products table, I'd run the following ALTER TABLE statement:

```
ALTER TABLE products add FULLTEXT(product_description);
```

Like all other indexes, FULLTEXT indexes can span more than one column. For example, if there was a second column you wanted to add to the FULLTEXT index with the ALTER TABLE statement, you can use a statement like the one below:

```
ALTER TABLE products add
FULLTEXT(product_description,product_other_column);
```

After you create a FULLTEXT index, you can run two types of searches against the index: a natural language search and a Boolean search.

Running natural language searches

A natural language search compares a string provided in a query against the indexed columns. MySQL goes through the indexed columns in each row and determines its *relevance*. Relevance is calculated by comparing the number of words the indexed columns and the proved string have in common. After this comparison is conducted, MySQL rates the relevance with a floating-point number. The higher the number, the greater the relevance.

To conduct a natural language search, you need to use the MATCH ... AGAINST ... syntax, as seen in the following example:

```
SELECT * FROM products
WHERE  MATCH (product_description) AGAINST('technical introduction');
```

When MATCH ... AGAINST is used in the WHERE clause, MySQL automatically returns rows in order, with the greatest relevance first.

You can also see the calculated relevance by including MATCH ... AGAINST in the column listing. For example:

```
mysql> SELECT product_name,
    -> match (product_description) against('technical introduction')
    -> as relevance
    -> from products;
+---------------------------------+------------------+
| product_name                    | relevance        |
+---------------------------------+------------------+
| MySQL Weekend Crash Course      |                0 |
| PHP for the Web                 | 0.64150596353055 |
| MySQL/PHP Database Applications  |                0 |
+---------------------------------+------------------+
```

You can use an ORDER BY statement or include the same MATCH ... AGAINST phrase in the WHERE clause to get these rows in order of the greatest relevance.

Using Boolean searches

Starting in version 4.0.1, MySQL supports Boolean searches against FULLTEXT indexes. With Boolean searches, you can easily determine what strings should or should not appear in query results. For example, the following query returns all rows where product_description contains "MySQL" but not "PHP."

```
SELECT product_name, product_description
WHERE match (product_description) against ('+MySQL -PHP' IN BOOLEAN MODE)
```

The plus sign indicates the following string must appear in matching rows. The minus sign indicates the following string must not appear in matching rows. In addition to the plus and minus signs, five other operators can be used with Boolean searches.

- < and >: Used to indicate increased or decreased importance of specific strings. For example '+MySQL +(>PHP <Perl)' matches all rows where the column contains MySQL and either PHP or Perl, but will rank those with PHP higher than those with Perl.

- (and): Used to group portions of a match phrase. Notice that parentheses were used with the previous example.

- * (asterisk): Has the same meaning as an asterisk in regular expressions: match zero or more characters.

Done!

REVIEW

In this session, you learned how regular expressions and FULLTEXT indexes can be used to match sophisticated and complex patterns. You saw that the LIKE predicate, while useful, does not offer enough power in all occasions. Then you saw how regular expressions make up for the limitations of LIKE predicate by offering character classes, multiple occurrences, and other features. You also saw that natural language and Boolean searches provide another method for string matching.

QUIZ YOURSELF

1. What keyword tells MySQL to run a regular expression comparison? (See "Regular expression basics.")
2. What are the two meanings of the carat (^) mark? (See "Special characters" and Expressing "Not.")
3. What predefined character class is equivalent to [0-9]? (See "Character classes.")
4. Using curly braces and numbers, how would you express the same meaning as the plus sign (+)? (See "Multiple occurrences.")
5. How would you write a regular expression that matches "jay" or "john"? (See "Grouping characters.")

Transactions with MyISAM and BDB Tables

Session Checklist

✔ Understanding potential dangers

✔ Understanding ACID properties

✔ Working with MyISAM tables

✔ Working with BDB tables

✔ Configuring BDB tables

**30 Min.
To Go**

At this point, you've learned just about everything you need to create MySQL-powered applications. And, if you're writing some small application for personal use, or if you're working with data that isn't especially sensitive, what you've learned so far should get you a long way. However, if you are working with vital data, you need to make sure that you interact with MySQL in a manner that ensures your data's integrity.

Understanding Potential Dangers

Remember that MySQL is a multi-threaded database server. Different threads can work on the same tables simultaneously. In the case of a Web-based application, it's possible that on a busy site, 50 or more users will be viewing, inserting, and altering data at the same time. This leads to some potentially tricky situations.

The problem

Consider the SQL statements needed to complete a new order. After a user goes through various pages and enters her name, address, and contact information, as well as the items she wants, several commands are required:

1. INSERT data into users table.
2. INSERT data into addresses table.
3. Check quantity of items in the inventory table with a SELECT.
4. Reduce quantity from inventory table by one.
5. INSERT data into orders table.
6. INSERT data into order_items table.

It may seem reasonable to simply run these commands serially in your application. But imagine what would happen if a power failure hit your database server between steps 5 and 6. You'd have a row in the orders table that had no associated rows in the order_items table. The information for that order is then incomplete.

There's also a potential problem between steps 3 and 4. With multiple threads working simultaneously, it's possible that two people can place an order for a book at nearly the same time. When I'm down to one copy of a book, the gap in time between steps 3 and 4 can leave a split second where one user is told that a book was available when in fact it is not.

Plus, if the inventory for an item is 0, I want all the preceding commands cancelled.

The usual solution: Transactions

Most databases solve this problem by implementing *transactions*. A transaction is comprised of a series of SQL statements. Within a transaction, you have a guarantee that either all the statements will be executed or none of them will. If you had the previous statements within a transaction, you wouldn't have to worry of a power failure between steps 5 and 6. You could be sure that none of these statements would be executed. You may lose data on an entire order, but you wouldn't be in a situation where the orders had no related rows in order_items.

But there's a little more to transactions than that, as you'll see in the next section.

Understanding the ACID Properties

A database that supports transactions must support four distinct properties. These are know by the acronym ACID. The properties are

- **Atomicity.** SQL statements will be executed as one unit. Either all the statements will be enacted completely, or none will be enacted at all.
- **Consistency.** Each transaction will transform the data from one consistent state to another. There will never be a case when your data is internally flawed.
- **Isolation.** Each transaction is conducted independently from others. The effects of transaction A are not visible to transaction B until transaction A is complete. If a transaction is not completed, the effects will not be seen by other transactions.
- **Durability.** When a transaction is complete, the changes are permanent. Even if the database crashes, the information from that transaction will be available and complete.

For a long time, the largest single reason developers avoided MySQL was because it lacked true ACID transaction support. However, that is no longer the case. In MySQL, transaction support is tied not so much to the server engine but to the type of table you choose for your data. If you remember back to Session 4, MySQL offers several table types and some of these (BDB, Gemini, and InnoDB) are transaction safe. In this session and the next, I describe the difference between these tables and show how they work with transactions.

A good first step is to see what table types are available to your server. To see what table types are available, look at MySQL's variables with the SHOW VARIABLES command. SHOW VARIABLES lists quite a few configurable properties, some of which you'll see later in this book. To see what table types are available, add a LIKE clause to SHOW VARIABLES: SHOW VARIABLES LIKE 'have%'. From the command-line client, you'll get a listing like this:

```
mysql> SHOW VARIABLES LIKE 'have%';
+---------------+----------+
| Variable_name | Value    |
+---------------+----------+
| have_bdb      | YES      |
| have_gemini   | NO       |
| have_innodb   | DISABLED |
| have_isam     | YES      |
| have_raid     | NO       |
| have_ssl      | NO       |
+---------------+----------+
```

On the server where I ran this command, I have access to MyISAM and BDB tables. Additionally, the DISABLED indicator lets me know that I can get InnoDB tables working if I make a couple of configuration tweaks. (I cover these in the next session.) If you use the NuSphere install, you'll have support for Gemini tables, and if you installed MySQL Max, you'll have BDB and InnoDB support. You can add support for different table types by downloading the source and recompiling MySQL with different configure flags. I discuss installation of different table types when I cover those tables.

> A lot of people end up deploying MySQL-powered applications on a server they don't control (like at an ISP. Make sure you check that your sever supports the tables you want to use in your application before you develop your application.

Working with MyISAM Tables

20 Min. To Go

MyISAM tables do not support ACID transactions. However, if you are hosting your application at an ISP, there's a chance that this will be the only table type available to you.

Applying table locks

You can get some of the functionality of transactions by using table locks. As you'll see in the coming sections, different MySQL tables have differing locking abilities.

MyISAM's locking abilities are fairly basic. You can obtain either a READ or a WRITE lock on an entire table or series of tables. A READ lock leaves a table in a state where other users (that is, threads) can run SELECT statements against the table, but cannot run INSERTs or UPDATEs. The syntax for a READ lock is

```
LOCK TABLES table_name READ;
```

A WRITE lock assumes that the current user is going to be making a change to a table and prevents other users from running any queries — SELECTS, INSERTS, UPDATES, DELETES — against the table.

If you want to see locks in action, you can open two copies of the MySQL command-line client. On a Unix machine, you need to open a second shell, and on Windows, you need another DOS window. In the first window, switch to the store database and run the following command:

```
LOCK TABLES users WRITE;
```

Then go to the second window and attempt to run a query, any query, against the users table. You'll see that the database does not respond. It just sits there. Now go back to the first windows and run the command:

```
UNLOCK TABLES;
```

Suddenly, the second window executes its query.

Using locks in applications

Listing 13-1 contains pseudo-code that shows how I'd likely structure a script that processes orders without transactions. I've provided a bit more detail than in the previous list. In this listing, I have not provided locks.

Listing 13-1   *Basic order processing code*

```
//assume user data are in a series of scalar variables
//assume items to include for the order are stored in
//an array
INSERT query into users table.
run last_insert_id() to get user_id
INSERT query into addresses table
INSERT into orders table
run last_insert_id() to get order_id
for each of the items in the order
    get quantity from the inventory table
    if quantity is > 0
        insert into order_items table
        update inventory table subtracting the ordered item
    elseif quantity = 0
        delete all items from order_items with current order_id
        delete item from orders table with current order_id
        update inventory table to replenish items now that this is
cancelled
        output error, telling of the inventory problem
if no inventory problem
    update orders table with the current order_id, adding the order_total
```

If ACID transactions were available, a lot of this code wouldn't really be necessary, as you will soon see. The major problem with this code is that, as it stands, I can't be absolutely sure that the quantity I get from the inventory table is reliable. I can't be sure that another thread won't grab the final copy of an item between the time I get the number in the inventory and the time of the insert into the order_items table that updates the inventory table.

To fix this with MyISAM tables, I'm going to apply a WRITE lock. A WRITE lock keeps any other threads from getting at the table, which saves all other threads the possibility of bad data. Other threads should be able to see the value only after I have updated the table. With the addition of locks, the listing looks like that shown in Listing 13-2.

Listing 13-2 *Orders page improved with table locks*

```
INSERT query into users table.
run last_insert_id() to get user_id
INSERT query into addresses table
INSERT into orders table
run last_insert_id() to get order_id
for each of the items in the order
    get write lock on inventory table
    get quantity from the inventory table
    if quantity is > 0
        insert into order_items table
        update inventory table subtracting the ordered item
        unlock tables
    elseif quantity = 0
        delete all items from order_items with current order_id
        delete item from orders table with current order_id
        update inventory table to replenish items now that this is
cancelled
        output error, telling of the inventory problem
if no inventory problem
    update orders table with the current order_id, adding the order_total
```

At this time, you may be thinking that locking an entire table is a bit of overkill. After all, only a few rows contain data that will be subject to change. For example, there may be hundreds of rows in the inventory table, but I really need only to isolate one row at a time. In fact, the other MySQL table types offer more granular levels of locking. A more specific locking mechanism is a key to transaction support — more on this later.

You may be wondering why, if you can use tables that support transactions, you should bother with MyISAM tables at all. The reason is because MyISAM tables are extremely fast for SELECTs. For tables where the primary actions will be INSERTs and UPDATEs (such as the order_items table) a table capable of transactions is a good choice and will be faster. However, for tables that will be used primarily with SELECT statements, MyISAM tables are a better choice.

10 Min.
To Go

Working with BDB Tables

Sleepycat Software, which does a lot of excellent open source database work, provided MySQL with its first transaction-capable table — the Berkeley DB, or BDB, table. If you installed MySQL-Max, you should see BDB table support when you run SHOW VARIABLES LIKE 'have%'. If you don't have support for BDB tables and want to use them, you need to reinstall MySQL. The easiest way to go about this to get MySQL Max from www.mysql.com. There are binaries for Windows and most UNIXs. Note that at the time of this writing, BDB tables did not work on MacOS X.

Creating BDB tables

To create BDB tables, you need to indicate that you want to in your CREATE table statement. For example:

```
CREATE TABLE my_table(
    col1 int not null primary key,
    col2 char(255)
) type=BDB
```

And you can change a MyISAM table to BDB with the ALTER TABLE statement.

```
ALTER TABLE my_table TYPE=BDB
```

Applying transactions

In just about all databases and table types, you can use the keywords BEGIN WORK, COMMIT, and ROLLBACK to signify different portions of a transaction. BEGIN WORK, as you can probably guess, indicates the start of a transaction. The SQL statements executed within a transaction will be available to other threads only after the COMMIT command has been executed. Alternatively, you indicate that you want all the actions within a transaction aborted by executing a ROLLBACK.

To see how this works, try this exercise. If you are working on Windows, open two DOS windows; if you're on Unix, open two shells. In each of them, start the MySQL command-line client.

In the first window, create a simple table, making sure to use a BDB table type.

```
mysql> CREATE TABLE my_table(
    ->     col1 int not null,
    ->     col2 char(255)
    -> ) type=BDB;
```

Following that, run the following three commands in the first window:

```
mysql> SET AUTOCOMMIT=0;
mysql> BEGIN WORK;
mysql> INSERT INTO foo (col1, col2) VALUES (1, 'my first value');
```

At this point, you can do a SELECT * FROM foo from both windows. In the first window, where you started the transaction, you see the inserted data in the table. But the second window doesn't respond. Now in the first window, run

```
mysql> COMMIT;
```

Immediately, the second window responds. The second thread was shielded from data from the transaction until it was complete. Now try this process again, but instead of executing COMMIT, run the following:

```
mysql> ROLLBACK;
```

When you run the ROLLBACK, the row created by the INSERT command is removed. The other threads were never aware of its existence.

> **By default, MySQL works in** AUTOCOMMIT **mode, meaning that all SQL commands are immediately made to the database. In order to use transactions, you'll need to turn off** AUTOCOMMIT **mode with the following command.**
>
> ```
> SET AUTOCOMMIT=0
> ```
>
> **If you fail to set** AUTOCOMMIT **to 0, each statement is treated as a transaction and committed immediately.**

Rewriting code using transactions

Now, take a look at Listing 13-3 to see how I improved the pseudo-code from Listing 13-2 by applying transactions.

Listing 13-3   *Orders page improved with table locks*

```
INSERT query into users table.
run last_insert_id() to get user_id
INSERT query into addresses table
BEGIN WORK
INSERT into orders table
run last_insert_id() to get order_id
for each of the items in the order
    get quantity from the inventory table
    if quantity is > 0
        insert into order_items table
        update inventory table subtracting the ordered item
    elseif quantity = 0
        set error variable
if error variable is not set
    update orders table with the current order_id, adding the order_total
    COMMIT
else
    ROLLBACK
```

The most obvious thing to notice here is that the code is a lot cleaner. There was no need to run the DELETE and UPDATE queries to get rid of unwanted rows. Remember that this method is also safer. Because BDB tables offer all the ACID properties (including the D for Durability), you can be sure that your data will be in a reasonable state even if there is a catastrophic disk failure or a power failure. If a backhoe goes through your power grid in the midst of this transaction, all of these statements will be rolled back.

Whereas MyISAM tables offered only table-level locking, BDB tables work with page-level locks. In the world of relational databases, "pages" are sets of rows. When running transactions, BDB can lock individual sets, leaving most rows unaffected by locks and ready for any queries you throw at them. In Session 14, you'll see yet another level of locking.

Configuring BDB Tables

There are a series of variables associated with BDB tables that you should be aware of. You can get a listing of these by running SHOW VARIABLES LIKE '%bdb%'. Table 13-1 shows some of the BDB-related variables.

Table 13-1 *BDB Configurable Options*

Variable	Meaning	Configuration Method
bdb_cache_size	RAM dedicated to holding rows and indexes	--set-variable bdb_cache_size=VALUE
bdb_max_lock	The maximum number of locks available. Locks take resources so by default BDB tables are limited to 10000 locks. If you get errors that locks are unavailable adjust this number	--set-variable bdb_max_lock=VALUE
bdb_home	default location of bdb tables	--bdb-home=/dir/to/tables
bdb_logdir	location of bdb log files	--bdb-log=/dir/to/log

Log files are extremely important and need to be placed carefully. Session 24 discusses logs in greater detail.

These variables, like all other configurable MySQL variables, can be set when starting the MySQL daemon. When starting MySQL, you normally run something simple like this from the `mysql/bin` directory:

```
shell> safe_mysqld &
```

But you can also indicate specific options by applying the flag noted in the Configuration Method column in Table 13-1. For example, if I needed 15,000 locks for my very busy server, I'd use the following at startup:

```
shell> safe_mysqld --set-variable=15000 &
```

In addition to these options, if you've installed MySQL with BDB support but end up not using BDB tables, you should start the server with the `--skip-bdb` option. This saves some resources that would be put toward BDB.

Done!

REVIEW

In this session, you learned the importance of transactions. You saw that without transactions, it is possible some threads will view inaccurate data. Additionally, you saw that without transactions, a crash can lead to a situation where your tables contain orphaned rows and inconsistent data. Then you went on to see how to address some problems associated with transactions with MyISAM tables. MyISAM tables don't support transactions, but you can prevent some data-integrity problems by applying locks. Then you saw how to work with one of MySQL transaction-capable tables: BDB. You learned the BEGIN WORK / COMMIT / ROLLBACK syntax and saw how to rewrite applications by making use of transactions.

QUIZ YOURSELF

1. What are the two potential dangers that lurk when applications don't use transactions? (See "Understanding Potential Dangers.")
2. What does each letter in the acronym ACID stand for? (See "Understanding the ACID Properties.")
3. What two methods of locking are available in MyISAM tables? (See "Applying table locks.")
4. What is the correct setting for AUTOCOMMIT for working with transactions? (See "Applying transactions.")
5. On starting the MySQL daemon how would you indicate that the sever should skip all BDB properties? (See "Configuring BDB Tables.")

Using Gemini and InnoDB Tables

Session Checklist

✔ Understanding row-level locking

✔ Using Gemini tables

✔ Using InnoDB tables

**30 Min.
To Go**

The table types examined in Session 13 are well designed and very useful. If you have a table that is almost always used for SELECTs, there's nothing better than MyISAM. For tables that make use of heavy INSERTs and UPDATEs — tables that are used in transactions — BDB tables works just fine. But in addition to BDB tables, MySQL has two other table types that offer ACID transaction properties. In fact, these tables are even more sophisticated than BDB tables in that they offer a finer level of locking.

In this session, I show you how to go about installing and using both Gemini and InnoDB tables. But before you get around to using these tables, you need to understand the locking mechanisms used by these table types. Note that if you installed MySQL from the binaries, RPMs, or source code, you will probably want to use InnoDB tables for your transactions, as these tables are pre-installed. If you used the NuSphere install, you will find the Gemini tables available to your system.

Understanding Row-Level Locking

Both Gemini and InnoDB offer row-level locking. If you remember back to Session 13, MyISAM tables offer only table-level locking, and BDB tables use page-level locking. Compared to these methods, there's a clear advantage to row-level locking. For example, consider a simple UPDATE statement that operates on a single row during the course of a transaction. Something like this:

```
UPADTE orders SET order_total=55.95 WHERE order_id=191
```

If the orders table were a MyISAM table, MySQL would internally apply a lock to the entirety of the orders table during the time it took to execute the UPDATE statement. This means that any other statements accessing this table — including SELECTs, INSERTs and UPDATEs that don't need access to this row — will be delayed until the above statement executes.

In a table that allows for row-level locking, MySQL would place a lock on only the row in orders where order_id=191. The lock would last the duration of a transaction — until the transaction is committed or rolled back. SELECT or other SQL statements working on the table that didn't access this row would not encounter a lock and therefore would execute immediately. You can probably imagine that in transactional environments, row-level locking is a great advantage. Because locks are so specific, actions are less likely to interfere with each other and therefore more statements can execute concurrently. Gemini and InnoDB implement row-level locking in different ways. You need to understand these implementations in order to write applications that properly use these tables.

Even if you plan on using InnoDB tables, please read through the sections on Gemini below. The explanation of InnoDB relies on definitions given during the discussion of Gemini tables.

Using Gemini Tables

20 Min.
To Go

Gemini tables were adapted for MySQL by NuSphere, which is a subsidiary of Progress Software. To install Gemini tables, you'll almost certainly want to use a version of the NuSphere installer. Aside from the installer that comes with this book, you can download a free version of the MySQL with Gemini from the NuSphere site (www.nusphere.com). I assume that you have used one of these installers rather than attempting to compile Gemini from source. Note that at the time of this writing, Gemini worked on a limited number of platforms, including Windows, Linux, and Solaris. Some potential users, such as those using OpenBSD or MacOS X, may be out of luck.

To check if Gemini is available on your MySQL server, check the system variables in the same way seen in the previous session. If it is not available, try reinstalling from the NuSphere installation disk.

```
mysql> SHOW VARIABLES LIKE '%have%';
+---------------+-------+
| Variable_name | Value |
+---------------+-------+
| have_bdb      | NO    |
| have_innodb   | No    |
| have_isam     | YES   |
| have_gemini   | YES   |
| have_symlink  | YES   |
| have_openssl  | NO    |
+---------------+-------+
```

The listing above shows that Gemini tables are available for use. In addition to the have_gemini variable, there are many configurable parameters for Gemini tables. You can get a list of these by running another query of system variables:

```
mysql> show variables like '%gemini%';
+--------------------------+--------+
| Variable_name            | Value  |
+--------------------------+--------+
| gemini_buffer_cache      | 128    |
| gemini_connection_limit  | 100    |
| gemini_io_threads        | 2      |
| gemini_log_cluster_size  | 32     |
| gemini_lock_table_size   | 4096   |
| gemini_lock_wait_timeout | 10     |
| gemini_recovery_options  | FULL   |
| gemini_spin_retries      | 1      |
| have_gemini              | YES    |
+--------------------------+--------+
```

If you're reading to deploy a large application that will make use of Gemini tables, you'll need to know what these variables mean. For that information, review the documentation that came with your NuShpere install. You can change any variable parameters at startup by including flags when starting the daemon. More likely, you'll be making changes to the my.cnf file. (You learn how to use the my.cnf file in Session 22.) For now, as you're getting to learn MySQL, spend the time for this session understanding the concepts that accompany Gemini and InnoDB and worry about configuration issues later.

Gemini tables use a two-phase transaction system. This may sound complicated, but all it means is that a piece of data is either committed or it is not. Within a transaction, until a INSERT, UPDATE, or DELETE is committed, the effect on the data will not be available to any other thread — and until such time as the data is committed, the thread conducting the update will maintain a lock on the rows being altered to prevent other threads from getting bad data. When the data is committed, the locks will be released, and the other threads will be able to use the data.

This is a fairly basic description, and it should make more sense when you understand the types of locks implemented by Gemini.

Share lock

When, during a transaction, a thread places a share lock on a row, all other threads will be able to read that row with SELECT statements, but they will not be able to alter the row with UPDATE or DELETE statements.

During transactions in Gemini tables, share locks are placed on rows that are the subject of SELECT statements. For example, if Thread 1 were to run the following statements at the start of a transaction, a share lock would be placed on a row:

```
SET AUTOCOMMIT=0
BEGIN WORK
SELECT * from orders_gemini WHERE order_id=191
```

Thread 2 can run another SELECT that accesses this row:

```
SELECT * from orders_gemini WHERE order_id BETWEEN 100 and 200
```

Conflict in the MySQL Development Community

At the time of the writing of this book, NuSphere, the company that creates the really nice MySQL installer and the Gemini table type, was involved in a legal dispute with MySQL AB, the Finnish company that originated MySQL and continues the development of the MySQL server engine. MySQL AB has a couple of grievances, including NuSphere's use of the mysql.org domain, which MySQL AB feels is in violation of a copyright agreement. The other area of disagreement concerns the GPL (GNU Public License), an open-source license intended to ensure that open source code remains open and free. MySQL AB feels that NuSphere has violated the GPL.

Things had gotten so acrimonious that when the MySQL 4.0 update was released, it was announced by MySQL AB that all Gemini hooks were removed from the code base. NuSphere then went about reinstalling them.

I point this out because as you get to know MySQL you may become aware of some enmity toward NuSphere in the development community. If you're a strong believer in open source licenses, you may want to look further into NuSphere's actions and decide for yourself whether or not you want to use their software. There's no doubt that the folks at MySQL AB would rather you use InnoDB when you have row-locking needs.

I have no opinions on the merits of either side's arguments. My only real thought on the matter is that the conflict is unfortunate, as I think that if these companies could work together, MySQL would become a stronger product.

But Thread 2 would be prevented from running the following statement until Thread 1 was either committed or rolled back:

```
UPADTE orders_gemini SET order_total=55.95 WHERE order_id=191
```

This type of lock makes a lot of sense. Often when a thread runs a SELECT, there's no reason to cut off other threads from read access to that row.

Exclusive lock

An exclusive lock cuts off all access to a row. When an exclusive lock is applied, no other threads will be able to read data from the row in question until the transaction that obtained the lock either commits or rolls back.

Within transactions, exclusive locks will be applied to all INSERT, UPDATE, and DELETE statements. So, for example, if one thread runs the following statements, no other thread will be able to execute any statements that access this row:

```
BEGIN WORK
UPADTE orders SET order_total=55.95 WHERE order_id=191
```

Again, this makes a lot of sense. Until the transaction performing the update is either committed or rolled back, the information in this row is unreliable — after all, the transaction can go either way.

Additionally, there may be cases when you need to get an exclusive lock when reading data with a SELECT statement. For example, if in my store database I had an inventory table that stored the number of items in stock for all items, when completing a sale I'd want to make sure I followed a process like the one shown in the following pseudo-code.

```
get all items selected for purchase
for each item
    check number in inventory
    if number in inventory > number purchased
        continue processing sale
    else if number in inventory < number purchased
        abort sale
        rollback all statements
        inform user that inventory is low
```

When it comes to checking the number in inventory, you need to be very careful. If you get the number with a standard SELECT, you will place a share lock only on the inventory information. As described earlier, the share lock allows other threads to view the data. But because you know that this number will almost certainly change, you're better off placing an exclusive lock on this row. That way, other threads do not risk getting an inventory number that is likely to be out of date in a matter of microseconds.

You can place an exclusive lock in a SELECT statement by adding the clause FOR UPDATE at the end of the SELECT statement. For example:

```
SELECT in_stock FROM inventory WHERE item_id=227 FOR UPDATE
```

Working with Gemini locks

So what does a Gemini table do when it encounters a lock? It waits. A lock, whether it's shared or exclusive, is released when a transaction is committed or rolled back. All other transactions that are prevented from accessing a row will wait until the locks are released. Keep in mind that transactions are a part of your applications and execute very, very quickly. So the wait is not going to slow down your applications.

How long will Gemini wait? This parameter is set in the gemini_lock_wait_timeout variable. The default value of this variable is 10 (meaning 10 seconds), but it can be changed at startup by setting the variable when starting the server daemon using something like

```
shell> mysqld set-variable gemini_lock_wait_timeout=5
```

To get an idea of how Gemini works with transactions and the different locks, try the following examples. First, open two copies of the command-line client on an installation that has Gemini available. In one client, create a simple table and insert some data.

```
mysql> CREATE TABLE gem_test (id int not null primary key auto_increment,
mysql> total int) type=gemini;
mysql> INSERT INTO gem_test (total) values (22), (33), (44);
```

Now in that same client, set AUTOCOMMIT to 0, start a transaction, and run a SELECT statement.

```
mysql> set AUTOCOMMIT=0;
mysql> begin work;
mysql> SELECT * FROM gem_test WHERE id=1
```

This applies a share lock to the first row. In your second client, try to run two statements: first a SELECT that involves row 1.

```
mysql> SELECT * FROM gem_test;
```

This runs without a problem. However, now try to run an UPDATE on the first row.

```
mysql> UPDATE gem_test SET total=100 WHERE id=1
```

The client doesn't respond. It's waiting for the lock in the first client to be released. So now go to the first copy of the client and commit the transaction. After you do that, the statement in the second client executes immediately.

You can try this again, this time obtaining an exclusive lock on row 1. Start a transaction in one copy of the client and run a statement that gets an exclusive lock — either an UPDATE or SELECT ... FOR UPDATE.

```
mysql> set AUTOCOMMIT=0;
mysql> begin work;
mysql> SELECT * FROM gem_test WHERE id=1 FOR UPDATE;
```

Now, in your second copy of the client, run any statement that involves row 1. You'll find that even SELECTs won't execute until the exclusive lock is released and when the transaction in the first copy of the client is committed or rolled back.

Here I have covered the default locking mechanisms for Gemini. It's unlikely that you'll ever have to change the default setting, but you should be aware that with Gemini, you can work with a variable the controls isolation levels. Please see the documentation that came with your NuSphere installation for more on isolation levels.

Using InnoDB Tables

10 Min.
To Go

InnoDB tables have a couple of distinct advantages over all other transactional table types. First, they work on a wide variety of platforms, including the BSD family and MacOS X. Second, it's the only table that offers foreign key constrains, which you learned about in Session 4.

In order to properly use InnoDB tables, you need to understand the locking and transactional model used by this table type. Before you try to understand these concepts, check to see that InnoDB is available on your server.

```
mysql> show variables like '%have%';
+---------------+-------+
| Variable_name | Value |
+---------------+-------+
| have_bdb      | NO    |
| have_innodb   | YES   |
+---------------+-------+
```

If the Value for InnoDB is DISABLED, you need to make some changes to your configurations in order to use InnoDB. The easiest way to change your configuration is to follow the following steps. The reasons for taking these steps may not make sense right now, but should become clearer later in this book.

Find the file named my-medium.cnf. It may be in your support-files/ directory. Rename this file my.cnf and copy it to the data directory of your server (usually mysql/data or mysql/var). Now open the my.cnf file and move to the section with InnoDB options; remove the hash marks at the beginnings at the each of those lines. Each of these lines relates to one of the following variables you can see when the server daemon starts:

```
mysql> show variables like '%inno%';
+--------------------------------+----------------------+
| Variable_name                  | Value                |
+--------------------------------+----------------------+
| have_innodb                    | YES                  |
| innodb_data_file_path          | ibdata1:64M          |
| innodb_data_home_dir           |                      |
| innodb_flush_log_at_trx_commit | OFF                  |
| innodb_log_arch_dir            |                      |
| innodb_log_archive             | OFF                  |
| innodb_log_group_home_dir      | /usr/local/mysql/var/|
| innodb_flush_method            |                      |
+--------------------------------+----------------------+
```

Now restart the MySQL server daemon. You should now see that InnoDB tables are available.

Understanding the InnoDB transactional model

InnoDB uses what's called a *multi-versioning concurrency model*. Essentially, this means that each transaction is locked to the data at a specific point in time. When a thread initiates a transaction, InnoDB gets a snapshot of the data based on the exact moment the transaction started. To understand how this works, take a look at the following example. You have a simple InnoDB table:

```
mysql> select * from orders;
+----------+-------------+
| order_id | order_total |
+----------+-------------+
|        1 |         192 |
|        2 |        3333 |
|        3 |          70 |
+----------+-------------+
```

In one copy of the command-line client, you start a transaction:

```
mysql> set AUTOCOMMIT=0;
mysql> begin work;
```

This thread now has a snapshot of the table seen above. If you were to then open another copy of the client and start another transaction, that second client would have the same snapshot of the same table. Say at this point the first client runs an UPDATE statement and commits the transaction.

```
mysql> UPDATE orders set order_total=35 WHERE order_id=3
mysql> commit;
```

Even after this commit, the second client will not see the results of this UPDATE. The second client receives a snapshot of the data at the moment its transaction began (with a begin work). Until the second client finishes its transaction (with a commit or rollback), it will not be able to view the changes implemented by other threads that took place while the transaction was active.

Things get really sticky if the second client was also running an UPDATE on the same row. If the first and second clients start their transactions at the same time, they would get the same snapshots of data. The first client would run an UPDATE WHERE order_id=3, but the second client would be unaware of the change. The second client could then run its own UPDATE WHERE order_id=3. After both of these clients commit their transactions, only one of the values can survive. As it turns out, the last one to commit wins.

Immediately, you should see that this is quite different from the two-phase model used by Gemini. If using Gemini with the scenario presented above, the client that ran the UPDATE would receive an exclusive lock, and the second thread would just have to wait until the first thread was finished. With InnoDB, the second thread does not have to wait. But as you can probably see, running a multi-versioning system can be dangerous if you're not careful. If you don't follow the instructions in the following sections, some users of your database may see out-of-date or inaccurate data.

Working with InnoDB locks

Of course, there are steps you can take to make sure the rows obtained by your transactions are up-to-date. It may not surprise you that staying current involves obtaining locks. With InnoDB, threads can apply the same types of locks that were available in Gemini.

In Gemini tables, when you run a SELECT within a transaction, a share lock is placed on the rows read by the SELECT. However, by default, InnoDB does not place any locks on rows during a SELECT. But you can let InnoDB know that you want to obtain a share lock by the adding the clause LOCK IN SHARE MODE at the end of a SELECT.

When a thread issues a SELECT with a LOCK IN SHARE MODE clause, InnoDB goes beyond the snapshot of data taken at the start of the transaction and looks for the latest committed data. By obtaining the share lock and receiving the latest data, the LOCK IN SHARE MODE clause ensures that the data read by a SELECT will be accurate and up-to-date.

If you'd like to see how this works, try the following, using the same table shown above. In one client, start a transaction and then select a row while issuing a share lock.

```
mysql> set AUTOCOMMIT=0;
mysql> begin work;
mysql> SELECT * FROM orders WHERE id=1 LOCK IN SHARE MODE
```

Now in another copy of a client, start a transaction.

```
mysql> set AUTOCOMMIT=0;
mysql> begin work;
```

Now in the second copy of the client, try issuing a SELECT.

```
mysql> SELECT * FROM orders;
```

Because the first client has only a share lock, this command will execute. However, if you try an update, the client will react differently.

```
mysql> UPDATE orders set order_total=35 WHERE order_id=1
```

Because of the share lock, the client has to wait until the first client either commits or rolls back its transaction.

Threads request exclusive locks from InnoDB tables in exactly the same way they do for Gemini tables: with SELECT ... FOR UPDATE statements. The earlier section of this session on using Gemini tables describes how to use SELECT .. FOR UPDATE.

With InnoDB tables, it's important that you keep the multi-versioning transactional model in mind. In particular, you need to be careful when writing SELECT statements. When writing a SELECT in your application, ask yourself if the statement needs to be protected from concurrent updates. If the answer is "yes," add a locking mechanism to your SELECT with the LOCK IN SHARE MODE or FOR UPDATE clauses.

Done!

REVIEW

In this session, you learned how to use MySQL's most sophisticated tables: Gemini and InnoDB. You saw that both of these tables implement row-level locking. However, they do it in slightly different ways. Gemini tables use a two-phase locking system that sets either exclusive or shared locks on rows based on the type of SQL statement run within transactions. All other threads have to wait until the thread owning the lock is either rolled back or committed. The InnoDB transactional system is a bit different, employing a multi-versioning transactional model. You saw that in this model you must take special care with your SELECT statements to ensure that your threads always receive the most up-to-date data.

QUIZ YOURSELF

1. A share lock prevents locked out threads from running which statements?
   (See "Share lock.")

2. An exclusive lock prevents locked out threads from running which statements?
   (See "Exclusive lock.")

3. What must be added to a SELECT statement in order to get an exclusive lock?
   (See "Exclusive lock.")

4. Why is there a danger of getting out-of-date data with SELECTs in InnoDB tables?
   (See "Using InnoDB Tables.")

5. How can you obtain a share lock from a SELECT statement with InnoDB?
   (See "Working with InnoDB locks.")

Working with MySQL and PHP

Session Checklist

✔ Installing PHP with MySQL support

✔ Installing on Windows

✔ Testing your MySQL installation

✔ Using PHP's MySQL functions

**30 Min.
To Go**

In all previous sessions, queries were sent to the database server through MySQL's command-line client. This client provides a nice way for viewing the results of queries and administering databases, but there's no way to use the client to write applications. You can write MySQL applications in pretty much any language, but the two most popular choices are Perl and PHP.

The next few sessions show you how to write applications using these languages. Note that these sessions assume some knowledge of the language being discussed. If you need to learn either PHP or Perl from scratch, please consult a book that is exclusive to the topic.

Installing PHP with MySQL Support

PHP is not a language like Java or C++, where the code can stand on its own. PHP, which is used for creating dynamic Web sites, needs to work with a Web server in order to process browser requests. There are two major Web servers that can work with PHP. The first is Apache. Like PHP and MySQL, Apache is an open source project and is most frequently used on Unix systems like Linux, FreeBSD, and Solaris, and Mac OS X.

The other major Web server come from Microsoft and is known as IIS, Internet Information Server. This works on server-grade operating systems from Microsoft (Windows NT Server, Windows 2000 Server). On other, consumer-class operating systems (Windows 98, WindowsXP), Microsoft provided a scaled-down version of IIS called PWS, Personal Web Server.

Which should you use? If you are planning on serving your live application off of a Unix/Linux box, you're probably going to be using Apache. Pretty much every ISP that offers MySQL and PHP hosting uses some sort of Unix variant with Apache. For this reason, I don't recommend using PHP and MySQL with anything but Apache, even though you can use PHP and MySQL with IIS and PWS. In the following sections, I show you how to install Apache with PHP and MySQL support on both Unix and windows systems.

 The NuSphere installation installs MySQL, Apache, PHP, and Perl on both Windows and Red Hat Linux. If you went that path with your installation, you can skip this section.

Installing PHP and Apache on Linux/Unix

There are a variety of ways to install Apache and PHP on your systems. If you are using Linux, you can choose to install from binaries, RPMs, or compiling from source. If you have a particular affection for any of these methods, feel free to continue with that course. Most every Linux distribution creates and distributes some binary distribution of PHP and Apache. Check the Web site of your distribution for specifics.

For the sake of providing something that is useful on a variety of operating systems, I'll show how to compile Apache and PHP with MySQL support from source files. I like using Apache's apxs feature, which allows for modules to be loaded into Apache without having recompiling Apache. For more on the dynamic loading of modules, see this page from the Apache manual: http://httpd.apache.org/docs/dso.html.

Go to http://httpd.apache.org/dist/httpd/ and download the latest source in the 1.3 releases. (By the time you're reading this, Apache version 2 may be available, but the 2.x version was unavailable for testing at the time of this writing.). You'll need to download a file with .tar.gz extension. It will look something like apache_1.3.22.tar.gz. Then go to http://www.php.net/downloads.php and get the most recent source files for PHP. At the time of this writing, the most current version was 4.1.1 and the source file was php-4.1.1.tar.gz. Place these in your home directory (on my Linux box, my home directory is /home/jay), and run the following commands:

```
shell> gunzip apache_1.3.22.tar.gz
shell> tar xf apache_1.3.22.tar
shell> gunzip php-4.1.1.tar.gz
shell> tar xf php-4.1.1.tar
```

These commands extract the source files from the compressed archives you downloaded. Then you should move into the Apache directory and run the configure command. In the command below I've specified the directory into which Apache will be installed with the --prefix flag. Feel free to choose a directory that best suits your own setup:

```
shell> cd apache_1.3.22
shell> ./configure --prefix=/home/jay/webserver --enable-module=so
shell> make
shell> make install
```

Now you will have a working copy of Apache on your machine. Note that the enable-module=so flag lets Apache know that you want to make use of dynamically loadable modules. Now you need to compile PHP with support for MySQL. If you are still in the Apache directory, move to the directory created for PHP.

```
shell> cd ../php-4.0.6
```

Now you need to configure PHP so that it recognizes MySQL. In the configure stage you need to supply a path to your MySQL installation. The path depends on the type of installation you chose. In all likelihood, you'll need to supply a directory of either /usr/local or /usr/local/mysql. To figure out which you should use, run the following command:

```
show variables like 'basedir'
```

You use the value returned by this query when configuring PHP. In the following instructions, I'm assuming the basedir is /usr/local/mysql. Now, in the php directory run the following commands, making sure to use the appropriate paths for the Apache and MySQL directories. Note that the --with-zlib flag may not be necessary on your system, but including it couldn't hurt.

```
shell> ./configure --with-apxs=/home/jay/webserver/bin
        --with-mysql=/usr/local/mysql --prefix=/home/jay/phpinstall
        --with-zlib
shell> make
shell> make install
```

Now, you need to let Apache know which files the PHP interpreter should parse. This and about all other configurable Apache attributes can be modified in the conf/httpd.conf file. Open this file in a text editor and uncomment (remove the hash marks) before the following lines:

```
AddType application/x-httpd-php .php
AddType application/x-httpd-php-source .phps
```

Installing PHP on Mac OS X

The installation on Mac OS X is really very easy. In fact, you don't have to make any changes to Apache. Simply download the latest source files from www.php.net/downloads.php, and then run the following commands in the Terminal application, making sure to use the correct path for MySQL:

```
shell> gunzip php-4.1.1.tar.gz
shell> tar xf php-4.1.1.tar
shell> cd php-4.1.1
shell> ./configure --with-apxs --with-zlib --with-mysq=/usr/local/mysql
shell> make
shell> sudo make install
```

In order to compile PHP from source on MacOS X, you have to install a compiler. The easiest way to do that is to install the Developer Tools CD that came with your OS X package.

You then need to open the /private/etc/httpd/httpd.conf file and uncomment the following lines:

```
AddType application/x-httpd-php .php
AddType application/x-httpd-php-source .phps
```

Installation on Windows

**20 Min.
To Go**

Installation on Windows requires little more than some double-clicking. Go to the Apache download site (http://httpd.apache.org/dist/httpd) and find the latest of the 1.3 versions with a .zip extension; for example, apache_1.3.22.zip. Unzip the file, and then double-click on the installer (setup.exe). All you really need to do is select a directory where you would like Apache to be installed. When it's completed, an Apache Group item is added to the Start menu.

Now on to PHP — go to www.php.net/downloads.php and get the latest Windows binaries. Unzip this file into a folder. In that folder, copy MSVCRT.DLL and PHP4TS.DLL to c:\windows\system. Then rename php.ini-dist to php.ini and keep it in the same directory were you have the php.exe file.

All you need to do at this point is make sure that Apache is aware of PHP and that PHP is aware of MySQL.

First go to the directory where you installed Apache, find the httpd.conf file within the \conf directory, and open it in a text editor. Add these three lines to the file:

```
ScriptAlias /php4/ "c:/php4/"
AddType application/x-httpd-php4 .php
Action application/x-httpd-php4 "/php4/php.exe"
```

The first line indicates the path where PHP resides. The second tells Apache what file extensions must be parsed as PHP, and the third gives the path to the php executable file. Note that when using this type of installation, PHP runs as an executable, not an Apache server module. Note that above I've used c:\php4\ as an example, but there is no requirement that you use that directory in your install. These lines in the configuration file must be relevant to your own configuration.

There are a couple of other alterations you may have to make to your httpd.conf file. If the server refuses to start, you may need to add something to the ServerName directive. If you are using TCP/IP in your local area network, you may need to add the IP address of your machine. For example:

ServerName 192.168.1.2

Or, if your machine is not networked, you may want to use the following ServerName:

ServerName 127.0.0.1

Testing Your Installation

To test your installation, open a text editor and create a simple file that looks like this:

```php
<?php

phpinfo();

?>
```

Place this file in the /htdocs folder of your Apache directory and name in info.php. Once again, open your httpd.conf file, and look for the Port directive. Make sure the value of this directive is 80. Now start your Apache Web server. On Windows, select the Start Apache item from the Start menu. On Linux/Unix, go to the /bin subdirectory of your Apache installation and run the following command:

```
./apachectl start
```

On MacOS X either start or restart Web sharing from System Preferences.

Now open your browser to http://localhost/info.php. You should see a screen that looks like Figure 15-1. Look through this file to make sure there is an entry for MySQL. In that portion, you will see that the client library matches the version of MySQL you have installed on your system.

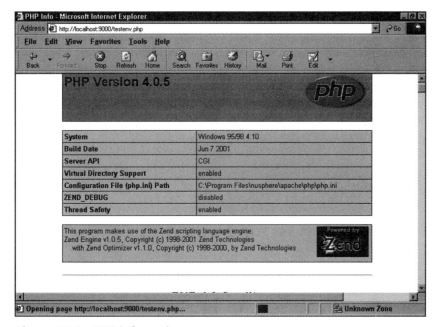

Figure 15-1   *PHP information page*

10 Min.
To Go

Using PHP's MySQL Functions

PHP has many MySQL-related functions. If you look at the list of these functions (at www.php.net/manual/en/ref.mysql.php), you may think that learning this API will take a great deal of time. After all, there are over 40 functions. But in fact, there are really only a few functions that you will use regularly. It's good to know that the others exist, and you should spend some time reading through the explanations of functions at the PHP site, although many of them you will never need to use.

Connecting to the server and choosing a database

PHP will not automatically connect to a MySQL database. Before you can process queries, you need to run either the mysql_connect() or mysql_pconnect() function to establish a connection. These functions take the form:

```
int mysql_connect(str host, str username, str password)
int mysql_pconnect(str host, str username, str password)
```

Both of these functions create connections between PHP and the MySQL server. The major difference is that mysql_pconnect() opens a persistent connection. In general, persistent connections are preferable because they're faster. When using a persistent connection, even when a thread closes, a connection to the database remains open. Then when another script attempts to connect, it can use that same connection, thereby saving some overhead that would occur during the connection process. However, there are some reasons to be wary of persistent connections. These are spelled out clearly in this page from the PHP manual: www.php.net/manual/en/features.persistent-connections.php.

The integer returned by these functions is a *resource identifier*. The host argument will be "localhost" if the database and PHP are installed on the same machine. Otherwise, you can specify a host by providing a URL here. The username and password will be those of the user you set up to handle your Web applications. You'll read more about creating users in Session 20. For now, use the username "root" and no password. So a working function looks like the following:

```
$conn=mysql_connect("localhost", "root", "");
```

The connection identifier is stored in the variable $conn. In your applications, you'll want to work with a database or two. You can select a specific database with the mysql_select_db() function, which takes the form:

```
int mysql_select_db(str db_name, [int connection])
```

The optional second argument would be the resource identifier gathered from the mysql_connect() function. This function usually looks like:

```
$db=mysql_select_d("store", $conn);
```

Sending and viewing queries

You can send arbitrary queries to MySQL with the mysql_query() function. It takes the form:

```
int mysql_query(str query, [int connection])
```

The optional second argument is the resource identifier from the mysql_pconnect() function. Normally, your query string is a combination of SQL keywords and variables that have been obtained from form values or URL querystrings. A basic use of this function may look like:

```
$result = mysql_query("SELECT * FROM users");
```

Once again the integer returned by mysql_query() is a resource identifier. You can extract rows from the results of the query with the mysql_fetch_array() function. It takes the form:

```
array mysql_fetch_array(int result_identifier, [CONSTANT])
```

This function returns a row from a query result as an array and advances the result set's pointer to the next row. So the next time you run this function, you'll get the next row in the result set. By default, mysql_fetch_array() returns each column in the row twice, first with a numeric array key and then with an associative key equal to the column name. When using MYSQL_ASSOC as the second argument, values in the row are returned only once, with column names as the associative keys. When using MYSQL_NUM as the second argument, PHP returns rows with only numeric array indexes. When PHP reaches the end of a result set, the function returns FALSE.

You will almost always use mysql_fetch_array() in a while... loop. That way, you can process every row in a result set. For example, to show all the databases associated with a server, you can run the following code after you make a connection to the MySQL:

```
$result=mysql_query("SHOW DATABASES");
while($row=mysql_fetch_array($result, MYSQL_NUM)){
    echo $row[0] . "<br>";
}
```

As of PHP 4.0.0, the mysql_fetch_assoc() **function returns a row as an associative array. Using this function saves you the trouble of including a constant in the second argument of** mysql_fetch_array(). **If you want to return a numeric array, you can use** mysql_fetch_row(). **Both** mysql_fetch_assoc() **and** mysql_fetch_row() **take a single argument, the resource identifier created with** mysql_query().

With the five functions you have learned so far, you can do some pretty sophisticated stuff. For example, the code in Listing 15-1 displays the contents of a query in an HTML table. In this listing, the database name and query string are hard-coded into the script, but these values can easily be constructed from variables.

Listing 15-1 *PHP script that displays a table*

```
<?php

//connect to server and choose database
$conn=mysql_connect("localhost", "root", "");
```

Continued

Listing 15-1 *Continued*

```
$db=mysql_select_db("store", $conn);

//run query and hold result identifier in variable $result
$result=mysql_query("SELECT * FROM users");

//the first time through I want to print the column names
//in the table header. This variable will be changed to
//FALSE once the table header is laid out
$layout_header=TRUE;

echo "<table border=1>\n";

//This while... loop will grab all results from the query.
//Using MYSQL_ASSOC, the column names are stored as array
//associative indexes.
while($row = mysql_fetch_array($result, MYSQL_ASSOC)){
    if($layout_header){
        $layout_header=FALSE;
        echo "<tr>\n";

        //print out each column name as the value of a row in the
        //table header
        while(list($col_name, $col_value)=each($row)){
            echo "<th>$col_name</th>\n";
        }
        //rewind the array pointer so that the values of this
        //row can be displayed in the table body.
        reset($row);
        echo "<tr>\n";
    }
    //now that the table header is in place, print
    //all the values for each row.
    echo "<tr>\n";
    while(list($col_name, $col_value)=each($row)){
        echo "<td>$col_value</td>\n";
    }
    echo "<tr>\n";
}
echo "</table>";
?>
```

Other helpful MySQL functions

Again, I'll mention that there are many MySQL functions available in PHP. There are functions like mysql_create_db() and mysql_list_dbs() that can be used, respectively, for creating databases and listing the existing databases. But why would you want to learn the syntax of these functions when you already know the CREATE DATABASE statement and the

SHOW DATABASES statement? When you need this type of information, you're better off using the familiar syntax and passing the query to MySQL with mysql_query().

Here are three functions that are very helpful when constructing applications.

mysql_error()

The mysql_error() is an absolute necessity. If, in your applications, a query fails, you'll want to know why. When a query does fail, MySQL produces an error, but in your application, you need to let PHP know that you want the cause of the error displayed. Normally, you use PHP's or die() operator along with mysql_query() so that a useful error is displayed when a query does not execute. For example:

```
mysql_query("SELECT * FROM foobar") or die
    mysql_error();
```

mysql_affected_rows()

This function returns the number of rows altered or deleted by an INSERT, UPDATE, or DELETE statement. It takes one optional argument, the resource identifier associated with mysql_connect() or myql_connect().

mysql_insert_id()

The mysql_insert_id() function is mapped to the MySQL last_insert_id() function, which you learned about earlier. It returns the last value created for auto_increment column for the active thread. This allows you to get the primary key of a column just after inserting a row.

Putting these functions to work

Listing 15-2 shows a PHP script that inserts, updates, and deletes records from the users table. Look through the script and its comments, and notice how I used mysql_insert_id(), mysql_affected_rows(), and mysql_error() to make a script that has decent error handling.

Listing 15-2 *PHP script using a variety of MySQL functions*

```php
<?php

//connect to server and choose database
$conn=mysql_connect("localhost", "root", "");
$db=mysql_select_db("store", $conn);

//the user has hit either the update or delete button.
if(!empty($submit)){

    //this is a new row an must be inserted
```

Continued

Listing 15-2 *Continued*

```
        if($submit=="update" && empty($user_id)){
            $query = "INSERT INTO users (fname, lname, email, home_phone,
                        work_phone, fax)
                    VALUES ('$fname', '$lname', '$email', '$home_phone',
                        '$work_phone', '$fax')";
            mysql_query($query) or die(mysql_error());
            if(mysql_affected_rows()==0){
                echo "INSERT FAILED, Please contact admin or try again";
                exit;
            }else{
                //get the primary key so I can display the
                //record in the form
                $user_id=mysql_insert_id();
            }
        }
        //now I know this row is form updating an existing record
        elseif($submit=="update" && !empty($user_id)){
            $query="UPDATE users SET
                    fname='$fname',
                    lname='$lname',
                    email='$email',
                    home_phone='$home_phone',
                    work_phone='$work_phone',
                    fax='$fax'
                    WHERE user_id=$user_id";
                    mysql_query($query);
            if(mysql_affected_rows()==0){
                echo "Warning, nothing changed in the submitted row.";
                exit;
            }
        }
        elseif($submit=="delete" && !empty($user_id)){
            $query="DELETE FROM users WHERE user_id=$user_id";
            mysql_query($query) or die(mysql_error());
            if(mysql_affected_rows()==0){
                echo "Warning, No rows deleted.";
                exit;
            }
        }

    }
    if(!empty($user_id)){
        $result2=mysql_query("SELECT * FROM users WHERE user_id=$user_id");
        $row2=mysql_fetch_assoc($result2);
    }



    ?>


    <table>
    <tr>
    <td>
```

```
<p>Click <a href="<? echo $PHP_SELF; ?>">here</a> for blank form.</p>
<?
//get listing of everyone in users table for printout
//user_ids will be included in querystring for so that when user
//clicks on one user_id, the results will be displayed in the form
$result1=mysql_query("SELECT user_id, concat(fname, ' ', lname) as username
                      FROM users
                      ORDER BY lname") or die(mysql_error());
while($row1=mysql_fetch_assoc($result1)){
    echo "<a href=$PHP_SELF?user_id=" .
        $row1[user_id] . ">" . $row1[username] . "</a><br>";
}



?>
</td>

<td>
<form>

    <input type="hidden" name="user_id" value="<?php echo $row2[user_id]?>"><br>
    <input type="text" name="fname" value="<?php echo $row2[fname]?>"> First Name<br>
    <input type="text" name="lname" value="<?php echo $row2[lname]?>"> Last Name<br>
    <input type="text" name="email" value="<?php echo $row2[email]?>"> Email<br>
    <input type="text" name="home_phone" value="<?php echo $row2[home_phone]?>"> Home
phone<br>
    <input type="text" name="work_phone" value="<?php echo $row2[work_phone]?>"> work
phone<br>
    <input type="text" name="fax" value="<?php echo $row2[fax]?>"> fax<br>
<input type="submit" name="submit" value="update">
<input type="submit" name="submit" value="delete"><br>
</form>
</td>

</tr>
</table>
```

Done!

REVIEW

In this session, you learned how to install PHP and Apache and how to make use of PHP's basic MySQL functions. This was the first session where you moved beyond the database server and wrote application code that interacts with the MySQL server. You saw how to establish a connection with the server, choose a database, and send arbitrary queries. The session ended by describing functions that provide useful information about the success of queries. You saw how all of these functions can be put together quickly in a simple but powerful application.

Quiz Yourself

1. What file holds Apache configuration information? (See "Installing PHP with MySQL Support.")

2. What flag in the Apache configure step enables dynamically loadable modules? (See "Installing PHP and Apache on Linux/Unix.")

3. What two functions establish a connection between PHP and MySQL? (See "Connecting to the server and choosing a database.")

4. What two functions can be used in place of mysql_fetch_row()? (See "Sending and viewing queries.")

5. What is the danger of not including or die() with your queries? (See "mysql_error().")

SESSION

16

MySQL and PHP: Best Practices

Session Checklist

✔ Cleaning user data

✔ Handling queries

✔ Establishing a connection

✔ Organizing files

**30 Min.
To Go**

There's no way to cover all you need to learn for writing applications with MySQL and PHP. (I did co-author an entire book on this topic, *MySQL/PHP Database Applications*, published by Hungry Minds, Inc., if you're interested.) In the course of this session, I can show you some tips, tricks, and ideas that may make your coding life a little easier. I start by assembling some functions that you can use in your applications. These are general utility functions and should save you a little bit of time in all of your applications that use MySQL.

Cleaning User Data

I'm going to start by creating a function that makes sure our user data is fit to be inserted in a MySQL database.

Escaping string

One of the first things you learned about MySQL was that certain characters, like single quotes, can cause problems within INSERT and UPDATE statements. Before you send any data that can contain single quotes to MySQL in a query, you'll want to make sure that those strings are properly escaped.

PHP has both universal settings and functions that make escaping strings extremely easy. The first thing to look at is the magic_quotes_gpc setting. *Magic quotes* — a PHP feature that automatically escapes single quotes, double quotes, and backslashes — and many other settings are stored in the php.ini file. The location of this file varies depending on the specifics of your installation; you can find out where yours is by looking at the results of the phpinfo() function. Toward the top, you see the path to this file. If the file is not in the location indicated in phpinfo(), copy the php.ini-dist from your PHP install directory to that location.

If magic_quotes_gpc is set to "on," the PHP engine automatically escapes single quotes, double quotes, backslashes, and NULs that come from GET, POST, or cookies. "On" is the default setting, and most people find that they like having magic_quotes_gpc enabled. But when you are writing applications, you want to make sure your code is as portable as possible. That is, you want applications to work in environments where magic quotes are enabled and disabled.

I'm going to construct a function that I can use to examine and scrub any user data. I can check to see if magic_quotes_gpc is on by using the ini_get() function. If magic quotes are not enabled, I'll use the addslashes() function, which escapes all relevant characters. For starters, the function may look like this:

```
function scrub_data($data){
    if(!ini_get("magic_quotes_gpc")){
        addslashes($data);
    }
    return $data;
}
```

But this simple function works only on *scalar* (single value) variables, and you're going to want to scrub all data, some of which may be passed to PHP in the form of an array. In fact, in PHP, all GET, POST, and cookie values are available, respectively, in the $HTTP_GET_VARS, $HTTP_POST_VARS and $HTTP_COOKIE_VARS arrays. And any one of these arrays can contain arrays itself.

PHP 4.1 contains other variables that contain POST, GET, **and cookie** DATA. **Please see** www.php.net/release_4_1_0.php **for more details.**

The most compact function I can write that would process these arrays involves some reasonably advanced PHP concepts. If you're brand new to PHP, or programming in general, this may be difficult to understand. For this reason, I'll briefly describe the concepts involved and provide links to more detailed explanations.

Any function that processes arrays that may contain other arrays must work *recursively*. A recursive function calls itself. When you want to process all scalar variables within multi-dimensional arrays, your function will have to call itself when a non-scalar variable (an array) is encountered. For more information on recursion see www.phpdev.com/articles.php?task=view&articleID=3.

You should also understand *passing by reference*. Normally when you call a function, you pass the function a value or set of values. Then at the end of the function, you return a new value. For example:

```
function add_stuff($val1){
    $newval=$val1+5;
    return $newval;
}
$val=5;
$val=add_stuff($val);
```

Normally, the PHP engine makes copies of variables within functions and operates on those copies. In the above example, PHP makes a copy of $val and operates on that within the function. However, if I pass by reference, I can operate on the values of the original variable within the function. I indicate that I'm passing by reference by prepending a variable name with an ampersand in the function's variable list. I'd rewrite the previous function in this way:

```
function add_stuff(&$val1){
    $val1=$val1+5;
}
$val=5;
add_suff($val);
```

In this example the variable $val is changed within the function. For more on passing by reference, see this page in the PHP manual (www.php.net/manual/en/language.references.pass.php).

I applied these concepts in my revised scrub_data() function. It makes use of the array_walk() function, which sends each value within an array to the indicated function.

```
function scrub_data(&$data){
    if(is_array($data)){
        array_walk($data, "scrub_data");
    }
    elseif(!ini_get("magic_quotes_gpc")){
        $data=addslashes($data);
    }
}
```

And, if I include the following lines at the top of all my applications, I know that all user-submitted data will be properly escaped and ready for processing in my applications.

```
scrub_data($HTTP_GET_VARS);
scrub_data($HTTP_POST_VARS);
scrub_data($HTTP_COOKIE_VARS);
```

Note that you may need to rewind the arrays if you want to cycle through them again.

Now I'll install some additional features in the scrub_data() function. Note that this function assumes you will be referring to GET, POST, and COOKIE data through these arrays. This function does not affect the global variables created by GET, POST, and COOKIE data.

Removing unwanted HTML

Imagine you had a form that loaded information for a discussion list (something like slash-dot). You wouldn't be able to approve every post because there would be too many to look at. But what if somebody included the following text within his post?

```
<img src=www.mydomain.com/image/of/michael_bolton.jpg>
```

You would end up with an unwanted image in your page. Happily, PHP has a single function that can remove all HTML tags: the `strip_tags()` function. It takes two arguments. The first is the string from which you want tags stripped. The second argument is optional and can contain any tags that are allowable in the final result.

You also may want to consider converting some characters to their HTML entities. By using `htmlspecialchars()`, PHP will convert the ampersand, double quote, greater than sign, and less than sign to their proper entities (&, ", >, and <). And, if you use ENT_QUOTES as the second argument in the `htmlspecialchars()`, single quotes will also be converted to the proper entity (&#039).

In Listing 16-1, I've added the `strip_tags()`function to my `scrub_text()` function. Note that I've decided that <b>, <i>, and <strong> tags can remain within the scrubbed strings.

Listing 16-1   *Final scrub_data() function*

```
function scrub_data(&$data){
    if(is_array($data)){
        array_walk($data, "scrub_data");
    } else {
        if(!ini_get("magic_quotes_gpc")){
            $data=stripslashes($data);
        }
        $data=strip_tags($data, "<b><i><strong>");
    }
}
```

Handling Queries

**20 Min.
To Go**

In the previous session, you learned that `mysql_query()` alone does not return useful error messages. To get error messages, you have to use `mysql_error()` in this manner:

```
$result=mysql_query($query) or
    die(myql_error());
```

But in your applications there will be dozens of queries, and there's really no reason to write the or `die()` portion with every single query. You're better off using a function. At the most basic level, a function to handle queries may look like:

```
function handle_query($query){
    $result=mysql_query($query) or
        die(mysql_error());
```

```
        return $result;
}
```

But when using a function, the error message created by `mysql_error()` will not be associated with a line number in your scripts. If you have a page full of queries all going through the `handle_query()` function, it may take you a while to find the offending query. So within the `die()` portion, you may want to include the text of the query:

```
function handle_query($query){
    $result=mysql_query($query) or
        die(
            "<b>Following query failed: $query</b><br>"
            . mysql_error()
        );
    return $result;
}
```

As it stands, this function should work well while you are developing your applications. However, when your application is live, you probably don't want the users of your applications to view errors created by `mysql_error()`. First of all, it doesn't help the user much. You may get an e-mail from the user saying there's a problem, but chances are the user won't spend the time to quote the error message when he or she contacts you to complain. Secondly, if your user happens to be a skilled hacker, it's possible that the information printed by this function will show an area of potential attack.

To handle these potential problems I'm going to add two key portions to my function. First, I'm going to split the query in half. One half works while running the query in debugging mode (during the development phase), and the other half runs when the script is not in debugging mode (when the application is live). The function determines which portion to run by means of a GLOBAL variable. If the variable, named `$query_debug`, is set to "on," the errors will be printed.

When `$query_debug` is set to "off," however, you want to know exactly what the error is, but you don't want it printed to the screen. You can get access to error information by printing it to an error log. The PHP `error_log()` function (`www.php.net/manual/en/function.error-log.php`) can either write errors to a specific file, or e-mail the results of an error to a known address. You can set the path and filename of the error log in the `php.ini` file (the `error_log=[path]` item), and you can find the current location of the error file using `phpinfo()`.

In the finalized version of `handle_query()` (see Listing 16-2), query errors are printed to the error log along with the text of the query and the page that on which the error occurred. The user sees only a generic error message.

Listing 16-2   *Final handle_query() function*

```
function handle_query($query){
    global $query_debug, $PHP_SELF;
    if($query_debug=="on"){
        $result=mysql_query($query) or
            die(
```

Continued

Listing 16-2 *Continued*

```
                    "<b>Following query failed: $query</b><br>"
                    . mysql_error()
                );
        }elseif($query_debug="off"){
            $result=mysql_query($query) or
                error_log(
                    $PHP_SELF . ", " . $query . ", " . mysql_error()
                    , 0);
            if(!$result){
                echo "Sorry, internal error encountered";
                exit;
            }
        }
    }
    return $result;
}
```

Using this function, an item printed to the error_log looks like this:

```
[22-Oct-2001 09:36:44] /jaygreen/test3.php, select * from bar, Table
'store.bar' doesn't exist
```

Establishing a Connection

**10 Min.
To Go**

As you saw in Session 15, creating a connection between PHP is not especially difficult. You can put the following lines at the top of a file that is included in all of your applications:

```
$conn=mysql_pconnect("localhost", "username", "password");
mysql_select_db("mydb", $conn);
```

But this isn't very robust. I prefer a function that I can reuse in a variety of applications — something that handles errors intelligently. Additionally, you should look at other alternate methods for connection to a MySQL database that may be necessary for some atypical configurations.

Creating a connection function

For starters, a function that handled a connection may look like this:

```
function make_connection($username="", $psswd="", $dbname="", $host="localhost"){
    $conn=@mysql_pconnect($host, $username, $psswd) or
        die("Connection to database server failed");
    $db=@mysql_select_db($dbname) or
        die("Couldn't select database");
    return $conn;
}
```

Notice that I used the @ symbol before `mysql_pconnect()` and `mysql_select_db()`. The @ symbol represses errors that would automatically be sent to the browser. In the function above, @ allows me to present an error message of my choosing, which I've put in the `die()` clause.

However, if the database server is unavailable, it's likely that there are some real problems on my server. In that circumstance, I'd want to immediately know that there's a problem. So again, I'm going to use the `error_log()` function, but this time I'm going to use it to send an e-mail to the site administrator. Again, a generic error message will be printed if the connection fails for any reason. Listing 16-3 shows my finalized connection function.

Listing 16-3 *Finalized connection function*

```
function make_connection($username="", $psswd="", $dbname="",
$host="localhost"){
    $conn=@mysql_pconnect($host, $username, $psswd) or
        error_log("gak, couldn't connect to MySQL server", 1,
"admin@msite.com");
    $db=@mysql_select_db($dbname, $conn) or
        error_log("gak, couldn't get db", 1, "admin@my.email.address");
    if(!$conn || !$db){
        echo "Encountered internal error. Administrator has been
notified.";
        exit;
    }
    return $conn;
}
```

Working with atypical configurations

In order to connect to the MySQL server engine, clients — all clients, including the simple command-line client — look for one of two ways to make a connection. Clients search for either the socket file (`mysql.sock`) or the available port. On most installations, the server engine is available through port 3306, and the socket file is created in the `/tmp` folder when the server daemon is started. However, depending on your installation, the location of the socket or the port may vary. In PHP, you may need to account for these variations.

You can change MySQL's port and socket file location. More on these configuration options are found in Session 25.

There are two ways to ways to indicate alternate MySQL ports or socket file locations in PHP: either in the `mysql_connect()` and `myql_pconnect()` functions or through the `php.ini` file. In the `php.ini` file, you can find the following lines:

```
; Default socket name for local MySQL connects.  If empty, uses the built-in
; MySQL defaults.
```

```
mysql.default_socket =

; Default host for mysql_connect() (doesn't apply in safe mode).
mysql.default_host =
```

If you have control of your server and the defaults don't apply, you're best off changing the values here and restarting your Web server. For example, if you kept a separate database server, you may change the host configuration like so:

```
; Default host for mysql_connect() (doesn't apply in safe mode).
mysql.default_host = mydbserver.mydoman.com
```

 You learn how to grant access to users from alternate hosts in Session 20.

If, for some reason or another, you don't have access to the php.ini file, you can indicate a port or socket location in mysql_connect() or myql_pconnect(). The following examples show how to connect to an alternate socket file location and alternate host, respectively:

```
mysql_pconnect("localhost:/path/to/mysql.sock", "username", "password");
mysql_pconnect("dbserver.mydomain.com", "username", "password");
```

Organizing your PHP Code

Different portions of PHP pages do very different things. For example, the parts of a php page that are not within the <? and ?> tags will not be parsed by the PHP engine. Beyond that, some portions of the page deal extensively with queries while others work through business logic. By separating your code into functions and includes, you can keep your PHP code in organized and reusable chunks. For example, you may want to take the handle_query() and make_connection() function and put those in a single file called myql_utils.inc.php. (Note that I've used an .inc.php extension to differentiate the file from the core files of my application. I've maintained the file .php extension so that just about any Web server will know to parse these as PHP files.).

If at all possible, it's best to keep include files out of the source tree of your application. For example, if your Web server is configured to serve all the pages below /home/apache/htdocs, you'd want to put the include files in a directory like /home/apache/phpincludes. That way you don't have to worry someone finding the contents of your include by typing a filename directly into a browser. If you have a path for includes, you can indicate that in the php.ini include_path directive and avoid typing a full file path each time you want to include a file.

In your includes, you want to try to put separate actions in separate files. For example, say that you had an application that was available only to authorized users. You'd want to make sure every page contained some code that made sure the user entered a correct username and password. So you could put all the authentication code in a single file, and then include that file in all pages in your application. The start of every file in your application may contain

```
<?
$query_debug="on";
include "mysql_utils.php";
$conn=make_connection("username", "psswd", "store");
include "authenticate.php";
...
?>
```

Listing 16-4 shows the authentication code I wrote. It validates against a simple MySQL table of two columns called username and psswd. Passwords are stored in the database using MySQL's password() function. This script works with PHP sessions. If a user has yet to enter a password, a blank form is presented. If the user enters a bad password/username combination, then a user form is printed along with an error.

However, if a user enters a valid username and password, the code creates a unique string with the md5() hash function. I store a copy of this hash on the server in a session variable, and I store another copy on the client (a browser) in a cookie. To be an authenticated user, the copy of the hash on the client must be identical to the hash on the server. If they are not identical, the user must login again.

A login form is kept in another simple file (see Listing 16-5).

Listing 16-4 *Authentication script*

```php
<?php
$query_debug="on";

include "test3.php";
$conn=make_connection("root", "mypass", "store");

session_start();


//see if user is submitting username/password data
if(!$PHPSESSID){
    include "loginform.inc.php";
    exit;
}
elseif(!empty($submit) && !empty($username) && !empty($psswd)){
    $result=handle_query("SELECT 1 FROM admins WHERE
                            username='$username' and
                            psswd=password('$psswd')
                    ");
    if($row=mysql_fetch_array($result)){
        session_register("myhash");
        $myhash=md5($username . "mystring" . $psswd);
```

Continued

Listing 16-4   *Continued*

```
            setcookie("hashcookie", $myhash, time()+(60*60), "/");
        }else{
            $error="No user with that username/password combination";
            include "loginform.inc.php";
            exit;
        }
    }
    else{
        session_register("myhash");
        if(empty($$HTTP_SESSION_VARS["myhash"]) ||
$HTTP_SESSION_VARS["myhash"]!=$HTTP_COOKIE_VARS["hashcookie"]){
            $error="Problem validating this user, please login again";
            include "loginform.inc.php";
            exit;
        }
    }
    ?>
```

Listing 16-5   *User login form*

```
<? echo "<b>$error</b>"; ?>

<form method="post">
<input type="text" name="username"> username <br>
<input type="text" name="psswd"> psswd <br>
<input type="submit" name="submit" value="submit"> <br>


</form>
```

Done!

Review

In this session, you saw some tips and tricks for using MySQL with PHP. You saw how basic PHP functions can be grouped within user-defined functions to provide a powerful means of processing MySQL connections and queries. In addition, you saw several MySQL-related parameters in the php.ini file. Finally, you saw that by separating your PHP code into includes, you can keep all of your PHP code in well-organized and easily maintained segments.

QUIZ YOURSELF

1. What PHP function escapes single quotes, double quotes, and NULs? (See "Escaping string.")
2. What symbol forces PHP to suppress errors? (See "Handling Queries.")
3. What two methods of delivering errors does error_log() offer? (See "Handling Queries.")
4. What is the default MySQL Port? (See "Working with atypical configurations.")
5. What is the default location of the MySQL socket file? (See "Working with atypical configurations.")

PART

III

Saturday Afternoon
Part Review

1. What two arguments does the ifnull() function take?
2. What are the three arguments for the if() function?
3. Which of the one-way cryptographic functions has an equivalent in most every programming language?
4. What function decodes the string created by md5()?
5. Which function is used to tack one string onto the end of another?
6. If you had mydomain.com as a value in a column named url, how would you write a LIKE predicate or a WHERE clause that matched db.mydomain.com?
7. What function returns the last auto_increment value created by a thread?
8. What does the question mark character stand for in a regular expression?
9. What are the two ways of writing a regular expression character class that matches all lowercase letters?
10. Write a regular expression that returns every character from the beginning of a string to the first occurrence of the letter z.
11. What does the acronym ACID stand for?
12. What two types of locks can be applied to MyISAM tables?
13. What key words signal the beginning of a transaction?
14. What key words signal the end of a transaction?
15. What is the name of the transaction scheme used by Gemini tables?
16. Within a transaction, how you do apply an exclusive lock with a SELECT?
17. What is the transaction scheme used by InnoDB tables?
18. When using InnoDB tables, how do you apply a share lock with a SELECT statement?
19. When working with MySQL through PHP, what is the preferred function for creating a connection?
20. When running a MySQL query in PHP with the mysql_query() function, how can you print out an error, should one occur?

21. What PHP function can either send an e-mail or add to a log should an error occur?

22. What php.ini setting and function can automatically escape characters so that they can be inserted into the database?

PART

IV

Saturday
Evening

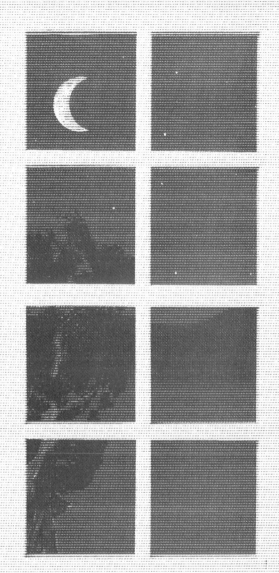

Session 17
Using MySQL with Perl

Session 18
MySQL and Perl: Best Practices

Session 19
Optimizing MySQL Queries

Session 20
Securing MySQL, Part I: The GRANT Tables

Using MySQL with Perl

Session Checklist

✔ Installing Perl with MySQL support

✔ Testing your installation

✔ Testing tour DBI and DBD installation

✔ Using Perl to communicate with MySQL

✔ Using Perl and MySQL to create Web applications via CGI

**30 Min.
To Go**

I n previous sessions, you learned how to send queries to the MySQL server in two ways: through the command-line interface and via PHP scripts running within the Apache Web server. In this session, you'll learn how to connect to MySQL via Perl, specifically via Perl's DBI and DBD modules. Please note again that the next two sessions assume some knowledge of Perl and Perl modules, as well as some basic knowledge of object-oriented Perl. If you need to learn Perl from scratch, please consult a Perl-specific book.

Installing Perl with MySQL Support

Unlike PHP code, Perl code can stand on its own. It does not have to be interpreted by a Web server like Apache. However, the most common use of Perl with MySQL is for Web development. The simplest way to use Perl and MySQL together is to write what's called a *CGI (Common Gateway Interface) script*. A CGI script is simply a program that is called by a Web server in response to a browser's request. It doesn't have to be written in Perl, although most CGI scripts are these days.

I'll start by going over the Perl modules necessary for Perl to connect to MySQL. Then I will create a simple Perl script that can send queries to MySQL. After that, I'll show you how to turn that script into a CGI script that can run under Apache.

In Session 18, I cover good coding practices with Perl and MySQL, show some of the drawbacks of using CGI scripts, and cover some other ways to use Perl with Apache and MySQL.

The NuSphere install package includes MySQL, Apache, PHP, and Perl for both Windows and Red Hat Linux. If you went that path with your installation, you can skip the installation sections of this session.

Installing Perl on Linux, Unix, and Mac OS X

There are a several ways to install Perl on your system. In fact, you are likely to have Perl installed already. Most modern Unix/Linux distributions ship with Perl as a standard component, as does Mac OS X. You can make sure you have a working installation of Perl by typing the following at your command prompt:

```
shell> perl -e 'print "hi \n"'
```

You may then see

```
hi
shell>
```

If you see a message similar to the following, you may not have a working installation of Perl:

```
perl: command not found
```

If this is the case, try this command:

```
shell> which perl
```

If you see something like

```
/usr/bin/perl
shell>
```

you can try running the test again with the full path to your Perl interpreter, like so:

```
shell> /usr/bin/perl -e 'print "hi \n" '
```

If you can't find a working Perl installation on your system, you need to install Perl in order to continue. Linux users can install Perl via RPM (check your Linux distribution's Website for a current Perl RPM). Other Unix users — or Linux users who prefer not to use the RPM system — can download the latest stable Perl distribution from www.cpan.org/src/stable.tar.gz and compile it.

To compile Perl on Unix after you've downloaded stable.tar.gz, follow this step:

```
shell> tar -xzf stable.tar.gz
```

This creates a new directory, called perl-X.XX (at the time of this writing, the latest stable Perl distribution was perl-5.6.1). This directory contains all the source code you need in order to compile Perl.

Now you can compile and install Perl on your system. Note that you need root (administrator) access in order to install Perl in its traditional location under the /usr/local/ directory. If you are a Mac OS X user with administrator privileges (by default, the first user created on an OS X system is an administrator) you can type **sudo sh** at the terminal prompt, followed by your password, in order to be logged in as an administrator.

If you don't have root access, you may need to ask your system administrator or ISP to make Perl available for your use. You can also install Perl under your home directory by following the directions at the installation prompts. Because Perl is so widely available on modern Unix-based systems, installing a personal version of Perl for Unix is not covered in this session.

Note for Mac OS X users: In order to compile programs on your system, you need to have installed the software on the Developer Tools CD that came with your OS X distribution. At the time of this writing, Mac OS X shipped with Perl installed, so you don't need to compile the source.

Compiling and installing Perl

You can install Perl with the following shell commands:

```
shell> cd perl-5.6.1/
shell> rm -f config.sh Policy.sh
shell> sh Configure -de
shell> make
shell> make test
shell> make install
```

You are presented with many questions during the compilation process. If you don't understand them, don't worry. The Perl defaults are quite sensible, and in almost all cases, following the default suggestions will work for your system. To accept the defaults, just hit <RETURN> at each question.

When you have a working version of Perl, you'll need to make sure you have the Perl modules that you need in order to connect to MySQL. These modules are called DBI and DBD::mysql.

DBI is a standardized database interface for Perl. It provides methods for programmers to connect to a variety of databases. In order to connect to different kinds of databases, DBI relies on a series of DBD (DataBase Driver) modules. So in order to use DBI with MySQL, you need to install the MySQL driver module, called DBD::mysql.

You may already have DBI installed on your system and not know it. To see if you have DBI installed, type the following command:

```
shell>perl -e 'use DBI'
```

If you get an error message like the following, you probably don't have DBI installed yet.

```
Can't locate Apache/DBI.pm in @INC (@INC contains:
/usr/lib/perl5/5.6.0/i386-linux /usr/lib/perl5/5.6.0
/usr/lib/perl5/site_perl/5.6.0/i386-linux /usr/lib/perl5/site_perl/5.6.0
/usr/lib/perl5/site_perl .) at -e line 1.
BEGIN failed--compilation aborted at -e line 1.
```

But installing DBI — or any other module, for that matter — is easy if you use Perl's CPAN module, accessed via the -MCPAN flag at the command line.

CPAN works best when you have the text-mode browser *lynx* installed. If your system does not have lynx installed already (OS X users in particular may not have lynx available), you should install it now.

To see if you have lynx installed on your system already, type the following:

```
shell> lynx
```

If you get a command not found error, you can install lynx by following these steps.

First, download the latest release from http://lynx.isc.org.

At the time of this writing, the latest version of lynx was 2.8.4, so the file I'll be using in the examples below is called lynx2.8.4.tar.gz.

```
tar -xzvf lynx2.8.4.tar.gz
cd lynx2.8.4
./configure
make
make install
```

Now you should be ready to use the CPAN module to install DBI.

```
shell> perl -MCPAN -e 'install DBI';
```

The first time you use the -MCPAN method to install a new Perl module, you are expected to answer a series of questions. Once again, don't worry. You can hit <RETURN> and use the sensible defaults. The big exception would be if you have installed Perl under your home directory. In that case, you should make sure that your modules are being installed in the same area as your private installation of Perl.

Installing DBD::mysql — the mysql drivers for DBI

Now it's time to install DBD::mysql, a Perl module that contains the drivers that let DBD communicate with MySQL.

```
shell> perl -MCPAN -e 'install DBD::mysql'
```

If you have an older version of Perl installed, you may find that installing the latest DBD::mysql module will cause CPAN to automatically upgrade your Perl installation. Once again, don't worry about the many questions you'll be asked during installation. Hitting <RETURN> at each prompt will allow you to accept the safe and sensible default options.

Installing for Windows

If you are planning on doing your Perl/CGI development under Windows, I emphatically recommend using the NuSphere to install Perl and its database modules. Otherwise you'll be faced with a fairly steep learning curve, as the compilation tools that come as standard features of Linux, Unix, and Mac OS X don't come built into Windows.

If you're an experienced developer, or extremely interested in learning to compile and install open-source programs for Windows, I recommend installing a free C compiler like gcc (available via http://gcc.gnu.org), and then visiting www.cpan.org for source code and instructions on compiling and configuring Perl and its database modules on your Windows system.

Testing Your Installation

**20 Min.
To Go**

After you have all the right components installed, connecting to your MySQL database from a Perl script is relatively simple. The DBI module provides a connect() method that returns an object that is referred to as a *database handle* (traditionally named $dbh). This object allows access to all the DBI methods for querying your database. To see the connect() method in action, create a file called test.pl with the following contents shown in Listing 17-1.

Listing 17-1 *Perl script that demonstrates DBI's connect() method*

```
#!/usr/bin/perl
# you may need to change the line above to reflect
# the path to your particular Perl installation.
# Windows users who have installed via the NuSphere disk
# can just use #!bash

use DBI;
use strict; ## always a good idea

my $host = 'localhost';
my $db = 'test';

## we're using the MySQL 'root' user for now
## just like we did in the PHP section.
## If you prefer to use another user account,
## or have created a password for your root user
## you will need to change the username
## and password variables below

my $user = 'root';
my $password = '';

my $dbh = DBI->connect("DBI:mysql:$db:$host",$user,$password)
          or die "Cannot connect to database.";

# if we made it this far, the script didn't die.
```

Continued

Listing 17-1 *Continued*

```
print "Cool, we connected to MySQL! \n";

$dbh->disconnect();
```

Now it's time to make sure everything works. Unix, Linux, and Mac OS X users need to make the script executable with the following command:

```
shell> chmod ugo+x test.pl
shell> ./test.pl
Cool, we connected to MySQL!
shell>
```

Now try to access a database that doesn't exist by changing the variable $db to 'testt" instead of 'test'. You should see the following connection error:

```
shell> ./test.pl
DBI->connect(testt:localhost) failed: Unknown database 'testt' at
./test.pl line 14
Cannot connect to database.
```

Turning Your Perl Script into a CGI Script

Now that you can connect to MySQL via the command line, it's time to try your script as a CGI script. Your Apache installation most likely came pre-configured with a cgi-bin directory. Files in this directory are expected to be scripts that can be run by Apache in response to a browser's request.

On many Unix systems, the directory will be /usr/local/apache/cgi-bin/. On Linux, the directory is often /var/www/cgi-bin/. If you are having trouble finding your cgi-bin directory, you can open your httpd.conf file and search for the string **cgi-bin**. If you prefer to place your scripts in a location other than cgi-bin, you can use the Apache configuration directive AddHandler cgi-script .cgi to make CGIs run from a particular location, or anywhere on your server.

When you've located or created your cgi-bin directory, you can copy your test.pl file into it. Next, I make some changes so the script will run in Apache's CGI environment. On my system, the copy command looks like this:

```
shell> cp /home/mydir/test.pl /usr/local/apache/cgi-bin/test.cgi
```

Now that I have a new file called test.cgi in the right place, I can alter the script so that it runs under Apache. First, I want to install another helpful Perl module, called CGI.pm.

By now, installing a module via CPAN should be no problem for you. First, see if it's installed already.

```
shell> perl -e 'use CGI'
shell>
```

In this case, no news is great news. If you don't see an error message, then you have the CGI module available already. If you see an error message (usually beginning with Can't locate CGI.pm in @INC), you can install CGI yourself.

Remember, please, that you need to be logged in as the root (administrator) user in order to install Perl modules in their traditional location, under /usr/local/.

```
shell> perl -MCPAN -e 'install CGI'
```

When you have the CGI module installed, you can modify your script as shown in Listing 17-2.

Listing 17-2 *Perl CGI script that connects to MySQL*

```perl
#!/usr/bin/perl

use DBI;
use strict; ## always a good idea
use CGI; ## note that we've added the CGI module here

my $host = 'localhost';
my $db = 'test';

## we're using the MySQL 'root' user for now. You may
## need to change the username and password
## variables below for this code to run on your system.

my $user = 'root';
my $password = '';

## set up a new CGI object

my $c = new CGI();

## Done setting up variables. Time to send the CGI
## header information and connect to MySQL

print $c->header();

print $c->start_html(-title=>'MySQL Test');
print "Trying to connect to MySQL now... <br><br>";

my $dbh =
 DBI->connect("DBI:mysql:$db:$host",$user,$password)
  or die "Cannot connect to database.\n";

print "Cool, we connected to MySQL! \n";

# disconnect from MySQL by calling the disconnect() method
$dbh->disconnect();
```

Continued

Listing 17-2 *Continued*

```
print $c->end_html();
```

Now Unix and Os X users will need to make the script executable with the following command:

```
chmod ugo+x test.cgi
```

With that, you can test the script via your Web browser. The URL will most likely look like http://www.yourdomain.com/cgi-bin/test.cgi.

If all is well, you'll see the following text:

```
Trying to connect to MySQL now...
Cool, we connected to MySQL!
```

Now let's see what happens when something goes wrong. Once again, change the variable $db from "test" to "testt" and reload your script in your browser. Now your browser window should say this:

```
Trying to connect to MySQL now...
```

So where are the error messages? In CGI programming, when a script dies, it sends its error messages to the server's error log. Error log locations vary with system types, but the file is often called error_log. In Linux, the file is often called /var/log/httpd/error_log. In other Unix systems, the file may be called /usr/local/apache/logs/error_log. As usual, when in doubt, check your httpd.conf file.

After you've located your error log, you can check it for errors relating to the last failed connection attempt. On my Unix system, the command to view the last two lines of my error log looks like this:

```
shell> tail -2 /usr/local/apache/logs/error_log

DBI->connect(testt:localhost) failed: Unknown database 'testt' at
/var/www/cgi-bin/test.cgi line 25
Cannot connect to database.
```

These are the same error messages we saw on the command line above, but this time the Apache server is logging the errors. This is nice for your site users because they don't see a screen full of incomprehensible (to them) error messages. But it can be annoying for you as a programmer to not see your errors onscreen. In the next session, I cover sensible error handling, including ways to display errors onscreen during development but send errors to the server logs after the site is available to the general public.

Some of DBI's Methods for Sending and Retrieving Data

**10 Min.
To Go**

So far this session, you have learned how to install Perl, Perl modules, and how to connect to MySQL. Now it's time to move on to some more useful functions that let you insert and retrieve data. Note that from now on, I'm going to present all scripts as CGI scripts because that's how you are most likely to be using Perl and MySQL together.

Retrieving data

The examples in this section assume that you have a table called `users` in your `test` database, which you can create as follows:

```
mysql> use test;
mysql> create table users (firstname varchar(80), lastname varchar(80),
users_id int auto_increment not null primary key);
```

Now put some test data into your new table.

```
mysql> insert into users (firstname, lastname) values ("Liz","Warner");
mysql> insert into users (firstname, lastname) values
("Elizabeth","Greenspan");
```

DBI lets you can retrieve data from MySQL in many ways.

Retrieving a scalar or array with selectrow_array()

For example, to retrieve one or more variables from a single row, you can use the `selectrow_array()` method. When called in a scalar context, it returns a single variable, which is the content of the first column of the first row returned by the query. When called in an array context, it returns an array of variables. For example:

```
my $firstname = $dbh->selectrow_array("select firstname from users where
users_id = 1");
```

or

```
my ($firstname, $lastname) =
  $dbh->selectrow_array("select firstname, lastname from users where
users_id = 1");
```

Protecting yourself from tainted variables with quote()

You may have noticed something missing in the examples above. Most scripts won't know the value of `users_id` in advance. For example, what if `users_id` was passed to your script through the CGI environment? Then it's a good idea to pass the variable through the DBI object's `quote()` method so that the proper quotation marks are added if necessary and any illegal characters are dealt with. For example:

```
my $users_id =
  $dbh->quote($c->param('users_id'));

my $firstname =
  $dbh->selectrow_array("select firstname from users where users_id =
$users_id");
```

Retrieving a two-dimensional array of rows with selectall_arrayref()

DBI also provides several ways in which you can retrieve many rows of data and iterate through them. One of the simplest ways to do this is with the `selectall_arrayref()` method, which returns a two-dimensional array of results. Here's an example:

```
my ($firstname,$lastname,$row);

my $rows =
  $dbh->selectall_arrayref("select firstname, lastname from users");

foreach $row (@$rows)
{
  ($firstname,$lastname) = @$row;
  print "Firstname is $firstname and lastname is $lastname <br>\n";
}
```

Selecting data with selectall_hashref()

The selectall_hashref() method returns query results as a reference to a hash of hashes. You specify the query and hash key as an argument.

```
# this example works with DBI version 1.20 or later

# if you are using a version of DBI prior to version 1.20, please see
# your local documentation, as selectall_hashref() has changed over time
# (in versions between 1.15 and 1.20 it returns a reference to an array of
#  hashes)

# note that I'm supplying two arguments for selectall_hashref()
# the query, and the key for the hash

my $hashref = $dbh->selectall_hashref('select * from users','users_id');

my $counter = 0;

while( $hashref->{$counter} )
{
  print $hashref->{$counter}{'firstname'} . ' ' .
$hashref->{$counter}{'lastname'} . '<br>';
  $counter++;
}
```

There are many other ways to retrieve data via DBI. Although `selectall_arrayref()` and `selectall_hashref()` may fill most, if not all, of your data retrieval needs, I encourage you to visit `http://dbi.perl.org/` to view the full documentation for DBI.

Now that you know how to connect to MySQL via a CGI script and retrieve data, you can use this knowledge to create a script (shown in Listing 17-3) that retrieves and lists all the rows in a table.

Listing 17-3 *Perl CGI script that displays all rows in a table*

```perl
#!/usr/bin/perl

use DBI;
use strict; ## always a good idea
use CGI;

my $host = 'localhost';
my $db = 'test';

# we're still using the MySQL 'root' user for example purposes.
# You may need to change the username and password variables
# below in order for this code to run on your system.

my $user = 'root';
my $password = '';
my $c = new CGI();

# Done setting up variables.
# Time to send the CGI header information and connect to MySQL

print $c->header();

print $c->start_html(-title=>'MySQL Test');
print "Trying to connect to MySQL now... <br><br>";

my $dbh = DBI->connect("DBI:mysql:$db:$host",$user,$password)
  or die "Cannot connect to database. Error: $DBI::errstr \n";

print "Cool, we connected to MySQL! <br><br>\n";

my ($firstname,$lastname,$row);

my $rows =
  $dbh->selectall_arrayref("select firstname, lastname from users");

foreach $row (@$rows)
{
  ($firstname,$lastname) = @$row;
  print "Firstname is $firstname and lastname is $lastname <br>";
}

$dbh->disconnect();

print $c->end_html();
```

Inserting data with do()

You can send any query to MySQL with DBI's do() method. This means that you can use the do() method to insert data into a table. For example, this code snippet can be used within a CGI script to insert a new user into the users table:

```
# make sure the variables are properly quoted,
# and don't contain any funny characters

my $fname = $dbh->quote($c->param('firstname'));
my $lname = $dbh->quote($c->param('lastname'));

# now insert the new row
$dbh->do("insert into users (firstname,lastname) values ($fname, $lname)")
or print "<br>Unable to insert data";
```

In the next session, I cover other ways to safely insert data without having to use the `$dbh->quote()` **method on each variable.**

Pulling It All Together

Now that you know how to send queries to MySQL and how to retrieve data, you can create a more complex CGI application that allows you to update, edit, and delete users from the test table you created earlier in this section. Note that this application is very similar to the PHP application you created at the end of Chapter 15, except that the Perl script is printing all the HTML dynamically. Unlike PHP, there is no built-in separation between HTML and Perl code. In the next session, however, I cover some more sophisticated uses of Perl with Apache that do allow for this handy separation.

The small application can be found on the CD in /session17/putting_it_together.pl.

Done!

REVIEW

In this session, you saw how to install Perl and several Perl modules: DBI, DBD::mysql, and CGI. You also learned how to send queries to MySQL via Perl, both from the command line and through CGI. Finally, you saw how to use this knowledge to create a Web-based application to create, update, and delete user records in a test table.

QUIZ YOURSELF

1. What modules does Perl use to connect to MySQL? (See "Compiling and installing Perl.")
2. What [MW1]DBI method can be used to write data to a MySQL table? (See "Inserting data with do().")
3. How do CGI scripts running under Apache keep track of error messages? (See "Turning Your Perl Script into a CGI Script.")
4. What DBI method can be used to retrieve a single variable from a single row in a MySQL table? (See "Retrieving a scalar or array with selectrow_array().")
5. How would you make sure that tainted data won't be sent to MySQL as a result of malicious or careless user input? (See "Protecting yourself from tainted variables with quote().")

MySQL and Perl: Best Practices

**30 Min.
To Go**

D uring this session, I show you some ways to help make your Perl and MySQL code safer and more efficient for the Web. I also provide some utility functions that you can use in your Web applications. Finally, I touch on some advanced uses of Perl with Apache that you may want to explore in the future.

Handling User Data

In the last session, you learned how to automatically clean and quote user data using DBI's quote() method. But calling quote() on a large number of variables can be overwhelming. So now I'd like to show you another way to handle user-provided variables safely by using placeholders and bind values.

DBI allows you to put placeholders in your MySQL queries and then supply the corresponding variables separately. These placeholders appear in your queries as question mark (?) characters, and the association of placeholders with variables is called *binding*. The variables to be associated are called *bind values*. When you use binding, the bind values are automatically provided with the appropriate quotes, and illegal characters are escaped properly. Here are a few examples:

```
# in these code snippets we are assuming that we have already created $c
as
# a CGI object, and $dbh as a database handle (DBI object).

# in this example, we're inserting the bind values into their own array.

my @bindvals = ($c->param('firstname'),$c->param(''astname'));

$dbh->do("insert into users (firstname, lastname)
values (?,?)",undef,@bindvals);


# here we're just supplying the bind values
# as arguments to the do() and select() methods

$dbh->do('update users set firstname = ? where users_id = ?',
undef,$c->param('firstname'),$c->param('users_id'));
my $lastname = $dbh->selectrow_array('select lastname from users where
users_id = ?',undef,$c->param('users_id'));
```

Removing Unwanted HTML

During the PHP sessions, you learned how to remove unwanted HTML using the PHP
strip_tags() and htmlspecialchars() functions. Unfortunately, Perl doesn't come
with any similar functions built in. If you want access to some sophisticated HTML parsing
functions, you can use the CPAN installation method you learned in the last session to
install the HTML::Parser module. (Search for **HTML::Parser** at http://www.cpan.org for
documentation on the latest version.) For now, however, I demonstrate a simpler function
to remove HTML from a single variable (see Listing 18-1).

Listing 18-1 *remove_html() function*

```
sub remove_html
{
  # this regular expression for removing HTML tags was lifted
  # from the Perl FAQ at http://cpan.org/doc/FAQs/FAQ/PerlFAQ.html
  my $item = shift();
  $item =~ s/<(?:[^>'"]*|(['"]).*?\1)*>//gs;
  return $item;
}
```

Handling Errors

In the last session, you learned that DBI/MySQL errors are silently logged to your Apache
error log. This is helpful for your site's users but can be annoying during development when

you may want to see your errors onscreen. You can easily take care of this by creating a simple error-handling function, which works along with a global variable called $debug.

If $debug is set to a true value (such as 1), your error function can print the MySQL error message to your HTML page. When you're ready to launch your site, you can set $debug to a false value (such as 0) and if there's a query error, your users see only a polite error message. I've created an example of such a function, called handle_error(). It's displayed in Listing 18-2 below. But first, here's a usage example:

```
my $query = "some query";

my $value = $dbh->selectrow_array($query)
    or handle_error("<br>Sorry! We were unable to retrieve your
data.<br>");
```

Listing 18-2 *handle_error() function*

```
sub handle_error()
{
    # assumes the existence of a global variable called $debug

    my $polite_message = shift();
    if ($debug)
    {
# print the query error to the HTML page
print "<b> Query Error: $DBI::errstr </b><br>";
    }
    else
    {
print "$polite_message";
            # remember, the DBI/MySQL error message is being
# logged to your apache error log already
    }
}
```

Optimizing Your Queries for the Web

**20 Min.
To Go**

When you're writing code for the Web, you may need to be aware of performance issues. When you select data from a MySQL table, that data needs to be stored in your server's memory while your script is running. On a lightly used site with small tables, this may not be an issue. But if you are planning on someday handling sites with many users and large tables, you'll want to think about how much data you are retrieving and whether you really need all the data.

The general rule is this: Never ask for more data than you need. This means avoiding queries that start with SELECT * unless you really need all the data in all the rows you're requesting. Especially for large tables, it can be much more efficient to retrieve only the variables you need.

Here's an example of a (possibly) inefficient query:

```perl
my $hashref = $dbh->selectall_hashref("select * from big_table where
big_table_id = 1000");

print $hashref->{1}{'somevar'} . " " . $hashref->{1}{'othervar'};
```

A more efficient query may be

```perl
my $hashref = $dbh->selectall_hashref("select somevar, othervar from
big_table where big_table_id = 1000");
```

Other Ways to Use Perl with Apache and MySQL

In the last session, you learned how to communicate with MySQL through CGI scripts. While CGI has historically been the most popular way to use Perl for the Web, it does have its drawbacks. First, your HTML code is printed by the script itself. You don't have the automatic separation of HTML from executable code that you do with PHP. Second, CGI can be inefficient for heavily used servers. This is because your Apache server needs to spawn a new instance of the Perl interpreter for every CGI request. PHP, on the other hand, runs entirely within Apache, which means that Apache doesn't need to start a new process with each PHP request.

As you may have guessed already, some clever Perl programmers have found ways around this problem. Most of these solutions are based on Apache's mod_perl module. If you used the included NuSphere disk to install Apache, you already have mod_perl available. Otherwise, you can visit http://perl.apache.org for download and installation instructions.

There isn't time in this session to cover all of the enhanced Perl/Apache tools available, but I'd like to offer a few tips for those of you who are interested learning more about enhanced Perl tools for the Web.

One of the most sophisticated mod_perl-based tools available at the time of this writing is HTML::Mason. It allows you to separate HTML from executable code just like PHP does, and it also allows you to create session-handling functionality, document templating, and highly sophisticated Web applications with relative ease. I show you some examples of code using HTML::Mason at the end of this session.

In addition to HTML::Mason, many Perl programmers use embedded Perl via the eperl and embperl tools. To learn about these and other tools that allow you to embed Perl in your HTML code, you can visit www.engelschall.com/sw/eperl/related/.

One major advantage of using a mod_perl-based tool like HTML::Mason is that you can take advantage of persistent connections through Apache::DBI. With CGI, you need to make a new connection to MySQL each time your script is called. This is, as you may have guessed, another way to overload your server. The Apache::DBI module behaves just like DBI, except that it automatically manages persistent database connections for you behind the scenes. Persistent database connections mean that your scripts load faster, and your server load is lighter.

**10 Min.
To Go**

A brief introduction to HTML::Mason

Installing HTML::Mason (also known as just Mason) on your system is fairly simple once you've got Apache's mod_perl installed. Again, if you used the NuSphere install, you already have mod_perl available. Otherwise, you can visit http://perl.apache.org for download and installation instructions for your system.

When you have mod_perl installed, you can install Mason via the CPAN technique you learned in the last session.

```
perl -MCPAN -e 'install HTML::Mason'
```

After you've installed Mason, you need to configure it. The instructions below worked at the time of this writing. Mason is a work in progress, however, so I recommend that you visit www.masonhq.com/d ocs/manual/Admin.html for the most current documentation.

Here are the directives that work on my Unix system. You will need to change the paths in the code below to reflect your personal configuration.

First, create a new directory for Mason's use and change it so that it is owned by "nobody" (or whichever username your Web server runs under). Depending on the path to your Apache installation, you may need to be logged in as the root (administrator) user for these commands to work:

```
shell> mkdir /usr/local/apache/mason
shell> chown nobody:nobody /usr/local/apache/mason
```

Now, in your httpd.conf file, add these lines. They tell Apache to handle .html files via the HTML::Mason module. (Advanced users can also set up a Mason-only directory or a virtual host where Mason handles all files. This is outside the scope of these examples.)

```
PerlRequire /usr/local/apache/mason/handler.pl

<Location />
    SetHandler perl-script
    PerlHandler HTML::Mason
</Location>
```

Finally, you must create your handler.pl file. I've provided an example handler.pl file (see Listing 18-3) that works with Mason at the time of this writing. Because Mason continues to be a work in progress, however, please see www.masonhq.com/docs/manual/Admin.html#configuring_via_a_handler_script if you have any trouble.

Listing 18-3 *Example handler.pl file*

```
#!/usr/bin/perl
package HTML::Mason;

use HTML::Mason;
use strict;
# use Apache::DBI instead of just plain DBI
# if you want persistent database connections
```

Continued

Listing 18-3 *Continued*

```perl
use Apache::DBI;


# List of modules that you want to use from components (see Admin
# manual for details)
{ package HTML::Mason::Commands;
}

# Create Mason objects
#
my $parser = new HTML::Mason::Parser;

# you may need to change the paths below to reflect your system config
my $interp = new HTML::Mason::Interp (parser=>$parser,
  allow_recursive_autohandlers =>undef,
  comp_root=>'/usr/local/apache/htdocs/',
  data_dir=>'/usr/local/apache/mason/data');

my $ah = new HTML::Mason::ApacheHandler (interp=>$interp);

# create a global DB handle
$parser->allow_globals(qw($dbh));

# set the appropriate tablename, username and password below

$interp->set_global(dbh => DBI->connect("DBI:mysql:test:localhost",
"Web_user","Web_password"))
|| die "Cannot connect to database";

# Activate the following if running httpd as root (the normal case).
# Resets ownership of all files created by Mason at startup. Change
# these to match your server's 'User' and 'Group'.
#
chown (scalar(getpwnam "nobody"), scalar(getgrnam "nobody"),
    $interp->files_written);

sub handler
{
  my ($r) = @_;

  # If you plan to intermix images in the same directory as
  # components, activate the following to prevent Mason from
  # evaluating image files as components.
  #
return -1 if $r->content_type && $r->content_type =~ /image/i;

  my $status = $ah->handle_request($r);
```

```
    return $status;
}

1;
```

Now you're ready to create some Mason files. First, you'll need to learn a few new syntax tricks. Like PHP, Mason lets you embed executable code (or include files containing executable code) within your HTML pages. Here are two ways to include Perl code directly in your HTML pages:

```
% print "this is a single line of perl code <br>";

Here is some HTML text outside the Perl areas.<br>

<%perl>

my $foo = "Hello";
print "$foo, this is a multi-line Perl block. <br>";

</%perl>
```

In the PHP sessions, you saw the utility of dividing your code into multiple reusable bits and including the files you need within your main documents. Using Mason, you can use the same technique. Here's a way to include another file (also called a *component*) within your HTML file.

```
<& "myfile.cmp", %ARGS &>
```

You can also include other files (components) within a Perl block by using the $m-comp() method. (The variable $m is provided to you by Mason as a helper object. See the documentation at www.masonhq.com for more on the $m variable and other useful objects Mason provides.)

```
% $m->comp('myfile.cmp',%ARGS);
```

Finally, Mason provides a way for you to display a single variable within your html code, like so:

```
<% $foo %>
```

You've probably been wondering about the %ARGS hash that keeps showing up in these code snippets. Mason creates this hash for you and puts CGI form variables into it, ready for use. So, for example, if you knew your user had just submitted a form containing the variables 'firstname' and 'lastname', you could use this syntax to write those two variables into a MySQL table:

```
# recall that the global database handle, $dbh, was created by handler.pl
# and is available to all components

if ($ARGS{'submit'})
{
```

```
$dbh->do("insert into users (firstname,lastname)
values (?,?)",undef,$ARGS{'firstname'},$ARGS{'lastname'})
or $m->out("Error inserting data");
}
```

Using Mason's autohandlers

Now that I've covered some basic syntax, I can get into one of the really interesting things about Mason. This is Mason's *autohandler* capability. If Mason sees a file called "autohandler" in the current directory, it automatically executes the code in that file before the file request is handled. This means you can do all kinds of neat things like handle sessions, handle form submissions, and create custom headers and footers — all without touching your HTML content files.

Listing 18-4 is an example autohandler that handles custom header and footers for two different virtual hosts.

Listing 18-4   *Example HTML::Mason autohandler*

```
%##### write the page header (the variable $header is defined below)

<& $header, %ARGS &>

%##### write the page body. This is the URI requested by the browser
%##### made available via the Apache Request Object, $r (see the Mason
manual)

<& $r->uri(),%ARGS &>


%#### write the page footer

<& 'footer.cmp', %ARGS &>

%##### Done With Display Code #######


%##### A component's "init" section always gets called first by Mason.
%##### It is traditionally placed at the bottom of the page,
%##### after all display code.
%##### This is where you can set up variables used by the display
components,
%##### and do any processing that must be done for each page.

<%init>

# let's get the name of the current virtual host, and serve a different HTML
# header for each of two different virtual hosts

# first, we can use the Apache Request object, $r, to get a hash of
headers
```

```perl
my %hheaders = $r->headers_in;

# now we can set a key in the %ARGS hash called 'server' for future
reference
# (the %ARGS hash is automatically filled with all CGI variables, and we
# can add extra parameters to it and pass it to our sub-components)

$ARGS{'server'} = $hheaders{'Host'};

my $header;

if( $ARGS{'server'} =~ /myexamplesiteone\.com/ )
{
    $header = "header_one.cmp";
}
else
{
    $header = "header.cmp";
}

</%init>
```

Now let's look at the header and footer files. For example, the contents of header_one.cmp could be very simple HTML, like this shown here in Listing 18-5.

Listing 18-5   *Example HTML::Mason component: header_one.cmp*

```html
<html><head><title>Welcome to examplesiteone.com</title></head>
<body bgcolor="white">
<h1>Welcome to Example Site One</h1>
```

Then the contents of header.cmp can include more complex Mason components (see Listing 18-6).

Listing 18-6   *Second Example HTML::Mason header component: header.cmp*

```html
<html><head><title>Default</title></head>
<body bgcolor="white">
<%perl>

    # now you could include, say, a global navigation component
      # that examines the value of $r->uri() and turns navigation images
      # on and off dynamically

    $m->comp("/global/my_custom_navigation.cmp",%ARGS);
</%perl>
```

The file footer.cmp, then, includes any text you want to appear at the bottom of each page, plus your closing HTML tags (see Listing 18-7).

Listing 18-7 *Example HTML::Mason footer: footer.cmp*

```
<br>
Copyright 2001, MyExampleSitesGalore, Inc.
</body></html>
```

Now take a look at the `index.html` file (see Listing 18-8). It has no starting or ending HTML tags, and no custom navigation elements. These were all placed in the header and footer components and automatically printed at each request by your autohandler. The current page includes only relevant content. (It can, of course, include embedded Perl code for things like MySQL selects and the like.)

Listing 18-8 *Example HTML::Mason index.html file for use with above*

```
<!-- note that there are no beginning or ending HTML tags on this or
     any page on this site -->

<table border="0">
    <tr><td> Here is the copy for the home pages of my sites. </td></tr>
</table>
```

Now when you request your new index.html file for www.myexamplesiteone.com from a browser, you should see the following (see Figure 18-1).

Figure 18-1 *Rendering of Sample HTML::Mason Files*

Done!

REVIEW

In this session, you saw some utility functions for using Perl with MySQL in a CGI environment. You also learned a bit about optimizing your scripts for the Web. Finally, you were introduced to some advanced concepts for future reference, including a brief overview of HTML::Mason.

QUIZ YOURSELF

1. What are two ways to make sure your queries aren't tainted by bad user-supplied data? (See "Handling User Data.")

2. What are some of the disadvantages of using CGI scripts? (See "Other Ways to Use Perl with Apache and MySQL.")

3. How could you optimize your queries for a heavily utilized Web server? (See "Optimizing Your Queries for the Web.")

4. How would you remove unwanted HTML tags from user-submitted text? (See "Removing Unwanted HTML.")

5. What are some of the advantages of maintaining persistent database connections? (See "Other Ways to Use Perl with Apache and MySQL.")

Optimizing MySQL Queries

Session Checklist

✔ Logging slow queries

✔ Looking at indexes

✔ Applying and testing indexes

✔ Other ways of applying indexes

**30 Min.
To Go**

In the previous four sessions, you saw how to write applications in PHP and Perl that use MySQL data. You're going to want your applications — no matter what language they're written in — to run as quickly as possible. While you may find that tweaks to your code speed a script's execution, nothing you can do to your scripts fixes a slow query. If a query doesn't execute at an acceptable speed, the application will be stuck, waiting for MySQL to respond to a query request. A pokey query can slow an application far more than a few lines of poorly written code. However, in MySQL, diagnosing and fixing queries that are not performing well is fairly easy. In almost all cases, you will be able to fix your queries by altering your indexes.

Logging Slow Queries

There is more information on logging in Session 24, but in this session you should know that there is one MySQL log whose sole purpose is to help the database administrator identify queries that are not performing well. It's called, aptly enough, the *Slow Query log*. You can start this log by starting the MySQL daemon with the `--log-slow-queries` flag. If you have multiple hard disks on your system, your log files should be put on a different physical disk than the one that holds the MySQL tables. In the commands below, I've started the MySQL daemon indicating the path and name of my Slow Query log. The first was run on Unix, the second on Windows.

```
shell> mysqld_safe --log-slow-queries=/home/mysql/slow.log
c:\Program Files\mysql\bin> mysqld --log-slow-queries=c:\myslowlog.log
```

The MySQL variable long_query_time determines how slow a query must be in order to be included in this log. The default value, as seen in the query below, is 10 (meaning 10 seconds).

```
mysql> SHOW VARIABLES LIKE 'long%';
+-----------------+-------+
| Variable_name   | Value |
+-----------------+-------+
| long_query_time | 10    |
+-----------------+-------+
```

Ten seconds is a very, very, very long time for a query to run; so, you may want to set this to a lower value. You can change the value of this variable by adding a line like the following to your my.cnf, file.

```
set variable = long_query_time=5
```

You see more about the my.cnf file in Session 22. Beyond the queries that end up being logged, you may have suspicions that other queries can be improved. Generally, you should be suspicious of queries that require many joins or return very large data sets.

Looking at Indexes

About 90 percent of your slow query problems with SELECT statements can be fixed by properly applying indexes. Remember that an index is a memory-resident representation of column values that stores values in a highly-optimized way. You can think of an index as a triangle, where, at the peak of the triangle, the index holds the median value. If the value being searched for is less than the median, MySQL searches the index in one direction. If the value is higher, MySQL searches the other direction. This continues down the triangle so at every level, MySQL can half the rows that potentially match. It works a lot like Beat the Clock on "The Price is Right." If you had to guess the value of an item that was somewhere between 0 and 10,000, you'd start with $5000, and then if the Bob said the value was higher, you'd say $7500. And you'd continue narrowing it down this way until you got the correct value.

Whenever possible, you want to make sure that your application is using indexes to find results of frequently used SELECT statements. Moreover, if you can be sure that a column for each row contains unique values, you're better off creating a UNIQUE index or assigning the column as the primary key (if the table doesn't have a primary key already).

To give you a firm idea of the importance of using SELECT with an index, consider this example:

I created a table with two columns, each with a 32-character char() type. The only difference between these columns is that the first column was declared the primary key and was therefore indexed; no index was applied to the second column.

```
CREATE TABLE tbl (
    col1 char(32) not null primary key,
    col2 char(32) not null
)
```

I loaded 30,000 rows into the table and then ran two nearly identical queries, changing only the column used in the WHERE clause. The two queries looked like

```
SELECT col1, col2 FROM tbl WHERE col='mystring';
SELECT col1, col2 FROM tbl WHERE co2='mystring';
```

In the first query, MySQL was able to use an index to resolve the WHERE clause; however, no index was available for col2, and thus MySQL had to read the table off disk. In my small test, the second query ran seven to nine times slower than the first. Though both queries executed quickly, this speed difference can be quite meaningful on a busy server where MySQL handles hundreds of queries per second. As your tables and queries increase in size, the speed difference between properly indexed tables and those that are not properly indexed grow even larger.

The above example shows one case where MySQL attempts to use an index (when searching for a single or multiple values in a WHERE clause). Here are some other occasions where MySQL will use an index if one is available:

- To discover what rows from different tables should be joined.
- To find the value of the aggregate functions min() and max().
- When ordering values with the ORDER BY clause.
- When resolving a LIKE comparison, if the matching string does not start with a wildcard (for example, SELECT fname FROM users WHERE fname LIKE '%jay' will never use an index).
- When searching for null values with the IS NULL predicate.

The good news is that MySQL makes it very easy to discover when and how indexes are used in SELECT statements.

 At this point you may be wondering what the big deal is. If using indexes are so advantageous, why not just create indexes for all columns? There's a very good reason, actually. Indexes require resources. Every time an INSERT or UPDATE executes, MySQL must update not only the rows within the table, but also the indexes on that table. On a table that is used primarily for INSERTs, unnecessary indexes can slow you down. Indexes also take up RAM.

Applying and Testing Indexes

**20 Min.
To Go**

In the store database, there are several tables where I can improve upon the indexes made by my original CREATE statements. I show a few examples of how I can examine and fix potential query problems. Along the way, you learn about some very sophisticated MySQL commands.

Creating multicolumn indexes

To start with, take a look at the original users table. When examining indexes, I don't want to see the data. I don't even want to see all the details I'd get from the SHOW COLUMNS FROM users command. I want to see only the details of the indexes. For that, I run a SHOW INDEX command. (Note that the \G option at the end of the query signifies that I want the results of the query in the layout seen below, rather then in tabular form).

```
mysql> show index from users \G
*************************** 1. row ***************************
        Table: users
   Non_unique: 0
     Key_name: PRIMARY
Seq_in_index: 1
  Column_name: user_id
    Collation: A
  Cardinality: 5
     Sub_part: NULL
       Packed: NULL
      Comment:
*************************** 2. row ***************************
        Table: users
   Non_unique: 1
     Key_name: index_on_email
Seq_in_index: 1
  Column_name: email
    Collation: A
  Cardinality: NULL
     Sub_part: NULL
       Packed: NULL
      Comment:
2 rows in set (0.01 sec)
```

This listing gives me a lot of information. For details on what each of these entries means, see the MySQL manual (www.mysql.com/doc/S/H/SHOW_DATABASE_INFO.html). For now, it's enough to understand that the users table contains two indexes, one for the primary key (users_id) and one for the email column. So any time I use the user_id or email as columns for ordering or as the criterion in the WHERE clause, an index will be used. But you don't have to take my word for it. You can use the EXPLAIN command.

MySQL's EXPLAIN command describes in great detail how the MySQL engine determines the results of a query. To run the command, all you need to do is prepend a SELECT query with the keyword EXPLAIN. For example, to make sure a query on the users table makes use of an index while using searching for a user_id, I'd run the following:

```
mysql> EXPLAIN SELECT user_id FROM users WHERE user_id=1 \G
*************************** 1. row ***************************
        table: users
         type: const
possible_keys: PRIMARY
          key: PRIMARY
      key_len: 4
          ref: const
         rows: 1
        Extra:
```

Some of the information here is pretty much self-explanatory. The result lists the table name, name of indexes, and estimated rows in the result. The most important part of this listing is type (the item just below table). Below you can see a list of the possible values for the type item and what the values mean. The items are listed in order from fastest to slowest.

- **const:** MySQL determines that there is only one possible matching row. Thus, MySQL views the values of this row as constants. That is, because there's only one row, there are no potential alternate values. (Note that the query above returns a type of const because I searched for a single value on a primary key index, where all values must be unique.)
- **eq_ref:** This is used during joins, and in fact, is the best possible value of type for joins. In this type of join, only one row is read from each table. An eq_ref is only possible when the indexes used for joins are UNIQUE or PRIMARY keys.
- **ref:** You see a ref value when indexes are used but at least one of the indexes is not unique. This is still fast and should be a common type value for your joins.
- **range:** Rows within a given range are retrieved while still using an index.
- **index:** The whole index tree must be scanned.
- **all:** A full table scan is needed for each combination of rows. You should endeavor to avoid this situation in all queries that are run with any frequency.

Aside from queries on the primary key of the users table, there's another query that I can see running frequently: searches on names. The users table may grow to be quite large, and you may want to search the table based on last name and first name (the lname and fname columns). Specifically, within my application, the query is likely to be something like one of these (assume that the dollar sign indicates a variable):

```
SELECT lname, fname, user_id FROM users WHERE lname='$lanme';
SELECT lname, fname, user_id FROM users WHERE lname LIKE 'lname%';
SELECT lname, fname, user_id FROM users WHERE lname='$lname' and
fname='$fname';
```

Given the existing indexes, you can run EXPLAIN on any of the above queries (with strings in the WHERE clause rather than variables) and see that the type item would be all — and that's no good. I can address each of these queries by applying an index on the lname and fname columns, with the following ALTER statement:

```
ALTER TABLE users ADD INDEX index_on_names(lname, fname)
```

MySQL will be able to use this index on any of the above three queries. To test this, you can run the following EXPLAIN:

```
EXPLAIN SELECT lname, fname, user_id FROM users WHERE lname='greenspan'
and fname='jay'
```

You see that the value of type is ref, which is acceptable. However, you need to be aware that this index will not be used on the following query:

```
SELECT lname, fname, user_id FROM users WHERE fname='jay'
```

This is because in MySQL, indexes work from left to right. If in a query, the left-most portion of an index is not used, MySQL is not able to use any remaining parts of the index. In the case of my application, I'm willing to live with this, because I feel that searches on fname alone will be quite rare.

In the previous queries, I retrieved not only the name information, but the primary key, user_id. And though user_id is indexed, a separate index exists for this column. So in order for MySQL to retrieve all column values for these queries, it must use an index to determine which row or rows to return and then fetch additional column value from the table itself. However, if all the values to be returned are within an individual index, MySQL will never have to check with the table at all. For example, if I remove the user_id column from one of the previous queries and run EXPLAIN on it, you'd see the following:

```
mysql> explain SELECT lname, fname FROM users WHERE fname='jay' and lname='greenspan'\G
*************************** 1. row ***************************
        table: users
         type: ref
possible_keys: index_on_names
          key: index_on_names
      key_len: 51
          ref: const,const
         rows: 1
        Extra: where used; Using index
```

Look at the Extra item. Here it's telling you two things. First, where used indicates that MySQL was able to eliminate many rows from the result, which is a good thing. Secondly, Using index lets you know that MySQL was able to return all possible values from the index and never had to read from the table. This should be a blazingly fast query. You can find all potential values for the Extra item of the EXPLAIN command in the MySQL manual (www.mysql.com/doc/E/X/EXPLAIN.html).

10 Min.
To Go

Using indexes on joins

The previous example used only a single table, but the fact of the matter is that nearly all of the queries you write within your applications will be joins of some sort. If you are not careful, a poorly executed join can slow your application to a near halt.

In my store database, it takes quite a few tables to get all the information relevant to a single order. I may need all the following columns: user_id, fname, lname, email, addr_1, city, state, zip. And then for each item in the order: order_items_id, item_id, format, product, product_description.

It takes six tables to put all of this together (users, addresses, orders, order_items, items_for_sale, and products). The query for a specific order may look like this:

```
SELECT fname, lname, email, addr_1, addr_2, city, state, zip,
    orders.order_id, order_total, order_items_id,
    order_items.item_id, order_items.price
    product_id, format, product_name
FROM users, addresses, orders, order_items, items_for_sale, products
WHERE orders.order_id=1
    and orders.address_id=addresses.address_id
    and users.user_id=orders.user_id
    and orders.order_id=order_items.order_id
    and order_items.item_id=items_for_sale.item_id
    and items_for_sale.product_id=products.product_id
```

If I run an EXPLAIN query on this table without enhancing the indexes, I get the following results:

```
*************************** 1. row ***************************
        table: orders
         type: const
possible_keys: PRIMARY
          key: PRIMARY
      key_len: 4
          ref: const
         rows: 1
        Extra:
*************************** 2. row ***************************
        table: users
         type: const
possible_keys: PRIMARY
          key: PRIMARY
      key_len: 4
          ref: const
         rows: 1
        Extra:
*************************** 3. row ***************************
        table: addresses
         type: const
possible_keys: PRIMARY
          key: PRIMARY
      key_len: 4
          ref: const
         rows: 1
        Extra:
*************************** 4. row ***************************
        table: order_items
         type: ALL
possible_keys: NULL
          key: NULL
      key_len: NULL
          ref: NULL
         rows: 5
        Extra: where used
*************************** 5. row ***************************
        table: items_for_sale
         type: ALL
possible_keys: PRIMARY
          key: NULL
      key_len: NULL
          ref: NULL
         rows: 3
        Extra: where used
```

```
*************************** 6. row ***************************
        table: products
         type: eq_ref
possible_keys: PRIMARY
          key: PRIMARY
      key_len: 4
          ref: items_for_sale.product_id
         rows: 1
        Extra:
```

The first thing to understand is that the order of the rows matches the order in which MySQL examines tables. I can be pretty happy with the first three rows. Any time I see const in type, I know it's going to be fast. Similarly, row 6 is about as fast as I can make it. However, the rows involving order_items and items_for_sale don't work well. The easiest way to fix this join is to go back to the query and look at the columns that are used as the basis for joins. If you were to run the SHOW indexes statement on each of these tables, you'd see that order_items and items_for_sale contain foreign keys that are used in this query but are not indexed. So I'll add indexes to these two tables with the following commands:

```
ALTER TABLE order_items ADD INDEX index_on_order_id(order_id);
ALTER TABLE items_for_sale ADD INDEX index_on_item_id(item_id);
```

When these indexes are available for joins, the EXPLAIN shows the following results. (I've eliminated some of the results in this listing to conserve space.)

```
*************************** 1. row ***************************
        table: orders
         type: const
        Extra:
*************************** 2. row ***************************
        table: users
         type: const
        Extra:
*************************** 3. row ***************************
        table: addresses
         type: const
        Extra:
*************************** 4. row ***************************
        table: order_items
         type: ref
        Extra: where used
*************************** 5. row ***************************
        table: items_for_sale
         type: eq_ref
        Extra:
*************************** 6. row ***************************
        table: products
         type: eq_ref
        Extra:
```

There is one other piece of information from EXPLAIN that deservers careful consideration: the row item. As mentioned above, row tells approximately how many rows MySQL will have to examine in order to complete a join. If two tables are being joined and one table shows 3000 for row and the other shows 100, that does not mean MySQL will have to examine 3100 rows in total. Rather, it will have to look at 300,000. It will have to examine each of the 3000 rows 100 times. If you're seeing unexpectedly high numbers of rows, look at the WHERE clauses of your query and try to narrow down the result.

Other Ways to Use Indexes

The output of the EXPLAIN statement is rather complex and can not be covered in full detail in this book; so, I encourage you to read everything the MySQL manual has to say on the topic (www.mysql.com/doc/E/X/EXPLAIN.html). Before you start pulling out your hair wondering why your queries refuse to make use of the indexes you've created, keep the following in mind: If MySQL determines internally that it's faster to read directly from the table, it will ignore the index and use the table instead. This happens if, for example, there are very few rows in a table. Additionally, MySQL will not be able to use indexes for joins if the indexed columns do not have identical types. If one column is char(10) and the other is varchar(10), you will not be able to use indexes to join these tables.

If you are having some particularly nasty problems, you can rewrite your queries so that they are joined in the order you request and using the indexes you request. Note that you will rarely, if ever, need to rewrite queries in the ways shown below. Play with your indexes for a while before resorting the rewriting with this syntax.

A simple equi-join, where join fields are enumerated in the WHERE can be rewritten using a STRAIGHT JOIN syntax. The advantage of the STRAIGHT JOIN syntax is that you can specify the order of the joins. For example, to join three tables in a very specific order, I can use

```
SELECT orders.order_id, order_total,
       order_items.item_id, format
FROM orders
     straight_join order_items
     straight_join items_for_sale
WHERE orders.order_id=order_items.order_id
     and order_items.item_id=items_for_sale.item_id
     and orders.order_id=1;
```

I know that MySQL will start this query with orders table and then move on from there.

If you think that an index is available that MySQL refuses to use, you can force the query to work with the index by using the USE INDEX syntax. For example:

```
SELECT lname FROM users USE INDEX(index_on_names) WHERE lname='Greenspan';
```

Done!

REVIEW

In this session, you learned how to speed queries by using indexes. You learned first that indexes can make for dramatic differences in the speed of queries. Then you saw how to apply an index on a pair of columns in order to optimize a SELECT statement that is likely to be used often in the course of your application. You learned about MySQL's EXPLAIN statement and saw how the values returned by EXPLAIN can provide valuable information (including the ref item) that will help you determine where a query is failing. Finally, you saw some alternate syntaxes for the SELECT statement that enable you to determine table join order or the indexes that will be used when searching a table.

QUIZ YOURSELF

1. What flag for starting the mysql daemon will start the Slow Query log? (See "Logging Slow Queries.")
2. What variable determines how long a query must run for it to be logged? (See "Logging Slow Queries.")
3. What command lists the indexes available for a table? (See "Creating multicolumn indexes.")
4. True or False: MySQL can use indexes when the comparison string within a LIKE predicate starts with a wildcard? (See "Looking at Indexes.")
5. What SQL syntax enforces the orders in which tables are joined? (See "Other Ways to Use Indexes.")

SESSION

20

Securing MySQL, Part I: The GRANT Tables

Session Checklist

✔ Understanding the GRANT tables

✔ Using the GRANT and REVOKE statements

✔ Logging in from clients

*30 Min.
To Go*

So far in this book, I have asked you to run all your queries as MySQL's root user. When you logged in to the MySQL command-line client with the -u root option, you were saying that you want to log in as the user known as root. In this case, you didn't use a password, either. It's a very, very bad idea to do most of your work as root. root has privileges to delete any rows in any tables in any database or can simply run the DROP command on any database

If you are administering MySQL, you're going to want to create users with very specific permission. For example, an application that interacts only with the store database doesn't need access to any other tables or databases. In fact, the store application doesn't even need full access to the store database. There's no reason in the world the application should have the rights to, say, DROP the users table.

This session teaches you to work with MySQL's GRANT tables, which control permissions in MySQL.

Understanding the GRANT Tables

MySQL user rights are stored in a series of tables that are automatically created with the MySQL installation. These tables are kept in a database called mysql. In the MySQL command-line client, you can run the SHOW DATABASES command and see a database named mysql.

```
mysql> SHOW DATABASES;
+----------+
| Database |
+----------+
| mysql    |
| store    |
| test     |
+----------+
```

Running the SHOW TABLES query on the mysql database lists the tables that store user permissions.

```
mysql> show tables;
+-----------------+
| Tables_in_mysql |
+-----------------+
| columns_priv    |
| db              |
| func            |
| host            |
| tables_priv     |
| user            |
+-----------------+
6 rows in set (0.16 sec)
```

Each of these tables corresponds to a level of access control. You can create any number of users, and users can be allowed access from any variety of hosts. A host is either a URL or an IP address. For each user/host combination, you can grant access to an entire database, to specific tables within a database, or to a number of columns within a table. Additionally, these tables grant administrative privileges. Users can be given permission to add and drop databases or permission to grant other users permissions.

 When working with any sort of security issues, it's best to keep this axiom in mind: "That which is not allowed is expressly forbidden." Start with the idea that no one needs access to anything and offer only permissions that are deemed absolutely necessary.

In practice, you will want to grant no more permissions than are absolutely necessary. You want to protect your data from the overzealous and the incompetent. The best way to do this with MySQL is to use the proper grant table when assigning rights, keeping the following in mind: Rights are granted in a hierarchical way. Rights granted in the user table will be universal. If a user is granted drop privileges in the user table, that person will be able to drop any table in any database in that MySQL installation.

Then there is the db table, which grants privileges on a database-specific basis. Using this table, you can grant rights for an entire database. For any one table or set of tables, make use of the tables_priv table. Finally, the columns_priv table allows you to grant rights on specific columns within a table. If you don't need to grant rights to an entire table, see that rights are assigned in the columns_priv table.

Recent releases of MySQL make use of a couple of very convenient commands that make creating users and assigning rights fairly easy. I discuss these commands after a brief look at the user, db, tables_priv, and columns_priv tables.

Understanding the user table

Every user who needs to get at a MySQL installation must be listed in this table. Rights may be granted elsewhere, but without a listing here, the user will be refused a connection to the database server. Here is the listing of columns in the user table.

```
mysql> SHOW COLUMNS FROM user;
+-----------------+---------------+------+-----+---------+-------+
| Field           | Type          | Null | Key | Default | Extra |
+-----------------+---------------+------+-----+---------+-------+
| Host            | char(60)      |      | PRI |         |       |
| User            | char(16)      |      | PRI |         |       |
| Password        | char(16)      |      |     |         |       |
| Select_priv     | enum('N','Y') |      |     | N       |       |
| Insert_priv     | enum('N','Y') |      |     | N       |       |
| Update_priv     | enum('N','Y') |      |     | N       |       |
| Delete_priv     | enum('N','Y') |      |     | N       |       |
| Create_priv     | enum('N','Y') |      |     | N       |       |
| Drop_priv       | enum('N','Y') |      |     | N       |       |
| Reload_priv     | enum('N','Y') |      |     | N       |       |
| Shutdown_priv   | enum('N','Y') |      |     | N       |       |
| Process_priv    | enum('N','Y') |      |     | N       |       |
| File_priv       | enum('N','Y') |      |     | N       |       |
| Grant_priv      | enum('N','Y') |      |     | N       |       |
| References_priv | enum('N','Y') |      |     | N       |       |
| Index_priv      | enum('N','Y') |      |     | N       |       |
| Alter_priv      | enum('N','Y') |      |     | N       |       |
+-----------------+---------------+------+-----+---------+-------+
```

If you remember back to the sessions on PHP or Perl, you may recall that in order to connect to the database, you needed to provide three strings: username, host, and password. In the preceding listing, you can see the corresponding field names. MySQL identifies a user by the combination of the username and host. For example, user "jay" can have a different set of rights for each host that he uses to connect to MySQL. If you or your PHP scripts are accessing MySQL from the local machine, you usually assign a host of localhost — and rights can be granted from localhost. However, if you connect from another machine, a different set of rights can be granted from that location.

The other columns are intuitively named. As you can see, all but the Host, User, and Password columns use the enum column type and allow only the strings 'Y' or 'N' as column values. As I mentioned earlier, any of these rights that are set to 'Y' in this table are granted to every table of every database. Most of the columns' names correspond to SQL statements (for example, DELETE, CREATE, and so forth).

The user table also contains a set of columns that grant administrative rights. These columns are File_priv, Grant_pirv, Process_priv, Reload_priv, and Shutdown_priv. The following is a brief explanation of the meaning of these columns. If you are security-minded, grant these rights sparingly.

- File_priv — If granted, this privilege allows the database server to read and write files from the file system. You will most often use it when loading a file into a database table.

- Grant_priv — Users with this right will be able to assign his privileges to other users.
- Process_priv — This right gives a user the ability to view and kill all running processes and threads.
- Reload_priv — This privilege is most often used with the mysqladmin utility to perform flush commands.
- Shutdown_priv — This allows the user to shut down the daemon using mysqladmin shutdown.

Loading data from files is covered in Session 25 and reloading applications with the FLUSH command is covered in Session 23.

**20 Min.
To Go**

Understanding the db table

For database-specific permissions, the db table is where you will be doing most of your work. The following is a list of columns from the db table:

```
mysql> show columns from db;
+-----------------+---------------+------+-----+---------+-------+
| Field           | Type          | Null | Key | Default | Extra |
+-----------------+---------------+------+-----+---------+-------+
| Host            | char(60)      |      | PRI |         |       |
| Db              | char(32)      |      | PRI |         |       |
| User            | char(16)      |      | PRI |         |       |
| Select_priv     | enum('N','Y') |      |     | N       |       |
| Insert_priv     | enum('N','Y') |      |     | N       |       |
| Update_priv     | enum('N','Y') |      |     | N       |       |
| Delete_priv     | enum('N','Y') |      |     | N       |       |
| Create_priv     | enum('N','Y') |      |     | N       |       |
| Drop_priv       | enum('N','Y') |      |     | N       |       |
| Grant_priv      | enum('N','Y') |      |     | N       |       |
| References_priv | enum('N','Y') |      |     | N       |       |
| Index_priv      | enum('N','Y') |      |     | N       |       |
| Alter_priv      | enum('N','Y') |      |     | N       |       |
+-----------------+---------------+------+-----+---------+-------+
13 rows in set (0.01 sec)
```

This works like the user table, except that permissions granted here work only for the database specified in the db column. So, for example, if the value of the db column is store and the value of Update_priv is 'Y,' the user will have the permissions to perform SQL UPDATES on any table in the store database.

Understanding tables_priv and columns_priv

The tables_priv table and the columns_priv table are nearly identical, and to save a bit of space, I show only the tables_priv table.

```
mysql> show columns from tables_priv;
+-------------+----------------+------+-----+---------+-------+
| Field       | Type           | Null | Key | Default | Extra |
+-------------+----------------+------+-----+---------+-------+
| Host        | char(60)       |      | PRI |         |       |
| Db          | char(60)       |      | PRI |         |       |
| User        | char(16)       |      | PRI |         |       |
| Table_name  | char(60)       |      | PRI |         |       |
| Grantor     | char(77)       |      | MUL |         |       |
| Timestamp   | timestamp(14)  | YES  |     | NULL    |       |
| Table_priv  |set('Select','Insert','Update',|    |       |
|             |  'Delete','Create','Drop','Grant', |   |       |
|             |  'References','Index','Alter')     |   |       |
|             |                |      |     |         |       |
| Column_priv | set('Select','Insert', |      |     |       |
|             |  'Update','References') |      |     |       |
+-------------+----------------+------+-----+---------+-------+
8 rows in set (0.00 sec)
```

For users who only get access to a table or set of tables within a database, the exact rights are stored in this table. Note the use of the set column type for table_priv and column_priv tables. All the rights available to a specific user are crammed into these two cells.

For example, if the value of table is store, the value of Table_priv is Select, Insert the user will have only the authority to run INSERT and SELECT statements on that table.

 Normally, I advise against using the set column type. But the Tables_priv table is a good example of where set makes sense. Few potential values exist for the column, and the number of potential values is not likely to change.

Using the GRANT and REVOKE Statements

Because the tables discussed above are regular MySQL tables, you can alter them with the SQL statements you are already familiar with. But consider the nightmare that would be. If you wanted to grant a new user table-level access, you would first need to insert a row into the user table with an SQL statement that looked like this:

```
INSERT INTO user (Host, User, Password, Select_priv,
          Insert_priv, Update_priv, Delete_priv,
          Create_priv, Drop_priv, Reload_priv, Shutdown_priv,
          Process_priv, File_priv, Grant_priv, References_priv,
          Index_priv, Alter_priv)
VALUES ('localhost', 'juan', 'password', 'N', 'N', 'N', 'N', 'N',
    'N', 'N', 'N', 'N', 'N', 'N', 'N', 'N', 'N')
```

Then you'd need to grant specific rights with another INSERT statement to the db table and then other one to the Tables_priv table.

If you are thinking you can script these functions with a Web front end, that is definitely a possibility. But be very careful because the script would have the equivalent of root access to the database, which could be very unsafe.

Happily, the MySQL has built-in statements that make user administration a whole lot easier. Knowing the GRANT and REVOKE statements will save you from having to send individual queries.

Using GRANT

Before I get into specifics of the GRANT statement, take a look at the statement that grants all rights on the database named store to user "jim"; jim's password is pword.

```
mysql> GRANT ALL ON store.* TO jim@localhost IDENTIFIED BY "pword";
```

The first part of the GRANT statement can take the word all, or it can take any of the options listed in the user table. Most often, you will be granting rights to use SQL statements (SELECT, CREATE, ALTER, DELETE, DROP, INDEX, INSERT, and UPDATE).

The second portion (on store.* in the example) identifies where privileges will be applied: universally, to a single database, to tables, or to columns. Table 20-1 shows how to indicate where privileges should be applied.

Table 20-1 *Permission Levels*

Identifier	Meaning
grant all on *.*	Universal rights; inserted into the user table
grant all on database.*	Applies to all tables in a single database
grant all on database.table_name	Rights apply to a single table
grant all(col1, col2) on database.table_name	Rights apply only to specific columns in a specific database and table.

The third portion (to jim@localhost in the example) indicates the user to be given access. As I mentioned earlier, MySQL needs both a name and a host. In the grant statement, these are separated by the @ symbol.

Finally, the IDENTIFIED BY portion gives the user a password.

After running GRANT ALL ON store.* to jim@localhost IDENTIFIED BY "pword"; here is what the user and db tables would look like for the user 'jim':

```
mysql> SELECT * FROM user where user='jim' \G
*************************** 1. row ***************************
        Host: localhost
        User: jim
    Password: 4c69bf4e60fb765f
 Select_priv: N
 Insert_priv: N
```

```
        Update_priv: N
        Delete_priv: N
        Create_priv: N
         Drop_priv: N
       Reload_priv: N
     Shutdown_priv: N
      Process_priv: N
         File_priv: N
        Grant_priv: N
    References_priv: N
         Index_priv: N
         Alter_priv: N
          ssl_type: NONE
        ssl_cipher:
       x509_issuer:
      x509_subject:
1 row in set (0.01 sec)

mysql> SELECT * FROM db where user='jim' \G
*************************** 1. row ***************************
          Host: localhost
            Db: store
          User: jim
    Select_priv: Y
    Insert_priv: Y
    Update_priv: Y
    Delete_priv: Y
    Create_priv: Y
     Drop_priv: Y
     Grant_priv: N
References_priv: Y
    Index_priv: Y
    Alter_priv: Y
```

For my store database, the permissions granted by the above statement may be okay if Jim is the administrator of this application. He can run any queries he likes against the database, but for anybody else — for example, the PHP or Perl applications that will interact with the database — you'd want to grant a more limited set of permissions.

First think about the in-house user. There's probably going to be someone who needs to update the product listing, change prices, and the like. But there's no reason this user should be able to DROP tables or, for that matter, run DELETEs on the users table. To get the right permissions, it's going to take several statements. I can start by granting SELECT privilege on all tables and then additional rights where they are needed.

```
GRANT SELECT on store.* to storeadmin IDENTIFIED BY 'hispword'

GRANT SELECT, UPDATE, DELETE, INSERT ON
store.products to storeadmin@localhost identified by "hispword"

GRANT SELECT, UPDATE, DELETE, INSERT ON
store.items_for_sale to storeadmin@localhost identified by "hispword"
```

```
GRANT SELECT, UPDATE, DELETE, INSERT ON
store.formats to storeadmin@localhost identified by "hispword"
```

And for the live application, the pages that are viewable to the world at large, you'd want to be even more restrictive. You probably wouldn't want to grant universal SELECT statements, because there's a pretty good chance that eventually this application will contain a table that shouldn't be readable by the world at large.

```
GRANT SELECT, ON
store.products to storeuser@localhost identified by "hispword"

GRANT SELECT, ON
store.items_for_sale to storeuser@localhost identified by "hispword"

GRANT SELECT, INSERT ON
store.orders to storeuser@localhost identified by "hispword"

GRANT SELECT, INSERT ON
store.order_items to storeuser@localhost identified by "hispword"

GRANT SELECT, INSERT, Update ON
store.users to storeuser@localhost identified by "hispword"

GRANT SELECT, INSERT, Update ON
store.addresses to storeuser@localhost identified by "hispword"
```

In this case, there's really no place where I need to grant only column-level privileges.

**10 Min.
To Go**

REVOKE

If you want to remove some of a user's privileges, you can use the REVOKE statement. To remove shutdown privileges from a user who had been granted all privileges, like jim above, you can run the following:

```
revoke Shutdown on *.* from josh@localhost;
```

Notice that the word from is used in the revoke statement in place of to. Otherwise, REVOKE works just like GRANT.

Note that to remove a user entirely, you must run a DELETE statement against the user table. Because the user is identified by a name and host, the following should do it:

```
DELETE FROM user WHERE user='user' and HOST='host'
```

Make sure to run the DELETE statement after the REVOKE statements. That way you won't risk having rows in some of the GRANT tables but not in the users table.

Viewing GRANTS

Starting in version 3.23.4, MySQL incorporated the SHOW GRANTS statement, which allows you to see the exact grants available at a given time. All you need to know is the username and host.

```
mysql> show grants for storeadmin@localhost;
+-----------------------------------------------------------------------
--+
| Grants for storeadmin@localhost                          |
+-----------------------------------------------------------------------
--+
| GRANT USAGE ON *.* TO 'storeadmin'@'localhost' IDENTIFIED BY PASSWORD
'5f1ebcf231129e98' |
| GRANT SELECT, INSERT, UPDATE, DELETE ON store.items_for_sale TO
'storeadmin'@'localhost' |
| GRANT SELECT, INSERT, UPDATE, DELETE ON store.products TO 'storeadmin'@'localhost'    |
+-----------------------------------------------------------------------
--+
1 row in set (0.00 sec)
```

Reloading GRANTS

The GRANT tables are loaded into memory when the MySQL daemon is started. Changes made to the GRANT tables that did not make use of the GRANT command do not take effect until you restart the program or tell MySQL to reload the table with the flush command.

Simply run:

```
flush privileges
```

Logging In from Clients

Now that you have created users other than root, you should make sure that you and every-one else who use the database log in as one of those other users. To log in as an alternate user with the MySQL command-line client with a password, use

```
shell> mysql -u username -p
```

When you hit Return, you are prompted for your password. Enter it and you are ready to work. You can also apply these new usernames and passwords in your applications upon making a connection.

At the start of Session 21, you see how to assign a password to the MySQL root user.

Done!

REVIEW

In this session, you saw how to secure MySQL by limiting user access to databases, tables, and columns. You also saw that access can be limited by query type. That is, certain users can have authorities to run only certain queries. You saw that the grant information is key in the mysql database, in a series of tables where privileges correspond to a specific table. Then you saw how to easily manage GRANTs with MySQL's GRANT and REVOKE statements. You also learned how grants should be applied to users depending on their exact needs. Users who don't need to run specific queries should never be given the ability to run those queries.

QUIZ YOURSELF

1. True or False: A user with an established username and password can log in from a client on any host? (See "Understanding the user table.")

2. If a user has a value of "Y" in the Grant_priv column of the user table, what special actions will that client be able to perform? (See "Understanding the user table.")

3. What grant statement indicates that permissions are to be applied to all tables in a database? (See "Using GRANT.")

4. What statement allows you to view grants for a specific user? (See "Viewing GRANTs.")

5. What statement removes permissions that have been granted to a user? (See "REVOKE.")

PART

IV

Saturday Evening
Part Review

1. Which Perl DBI module is used to connect DBI to MySQL?
2. What Perl module eases the installation of other MySQL modules and their dependencies?
3. What DBI method is used to connect to a database?
4. What DBI method returns row values as a hash?
5. What DBI method prints an error if one occurs?
6. What Perl module allows you to mix Perl and HTML as it is done in PHP?
7. How can you go about finding out which queries are executing slowly?
8. What variable determines the number of seconds that must elapse before a query is considered slow?
9. What MySQL command will show how the MySQL engine will execute a SELECT query?
10. If indexes increase speed, why should you not index every column?
11. When executing an equi-join, what SYNTAX can you use to specify the order in which the tables are joined?
12. What SQL phrase can you use to mandate a query to use a specific index?
13. A MySQL user is determined by a username and what parameter?
14. Which MySQL privilege gives users the right to give other users access to MySQL.
15. What portion of the GRANT statement specifies a password for a user?
16. Write a GRANT statement that will give all privileges to a user named 'john' on localhost to the 'my_db' database with the password "foo."
17. What statement can be used to remove privileges given with the GRANT statement?
18. What statement can you use to view the grants given to john@localhost?
19. If you make changes to the grant tables with INSERT, UPDATE, or DELETE statements, how do you reload the grant tables?
20. Can privileges be granted to specific columns within tables?

☑ Friday

☑ Saturday

☑ **Sunday**

Part V — Sunday Morning

Session 21
Securing MySQL, Part II: Your Unix Environment

Session 22
Advanced Configuration Options

Session 23
MySQL Client Applications

Session 24
Backing Up and Exporting MySQL Data

Session 25
Transferring and Importing Data into MySQL

Session 26
Replication

Part VI — Sunday Afternoon

Session 27
Diagnosing and Repairing Table Problems

Session 28
MySQL GUI Clients

Session 29
Optimizing MySQL

Session 30
Answering Remaining Questions

PART

V

Sunday Morning

Session 21

*Securing MySQL, Part II:
Your Unix Environment*

Session 22

Advanced Configuration Options

Session 23

MySQL Client Applications

Session 24

Backing Up and Exporting MySQL Data

Session 25

*Transferring and Importing Data
into MySQL*

Session 26

Replication

Securing MySQL, Part II: Your Unix Environment

Session Checklist

✔ Shutting down your MySQL server

✔ Assigning permissions

✔ Restarting applications

✔ Examining your Unix/Linux environment

30 Min. To Go

I f you have decided to run MySQL on your own server that is connected to the Internet or even an intranet, chances are you will opt to run MySQL on some sort of Unix system — maybe FreeBSD, Solaris, some version of Mac OS X, or Linux. In fact, Linux is such a popular environment for MySQL-powered Web sites that an acronym is often used to described the tools: LAMP (for Linux, Apache, MySQL, and either PHP or Perl).

Unix/Linux systems are robust and extremely stable, and if at all possible, I recommend using one of these operating systems to host MySQL rather than opting for a Windows alternative. However, when you start working on a Unix/Linux system, you have to take into account the potential security risks that come with such systems. It's not that Linux or Unix are inherently insecure — far from it. These operating systems are designed for networks and are designed to be extremely flexible. Thus, there are more ways to attack these systems. But if you're security minded and you take the proper precautions, these systems will be sufficiently secure.

And if you're a die-hard Windows user who has no interest or plans in working with MySQL on any sort of Unix (including Mac OS X), you can skip this session, spend a half hour reading the Sunday paper and watching cartoons, and then return for Session 22.

This session assumes a basic understanding of Unix/Linux systems, including the files structure and permissions model. If you're new to these topics, please consult a Unix/Linux-specific book.

Shutting Down Your MySQL Server

If you currently have your MySQL daemon running or have any copies of the command-line client in operation, it's time to shut them down. But before you shut down the command-line client, you want to make sure that you assign the MySQL root user a password. Remember that, until now, you have been logging in as root without any password identification. But after you create a password, you have to give the password whenever you log into MySQL as root. This is as easy as applying the techniques learned in Session 19. Give a GRANT statement that updates the password. (Note that below, "mypass" is the password string; you can use something that you like instead.)

```
GRANT ALL on *.* to root@localhost identified by "mypass";
```

You can then close the command-line client by typing **exit;**. Then, the next time you log in to the command-line client, you have to give both the username and the password. Something like

```
shell> ./mysql -u root -pmypass
```

Or, alternatively, you can give nothing after your -p argument, and you will be prompted for your password.

```
shee> ./mysql -u root -p
Enter password:
```

When you enter the password, the command-line client starts right up.

When you have changed your password and closed the command-line client, you then need to shut down the MySQL daemon, which you can do with the mysqladmin utility. I talk in much greater detail about mysqladmin later, but for now, just know you should run the following command in the /bin directory:

```
shell> ./mysqladmin -u root -pmypass shutdown
```

Now you can make changes to your Unix/Linux or Mac OS X environment that ensure your database is safe from intruders.

Want to test if your MySQL daemon is up and running on Unix? At the shell, you can use the ps **and** grep **commands.** ps **is the process status command and returns a listing of all running processes;** grep **prints all lines it encounters that match a regular expression. The following command shows if the MySQL daemon (mysqld) is running:**

```
shell> ps -ax | grep 'mysqld'
```

If the daemon is running, this command returns results. For more information on ps **and** grep, **see the respective man pages.**

Assigning Permissions

The best way to make sure that MySQL is safe and reasonably well isolated from the rest of your system is to create a group and user that are specifically for running MySQL-related processes. If you were to run the MySQL daemon as the systems (not the databases) root user, the MySQL daemon would have the authority to write to or delete any file on the system — not a good state of affairs.

If you followed the instructions in Session 2 for a binary install, you should have already created a user and group for running MySQL. If you installed from source, you'll need to make some changes. In either case, review the sections below and check your system to make sure it is as it should be. You have to review your system to see the actual location of various folders.

Creating users and groups on Unix/Linux

In the commands below, I create both a group and a user with the name mysqlusr.

```
shell> addgrp mysqlusr
shell> useradd mysqlusr -g mysqluser
```

The -g flag on the useradd command assigns the user being created to the group specified after the flag. So the user mysqlusr is a member of the group mysqlusr.

Creating users and groups on Mac OS X

**20 Min.
To Go**

On this OS, you're not going to use the command-line tools. Rather, you open NetInfo Manager, which is in the /Applications/Utilities folder.

To add the group and system account, authenticate yourself using the lock in the lower left so you can make changes. Then highlight the "groups" entry, and the third column will fill with the list of Unix groups currently on the system. Click on the group "www" and then choose Duplicate from the Edit menu. This creates an entry titled "www copy." When you select that, the lower window then contains three entries: passwd, name, and gid. Change the name from "www copy" to "mysqlusr", and the gid from 70 to 401 (or whatever gid number you like; just be sure it doesn't match any other gid on your system). Then click on the users entry. You will be asked to confirm and reload the settings you have changed. Go ahead and accept the changes. (See Figure 21-1.)

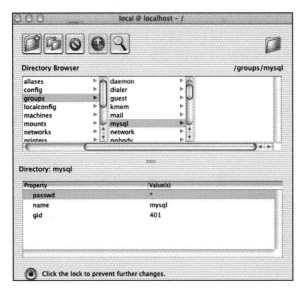

Figure 21-1   *Creating a group on Mac OS X*

When the users element is highlighted, select the "www" entry and duplicate it. Change the realname to something you like ("Mr. MySQL," maybe), and change the name entry to "mysqlusr," uid to 401, home to /usr/local/mysql, and gid to 401. The gid needs to match the gid you set for the mysqlusr group, and the uid must be unique — don't duplicate another account's uid. (See Figure 21-2.)

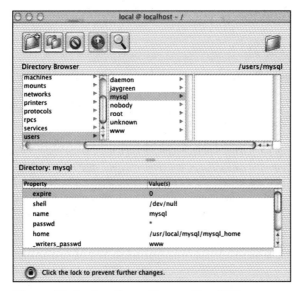

Figure 21-2   *Creating a User on Mac OS X*

Changing ownership of MySQL files and directories

Now that you have a user and group to whom you can assign file and directory ownership, you can use common Unix commands to assign ownership. Before running these commands, you should understand exactly what you're doing and why.

As already mentioned, the daemon should run as the newly created user (mysqlusr). This does not mean, however, that ownership for the MySQL daemon files (mysqld and mysqld_safe) need to be assigned to anyone but the system's root user. The system's root user can specify upon starting the daemon what system user the daemon should run as.

So for starters, when logged in as the root user, change ownership of the entire /usr/local/mysql directory to root.

```
shell> chown -R root /usr/local/mysql
```

If you're using Mac OS X, please keep in mind that the system by default does not have a root user, and this is a good state of affairs. Don't add a root user. Rather, start each command that needs to run as root with sudo. On OS X, the previous command would be changed to

```
shell> sudo chown -R root /usr/local/mysql
```

After entering this command, you'll need to enter an administrative password, which makes all of these files completely unavailable to anyone but root.

The folders that hold the database data need attention. They need to be available to the MySQL daemon but to no one else. If your database folders are readable by other users, it's possible that important data can be copied to another location or hacked into.

Because the MySQL daemon will run as mysqlusr, the folders that hold the databases must be available to only that user by changing their ownership. The database directory may be in /usr/local/mysql/data or /usr/local/mysql/var, depending on your system (run SHOW VARIABLES LIKE 'datadir' to check). As root, run the following command while choosing the correct directory for your installation:

```
shell> chown -R mysqlusr /usr/local/mysql/data
```

Now change the group ownership of the entire mysql directory to mysqlusr:

```
shell> chgrp -R mysqlusr /usr/local/mysql
```

When finished, a listing of the directory should look something like this:

```
shell> ls -Fla /usr/local/mysql
drwxr-xr-x 13 root    mysqlusr 1024 Jun 5 13:42 ./
rwxr-xr-x  11 root    root     1024 Jun 5 12:19 ../
drwxr-xr-x  2 root    mysql    1024 Jun 5 12:20 bin/
drwxr-xr-x  3 root    mysqlusr 1024 Jun 5 12:19 include/
drwxr-xr-x  2 root    mysqlusr 1024 Jun 5 12:19 info/
drwxr-xr-x  3 root    mysqlusr 1024 Jun 5 12:19 lib/
drwxr-xr-x  2 root    mysqlusr 1024 Jun 5 12:20 libexec/
drwxr-xr-x  3 root    mysqlusr 1024 Jun 5 12:20 man/
```

```
drwxr-xr-x  6 root     mysqlusr 1024 Jun 5 12:21 mysql-test/
drwxr-xr-x  2 mysqlsur mysqlusr 1024 Jun 5 13:42 run/
drwxr-xr-x  3 root     mysqlusr 1024 Jun 5 12:20 share/
drwxr-xr-x  7 root     mysqlusr 1024 Jun 5 12:21 sql-bench/
drwx------  4 mysql    mysqlusr 1024 Jun 5 13:37 var/
```

In addition to the daemon and the data files, there are two other portions of MySQL whose permissions you need to be aware of. First is the MySQL socket file, which is used by clients on the local machine to connect to the daemon. This is usually kept in /tmp (though the location can be changed). This needs to be world readable if clients are to connect. MySQL also has configuration files with the name my.cnf that need to be considered. I talk more about these files in Session 22.

Restarting Applications

Now that permissions are properly assigned, you need to restart the mysql daemon and have it run as mysqlusr. This is accomplished with the following command (run as either root or with sudo):

```
shell> /usr/local/mysql/bin/mysqld_safe --user=mysqlusr &
```

Now you're going to need access to the MySQL command-line client. But at this point, the command-line client is in the /usr/local/mysql/bin directory and is owned by root. It would be far easier if this application, which is likely to be used frequently and by a variety of users, was in a place that was a bit more accessible and carried permissions that made it easy enough to use. I recommend copying the client to /usr/bin and then giving it executable permissions for everyone.

```
shell> cp /usr/local/mysql/bin/mysql /usr/bin
shell> chmod +x /usr/bin/mysql
```

After running these commands, any user from anywhere in the file system can start the client by typing

```
shell> mysql -u username -p
```

Examining Your Unix/Linux Environment

**10 Min.
To Go**

The steps described above will keep MySQL about as safe as you can make it on a typical Unix/Linux box. However, if your box is full of gaping security holes, your data — and everything else on your system — is at risk. Unix/Linux security is a huge topic. There are very thick books written on this topic alone, and I couldn't possibly cover all possible security issues in a few pages. However, in the following pages, I suggest some simple ways of reviewing your system so that you can have an idea whether or not you're vulnerable to the most common attacks. The following sections pose security questions; if you answer "no" to any of them, you definitely have some work to do.

Note that out of the box some Unix systems are more secure than others. FreeBSD, for example, is pretty secure right after installation. Red Hat Linux, however, is very insecure right after installation, and you will have to make configuration changes prior to making the box available on the Internet.

Is your system up-to-date?

New security vulnerabilities are discovered all the time, and different Linux distributions post system updates when security issues are identified and fixed. Red Hat users should check the errata page regularly (www.redhat.com/apps/support/errata/index.html). Mandrake Linux posts updates at www.linux-mandrake.com/en/security/. SuSE posts security alerts at www.suse.com/us/support/security/index.html. See www.freebsd. org/security/index.html#adv for FreeBSD security advisories.

Are you enforcing good password policies?

All system logins on Unix/Linux systems should force everyone logging into the system to use passwords that are difficult to guess. Passwords should be of a reasonable length and should contain a mixture of uppercase, lowercase, numerals, and non-alphanumeric characters. There are a variety of ways to set these rules. On most Linux systems, you should look at Linuxconf. Normally, this can be started from the Start menu in you Windows manager. This program has a graphical interface for setting password policies. Check out the article at www.onlamp.com/pub/a/bsd/2001/01/17/FreeBSD_Basics.html for a good introduction to enforcing password policies on FreeBSD.

Even if you are enforcing good policies, it's an excellent idea to check your system against a tool that crackers are likely to use. The most popular of these is called Crack (www.users.dircon.co.uk/~crypto/download/c50-faq.html). Consider downloading it and running it against your own system.

Are unnecessary processes running?

The more processes that you have running, the greater the opportunity for crackers to attack your system. So you need to spend some time figuring out exactly what you have running, and if you find something you don't need, you should turn it off. In particular, you should be concerned about any process that runs using clear text protocols. You probably don't want to run Telnet and FTP daemons unless you absolutely need to; SSH and secure FTP are far better choices.

On Linux boxes, you can control what processes are initiated at startup by looking at the /etc/rc.d folders. In this folder, you find as series of subfolders, as shown below:

```
shell> ls /etc/rc.d -Fla
total 52
drwxr-xr-x  10 root    root      4096 Oct 30 08:32 ./
drwxr-xr-x  13 root    root      4096 Nov 1 10:36 ../
drwxr-xr-x   3 root    root      4096 Oct 30 08:42 init.d/
-rwxr-x---   1 root    root       539 Aug 8 2000 rc*
-rwxr-x---   1 root    root       159 Feb 17 2001 rc.local*
-rwxr-x---   1 root    root      2888 Oct 29 18:13 rc.sysinit*
drwxr-xr-x   2 root    root      4096 Feb 17 2001 rc0.d/
```

```
drwxr-xr-x  2 root    root      4096 Aug  7 2000  rc1.d/
drwxr-xr-x  2 root    root      4096 Sep 26 23:48 rc2.d/
drwxr-xr-x  2 root    root      4096 Oct 26 09:45 rc3.d/
drwxr-xr-x  2 root    root      4096 Aug 17 2000  rc4.d/
drwxr-xr-x  2 root    root      4096 Sep 26 23:48 rc5.d/
drwxr-xr-x  2 root    root      4096 Feb 17 2001  rc6.d/
```

Each of the rc.X folders is associated with a run level. Within these folders there are a series of files.

```
shell> ls /etc/rc.d/rc3.d/ -Fla
total 8
drwxr-xr-x  2 root    root      4096 Oct 26 09:45 ./
drwxr-xr-x 10 root    root      4096 Oct 30 08:32 ../
lrwxrwxrwx  1 root    root        17 Aug  8 2000  S15network -> ../init.d/network*
lrwxrwxrwx  1 root    root        17 Oct 21 11:10 S16getdate -> ../init.d/getdate*
lrwxrwxrwx  1 root    root        16 Aug  8 2000  S30syslog -> ../init.d/syslog*
lrwxrwxrwx  1 root    root        15 Aug 13 2000  S45named -> ../init.d/named*
lrwxrwxrwx  1 root    root        15 Aug 13 2000  S50inetd -> ../init.d/inetd*
lrwxrwxrwx  1 root    root        15 Aug 11 2000  S60crond -> ../init.d/crond*
lrwxrwxrwx  1 root    root        17 Aug 11 2000  S65proftpd -> ../init.d/proftpd*
lrwxrwxrwx  1 root    root        15 Aug 11 2000  S67mysql -> ../init.d/mysql*
lrwxrwxrwx  1 root    root        18 Feb 17 2001  S69postgres -> ../init.d/postgres*
lrwxrwxrwx  1 root    root        15 Aug 13 2000  S70imapd -> ../init.d/imapd*
lrwxrwxrwx  1 root    root        24 Sep 26 23:48 S71ravmail -> /etc/rc.d/init.d/ravmail*
lrwxrwxrwx  1 root    root        15 Aug 13 2000  S72qmail -> ../init.d/qmail*
lrwxrwxrwx  1 root    root        14 Aug 11 2000  S75sshd -> ../init.d/sshd*
lrwxrwxrwx  1 root    root        15 Aug 13 2000  S80httpd -> ../init.d/httpd*
lrwxrwxrwx  1 root    root        11 Aug 11 2000  S99local -> ../rc.local*
```

Each of the files that start with a capital *S* are started automatically at startup. Change the filename so that it starts with a lowercase *s* if you want the process to be off by default.

Additionally, you can turn processes on and off in Linux by using the ntsysv application. It provides a nice clean interface for turning processes on and off and determining if they start automatically at boot time. Many process can be started by inetd, so you need to check there as well.

In the process of determining what on your system is running, consider getting a utility that scans the ports of your system. If you see an available port that you were unaware of, you'll need to track it down.

Are your TCP Wrappers configured?

The /etc/host.allow and /etc/hosts.deny files control much of the remote access to your system. If you haven't spent time configuring your TCP Wrappers, making sure that you are denying access to all but the most trusted sources, you should do so now. Please consult a Unix/Linux book for configuration instructions.

Is your firewall watching out for MySQL ?

Are you working behind a firewall? If so, how are you treating requests to port 3306? That is MySQL's default port. Make sure that only the most trusted sources are allowed to attach to 3306.

Done!

REVIEW

This session continued the discussion of security that was started in Session 19. However, this session concentrated on the security of your Unix/Linux operating system. You started out by learning how to assign a password to the MySQL root user and then shut down MySQL clients and daemon. Following that, you saw that the MySQL daemon should run under its own username and group. You saw how to create a group and a user and then assign permissions, where needed, to that group and user (especially the directory holding the databases). The session ended by asking several questions about the overall security of your Unix/Linux system to flag what may be a glaring security risk.

QUIZ YOURSELF

1. What command shuts down the MySQL daemon? (See "Shutting Down Your MySQL Server.")

2. What flag in the adduser command assigns the new user to a group? (See "Creating users and groups on Unix/Linux.")

3. Which directory needs to be owned by the newly created mysql user? (See "Changing ownership of MySQL files and directories.")

4. When starting the daemon how do you indicate that MySQL should run as a specific system user.? (See "Restarting Applications.")

5. What files are involved with TCP Wrappers? (See "Are your TCP Wrappers configured?")

SESSION

22

Advanced Configuration Options

Session Checklist

✔ Understanding the my.cnf file

✔ Configuring the MySQL daemon

✔ Configuring the MySQL client

✔ Creating useful configuration files

30 Min. To Go

S o far in this book, I have only shown the most basic methods for modifying the configuration of the MySQL server. In previous sessions, you saw how to change a few
variables and settings when working with InnoDB and Gemini tables; in other places
you saw how to specify flags when starting the MySQL daemon. Most recently, you saw in
Session 21 the purpose and utility of the --user flag.

However, chances are you're not going to want to remember a long series of flags or variable settings every time you start up the server daemon. Furthermore, MySQL has many
options that have yet to be discussed. In certain circumstances, you may want to provide
different options to different users and clients. You may even need to manage multiple
installations of MySQL. This session introduces you to many of the settings and shows you
how to configure MySQL so it best suits your needs.

Understanding the my.cnf File

The my.cnf file gives on a central place to store all of possible variable setting and flags you'd
want to set when starting MySQL or its clients. It's easiest to understand the my.cnf file by
looking at a piece of one. Here is a fairly generic chunk you're likely find in a my.cnf file:

```
# The following options will be passed to all MySQL clients
[client]
port            = 3306
socket          = /tmp/mysql.sock
```

```
# Here follows entries for some specific programs

# The MySQL server
[mysqld]
port              = 3306
socket            = /tmp/mysql.sock
log-long-format
set-variable      = key_buffer=16M
```

Each of these items replaces a flag that you could include when starting either the MySQL daemon (`mysqld` or `mysqld_safe`) or any of the MySQL clients. By including this information in a `my.cnf` file, you save yourself from having to start the daemon with the following flags every time:

```
mysqld_safe --port=3306 --socket=/tmp/mysql.sock --skip-locking
--log-long-format --set-variable key_buffer=16M
```

Different MySQL clients have different configurable settings. In this session, I discuss settings for the MySQL daemon and the command-line client. You learn about a couple of other MySQL clients in future sessions.

my.cnf locations

When the MySQL daemon or any of the MySQL clients start up, they search for a `my.cnf` in one of three locations: in the MySQL data directory, in the `/etc` folder (on Unix/Linux) or `c:\` on Windows, or in a user's home directory on Unix/Linux. Each of the locations is associated with a specific level of control. The level of control determines exactly what you want to put in each of these files.

The first location on Unix/Linux platforms is `/etc/my.cnf` and on Windows `c:\my.cnf`. This file defines global preferences. Global preferences apply to all MySQL servers that may be running on the machine. For this reason, you may want to apply some general parameters, such as memory allocation, that make sense in every MySQL installation on your system. However, because these setting can affect a variety of MySQL servers, you don't want to set `port` or `socket` information here. You may end up with two servers clamoring for the same port.

Server-specific settings are best kept in the `my.cnf` file kept in the data directory. On Unix/Linux this is usually `/usr/local/mysql/data` or `/usr/local/mysql/var`. On Windows, it is something like `c:\program files\mysql\data`. Run SHOW VARIABLES LIKE `'datadir'` to find the proper directory on your system. This file applies only to the specific server that accesses the data directory. So this is a good place to indicate an alternate port or socket file location.

Finally, on Unix/Linux systems, you can place a `.my.cnf` (notice a dot is the first character of the filename) in a user's home directory, usually `/home/username`. This file will be read when the user starts a client application.

Later in this session, I show you how you may want to arrange each of these files. If you want to look at some samples, look at the installation directory of MySQL and find files named `my-small.cnf`, `my-medium.cnf`, `my-large.cnf`, and `my-huge.cnf` (usually in `/usr/local/mysql/shar/mysq` or `/support-files` directory, though your location may vary. You can open any of these in a text editor.

my.cnf sections

The my.cnf files are divided into several portions; each portion is identified by a bracketed word. As you just read, you can have a section for the daemon (identified by [mysqld]) and a section called [client]. The [client] section affects all of the MySQL clients that are used when working with MySQL. They include the MySQL command-line client, mysqldump, mysqlhotcopy, mysqlimport, mysqlshow, mysqlcheck, myisamchk, and myisampack. If you wanted to, for example, include a section specifically for configuring mysqldump, you can include [mysqldump] and your required settings in the appropriate my.cnf file.

Configuring the MySQL Daemon

**20 Min.
To Go**

There are many, many configuration options you may choose for your MySQL server. Some of these depend on your available hardware; others depend on your specific needs. For example, you saw in Session 14 that using either Gemini or InnoDB tables require very specific settings. When you use these table types, make sure that your my.cnf files account for these choices. Table 22-1 shows some of the options you can include when starting the MySQL server. These can be included when starting the server, using

```
shell> mysqld_safe --option
```

or by including the item in the my.cnf file. There are more options than I can include here. For a complete list of these options, see www.mysql.com/doc/C/o/Command-line_options.html.

Table 22-1 *MySQL Start-Up Options*

Option	Meaning	Example
base-dir	Path to the base of the installation. All other directories will be resolved from that base. This setting will be accurate after installation and will rarely, if ever, need to be changed.	base-dir=/path/to/mysql
bind-address	Specifies an IP address for the MySQL server.	--bind-address=192.168.1.2
data-dir	Specifies path for the data directory.	--data-dir=/usr/local/mydbs

Continued

Table 22-1 *Continued*

Option	Meaning	Example
default-character-set	MySQL by default uses a character set that is optimal for English. If you are working with another language, please see (www.mysql.com/doc/C/h/Character_sets.html).	--default-character-set=latin_de
default-table-type	Sets a default type. By default, MyISAM is the default table.	default-table-type=Gemini
language	Specifies a language for error messages.	--language=dutch
Log	Logs connections and queries to a file (more on this in a later session).	--log=/path/to/logfile
Log-slow-queries	Maintains a log file of slow queries.	--log-slow-queries=/path/to/slowlog
Log-bin	Tells MySQL to write all updates to a log file (more on this in a later session).	--log-bin=/path/to/log
myiam-recover	Specifies MyISAM recovery options. See Session 24 for more details.	myisam-recover=BACKUP
port	Specifies a port. Default is 3306.	--port=3309
skip-networking	All connections must be made through the socket file. This makes sense if all access to MySQL is through the local machine.	

Option	Meaning	Example
`--safe-show-database`	MySQL will show only databases to authorized users when running SHOW DATABASES.	`--safe-show-databases`
`skip-grant-tables`	Turns off all authentication. Everyone will be able to do everything. Normally, this is a very bad idea.	`--skip-grant-tables`
`socket`	Specifies location of a socket file.	`--socket=/usr/local/socket/mysql.sock`
`tmpdir`	Path for temporary files. Default is /tmp.	`--tempdir=/my/tmpdir`
`user`	Specifies system user name the daemon should run as.	`--user=mysqlusr`

In addition to these options, there are a host of variables that can be set at start up. The easiest way to see all the variables that can be set is to go to the MySQL daemon binary (`mysqld`), which is probably in the /libexec directory of your MySQL installation and run `mysqld --help`. You'll see a listing that looks something like this:

```
shell> ./mysqld --help
Possible variables for option --set-variable (-O) are:
back_log               current value: 50
binlog_cache_size      current value: 32768
connect_timeout        current value: 5
delayed_insert_timeout current value: 300
delayed_insert_limit   current value: 100
delayed_queue_size     current value: 1000
flush_time             current value: 0
ft_min_word_len        current value: 4
ft_max_word_len        current value: 254
ft_max_word_len_for_sort  current value: 20
innodb_mirrored_log_groups  current value: 1
innodb_log_files_in_group  current value: 2
innodb_log_file_size  current value: 5242880
innodb_log_buffer_size  current value: 1048576
innodb_buffer_pool_size  current value: 8388608
innodb_additional_mem_pool_size  current value: 1048576
innodb_file_io_threads  current value: 9
innodb_lock_wait_timeout  current value: 1073741824
```

The exact variables shown here will vary depending on the options included in your MySQL version. As you've already seen, different variables are associated with different table types. If you aren't using InnoDB tables, some of the listings from above will be missing from your installation.

In addition to the brief listing above, Table 22-2 shows many of the important variables you may alter configuring your MySQL server. To set them, you can either include `--set-variable var=value` when starting the daemon or

```
set-variable = var=variable
```

in a `my.cnf` file. Again, this is just a sampling. You should check `www.mysql.com/doc/S/H/SHOW_VARIABLES.html` for a complete list of variables and their meanings.

Table 22-2 *MySQL Configurable Variables*

Option	Meaning	Example
binlog_cache_size	Size of the cache that holds statements before the completion of a transaction. If you run large multistatement transactions, you can increase this size.	binlog_cache_size=64000
connect_timeout	Number of seconds the server waits for a connection.	connect_timeout=10
flush_time	If this is set to a non-zero value, tables will be closed after use to save resources. In most circumstances, you should keep this value at zero.	flush_time=5
interactive_timeout	Number a seconds the server will wait for an interactive connection.	interactive_timeout=28800
join_buffer_size	Size of the buffer that will be used for joins that do not use indexes. If indexing is not possible, you can add size to this variable.	join_buffer_size=13k

Option	Meaning	Example
key_buffer_size	The size of the buffer used for indexes. This is a key variable and you should allocate as much memory to indexes as possible — as much as a quarter of your system's total memory.	key_buffer=32M
long_query_time	Number of seconds before a query will be logged in the slow query log. (Discussed in Session 20.)	long_query_time=5
lower_case_table_names	If set to 1, all table names will be stored lowercase on the file system, and table name will be case-insensitive.	
max_allowed_packet	The maximum size of a single packet. If you are storing large BLOBs in the database, you may need to increase this size. Set in bytes.	max_allowed_packet=1M
max_binlog_cache_size	If a large transaction requires more memory than allocated in this setting, the client will receive an error.	max_binlog_cache_size=4M
max_binlog_size	If the size of the binary log (discussed in Session 24) exceeds this size, the log must be rotated.	max_binlog_size=1M
max_user_connects	Maximum number of connections for a single user.	max_user_connects=2

Continued

Table 22-2   *Continued*

Option	Meaning	Example
`max_connections`	Number of simultaneous connections allowed.	`max_connections=150`
`net_buffer_length`	The expected size of a query. This should normally not be changed.	`8k`
`query_buffer_size`	Size of buffer holding query contents. If inserting BLOBs, increase this size.	`query_buffer_size=1M`
`sort_buffer`	Sorts (ORDER BY and GROUP BY) require a buffer. Increase this size to give more space to the buffer.	
`table_cache`	Number of open tables for all threads. Increase this size to allow more space for open tables.	`table_cache=64`

Later in this session, I show you how you can apply some of these variables in the `my.cnf` files.

**10 Min.
To Go**

Configuring the MySQL Command-Line Client

There are far fewer options when it comes to the command-line client. As you've seen throughout the book, you can get about all the information you need by simply logging in with a username and password and sending queries. Table 22-3 shows most of the available options, including ones that I previously haven't used. To get a full list of options, from the `/bin` directory, run `mysql --help`.

Table 22-3 *MySQL Command-Line Client Start-Up Options*

Option	Meaning	Example
database	Specifies a database to use after starting the client.	database=store
execute	Execute the query and quit.	execute "show databases"
vertical	Print the output vertically (the same as using \G after queries).	--vertical
host	Connect to a specific host. If not specified the client will look for the local socket file.	--host=sqlserver.myhost.com
html	Outputs query results in HTML.	default-table-type=Gemini
xml	Outputs query results in XML.	--xml
port	Port number to use for connection.	--port=3309
i-am-a-dummy or (safe-updates)	Keeps you from running a DELETE or UPDATE statement without a WHERE clause.	
socket	Identifies location of the socket file.	--socket=/path/to/mysql.sock
--password	Identifies user password.	--password
User	Identifies username.	--user=myname
port	Specifies a port. Default is 3306.	--port=3309

Notice that many of these options can be very useful for parsing query results with, perhaps, a shell or Perl script. For example, if you had some data that needed to be processed in a quick and easy way by using a Perl script in the shell, you may run a query using the execute flag, so that the output was immediately printed and the client closed. If the result were put in XML, those results can be easier to parse. So from your Perl script, you may run a command like

```
mysql --user root -pmypass --xml --database="store" --execute="select *
from user"
```

Creating Useful Configuration Files

If you had only a single MySQL installation on your system, which was accessed by a variety of clients, you may have the following two my.cnf files. The first can be kept in the data directory.

```
[client]
port            = 3306
socket          = /tmp/mysql.sock

# Here follows entries for some specific programs

# The MySQL server
[mysqld]
port            = 3306
socket          = /tmp/mysql.sock
set-variable    = key_buffer=16M
set-variable    = max_allowed_packet=1M
set-variable    = table_cache=64
set-variable    = sort_buffer=512K
set-variable    = net_buffer_length=8K
set-variable    = myisam_sort_buffer_size=8M
```

Like everything else in the data directory, you'd want to assign ownership of this file to the MySQL daemon's user (in the previous session, mysqlusr).

Then you can have a separate file that makes life easier for all of your databases users. You can put this file (name .my.cnf) in a user's home directory and identify a username password in the file. Something like

```
[client]
user            = jack
password        = jack_password
port            = 3306
socket          = /tmp/mysql.sock

[mysql]
safe-updates
```

Then, if you've copied your MySQL command-line client to /usr/sbin, all the user will have to do after logging in to the system is type **mysql** at the shell, and the command-line client starts with the user's name and password. But before you give this option, you want to make sure you're following the security procedures discussed in Sessions 20 and 21. For starters, make sure that Jack has no more permissions within the database than he needs. So, if he's working heavily within the store database, you, the administrator, may allow him full access to that database — but only that database — from the command-line client.

```
mysql> GRANT ALL on store.* to jack@localhost IDENTIFIED BY
"jack_password"
```

You need to be very careful with the permissions of this file, as it is placed in Jack's home directory. No users other than the MySQL daemon (which now is running as mysqusr) should be able to read this file. Run the following commands. The first two assign user and group ownership of the file to mysqlusr, and the third says that only the file's owner has authority to read this file:

```
shell> chown mysqlusr /home/jack/.my.cnf
shell> chgrp mysqlur /home/jack/.my.cnf
shell> chmod 400 /home/jay/.my.cnf.
```

In addition the three locations of the my.cnf files discussed in the chapter, you can specify a configuration file by using the flags --defaults-file and defaults-extra-file. The former tells the application to use only the file you specified in the flag; the latter tells the application to read indicated file after reading the other files.

Done!

REVIEW

This session discussed MySQL's configuration files and configuration options. You saw that the MySQL daemon is highly configurable. Including specific directives in either the start-up command or the my.cnf file can change many settings. You saw that the my.cnf file can be placed in one of several locations and that the files in each of those locations have a specific task. In the tables in this session, you saw many of the options for both the MySQL daemon and for the command-line client. Finally, you saw how you can create two my.cnf files that would be useful for your installation.

QUIZ YOURSELF

1. In what three locations does MySQL search for my.cnf files? (See "my.cnf locations.")
2. What section of a my.cnf file affects all clients? (See "my.cnf sections.")
3. What option changes the daemons character set? (See Table 22-1.)
4. What variable determines the amount of memory available to keys? (See Table 22-2.)
5. What flags enables MySQL to use configuration files that are not in one of the three normal locations? (See "Creating Useful Configuration Files.")

MySQL Client Applications

Session Checklist

✔ Using `mysqladmin`

✔ Using `mysqlshow`

✔ Putting client applications to work

**30 Min.
To Go**

MySQL ships with several client applications. You can use these applications for a variety of tasks: repairing corrupted database tables, backing up databases, converting databases created in other applications to MySQL, and other processes. You see how to use some of these client applications in coming sessions. In this session, you see how to use two of the more important client applications you've yet to use: `mysqladmin` and `mysqlshow`. I'll also show you how to use these applications, along with the command-line client, in order to create helpful administrative shell scripts.

Using mysqladmin

A couple of sessions ago, you saw that to shut down a MySQL server, you need to apply the following command from your MySQL installation's `/bin` directory:

```
shell> mysqladmin -u root -p shutdown
```

The command makes use of `mysqladmin`. You can use `mysqladmin`, a command-line tool, for performing all sorts of administrative tasks on a MySQL server — everything from simple tasks like creating new databases to getting detailed information on the status of your MySQL server. In the following pages, I go over just about everything you can do with `mysqladmin`. But before you see the specific tasks, be aware that MySQL takes a number of fairly generic flags that you can apply to any of the processes you see below. These flags, like `-u`, `-p`, and `-h` (which indicate username, password, and host), show up in about every MySQL client, and you've seen their use repeatedly in previous sections when dealing with the command-line client. You can get a listing of these flags by running `mysqladmin --help`.

Basic administrative commands

Many of the tasks that you've seen performed within the MySQL command-line client can also be achieved with `mysqladmin`. The primary advantage of using `mysqladmin` for tasks like creating databases and setting passwords is that they can be entered from the shell or through a shell script without having to worry about entering and exiting the command-line client.

From `mysqladmin` you can perform the following basic administrative functions: create a database, drop a database, and change a password. The following examples show how to perform each of these actions. Note that for each of the examples, I'm performing the actions as the MySQL root user:

```
shell> mysqladmin -u root -p create store2
shell> mysqladmin -u root -p drop store2
```

The first command creates a database named `store2` and the second one drops the same database. Not that the DROP command gives a warning and asks you to confirm the DROP action:

```
Dropping the database is potentially a very bad thing to do.
Any data stored in the database will be destroyed.

Do you really want to drop the 'store2' database [Y/N]
```

This sort of response is fine, but it's something you'd want to avoid in an administrative shell script. You can ask `mysqladmin` to drop the database without confirmation by applying the `-f` or `--force` flag.

```
shell> mysqladmin -u root -p drop -f store2
```

You can also change passwords from `mysqladmin`. The following command changes the password for the MySQL root user from "mypass" to "hispass."

```
shell> ./mysqladmin -u root -pmypass password hispass
```

Status information commands

In previous sessions, you saw how to alter variables that control the number of threads able to access the server, the size of the log files, and many other parameters. But until now you haven't had a good way of determining the status and performance of your server. You can use `mysqladmin` to get a lot of information from your server.

mysqladmin ping

For starters, you can check that a MySQL daemon is alive and running by using `mysqladmin ping`. If the command is successful, it returns the message `mysqld is alive`. If it fails, you get an error message. Most often you will want to use `mysqladmin ping` when trying to establish that a connection is possible from a host other than `localhost`. In order to test the connection properly, you need to supply a host name, username, and password. Within your MySQL installation, make sure that a user with that name from that host is allowed.

```
shell> mysqladmin -u jay -pmypass -h mysqlserver.myhost.com ping
mysqld is alive
```

 If you simply want to test that the MySQL port is active, you can use a simple telnet client. If MySQL is running on the default port (3306), you can run telnet with the command:

```
telnet mysqlhost.myhost.com 3306
```

If the daemon is running, you get a response. You won't be able to connect through telnet, but you get a response rather than a time out.

mysqladmin version

You can get some interesting information about MySQL by running `mysqladmin version`.

```
shell> mysqladmin version
Server version          4.0.0-alpha
Protocol version        10
Connection              Localhost via UNIX socket
UNIX socket             /tmp/mysql.sock
Uptime:                 1 day 1 hour 15 min 10 sec

Threads: 73  Questions: 7168998  Slow queries: 119  Opens: 34482  Flush
tables: 1  Open tables: 64 Queries per second avg: 29.983
```

The beginning of the code shows very basic information. Below that, starting with Threads, you get some interesting information. Note that you can get just the information at the bottom of this listing (from Threads to Queries per second avg) plus some other goodies by running `mysqladmin status`.

mysqladmin status

There's some very important information available from this command.

```
/mysqladmin status -u root -pmypass
Enter password:
Uptime: 239352  Threads: 68  Questions: 7175296  Slow queries: 119  Opens:
34509  Flush tables: 1  Open tables: 64 Queries per second avg: 29.978
```

In this listing, you get the following information:

- **Uptime:** Number of seconds MySQL has been running.
- **Threads:** Number of clients connected to MySQL.
- **Questions:** Number of queries processed since the MySQL daemon was started.
- **Slow queries:** Number of queries that have taken longer to process than the value of the variable `long_query_time`. (See Session 19 for more on slow queries.)
- **Opens:** Number of table opens that MySQL has performed.

- **Flush tables:** Number of `flush`, `refresh`, and `reload` commands run. (More on flushes later in this session.)
- **Open table:** Number of tables open when `mysqladmin status` was run.
- **Queries per second avg:** Note that this is a simple measurement of the queries run divided by the time the server has been running. It is not a measure of your server's performance.

You can look at this information and start to make some decisions. If you have a high number of slow queries, it may be time to restart the server and log slow queries so you can see exactly what queries are problematic. If you find that the number of active threads is often close to the maximum number allowed by the `max_connections` variable, you may want to increase the number of available threads. If the `Opens` item is very large (as it is in the above listing), think about increasing the value of the `table_cache` variable.

Beyond these items, you can get far more information from your MySQL installation by running `mysqladmin extended-status`. This command returns a very long listing of system variables. You can get the definition for each of these items from the MySQL manual: `www.mysql.com/doc/S/H/SHOW_STATUS.html`.

mysqladmin processlist

Using `mysqladmin`, you can also view all of the server's active threads by running `mysqladmin processlist`. For example, in the following code, there are five threads active in the MySQL server, including the thread that is running `mysqladmin`.

```
shell> ./mysqladmin -u root -pmypass processlist
+----+------+-----------+-------+---------+-------+-------+---------------
---+
| Id | User | Host      | db    | Command | Time  | State | Info
|
+----+------+-----------+-------+---------+-------+-------+---------------
---+
| 44 | jayg | localhost |       | Sleep   | 12359 |       |
|
| 50 | jayg | localhost | store | Sleep   | 12166 |       |
|
| 77 | phps | localhost | store | Sleep   | 22    |       |
|
| 81 | root | localhost | mysql | Sleep   | 2     |       |
|
| 82 | root | localhost |       | Query   | 0     |       | show
processlist |
+----+------+-----------+-------+---------+-------+-------+---------------
-+
```

You can get the same listing by logging in to the command-line client and running SHOW PROCESSLIST. Note that you need proper permissions to get a full listing of threads. The `Process_privr` column of the `user` grant table stores these rights. If you don't have rights in this column, running `mysqladmin processlist` shows only the threads running with your username.

mysqladmin kill

When you have a listing, you can end a process with mysqladmin. Try a command like this:

```
./mysqladmin -u root -pmypass kill 44
```

You can see all MySQL variables by running mysqladmin variables. **This gives you the same listing you'd get by logging into the MySQL command-line client and running** SHOW VARIABLES.

Flush commands

**20 Min.
To Go**

The flush commands reload or reset files, tables, and logs. You probably won't have to use these commands very often, but they are important.

mysqladmin flush-hosts

The first flush command is mysqladmin flush-hosts. MySQL maintains a cached table of all the hosts connected to the MySQL server. If the connection from one of the hosts becomes problematic, MySQL registers the errors. When the number of errors exceeds the value of the variable max_connect_errors, MySQL cuts off access for that host. At that point, MySQL produces the error Host hostname is blocked. Some sort of TCP/IP networking error normally causes these errors. After the networking error is fixed, MySQL continues to block the given host until the cached host tables are flushed. You can run this command from the MySQL command-line client with the command FLUSH HOSTS.

If you want to completely do away with blocking errors, you can set the max_connection_errors **to 99999999999.**

mysqladmin flush-logs

The mysqladmin flush-logs command closes and re-opens all log files. You learn much more about log files in Session 24. You can also flush the MySQL logs by logging in to the command-line client and running FLUSH LOGS.

mysqladmin flush-privileges

You can use mysqladmin flush-privileges to reload the grant tables you saw in Session 20. Normally, you won't need to flush the grant tables. If you are using the GRANT statements, changes in permissions are updated immediately. However, if you decide to change the GRANT tables with standard UPDATE, INSERT, and DELETE statements, you need to flush the GRANT tables with this statements. You can also run this command from the command-line client by running FLUSH PRIVILEGES.

mysqladmin flush-tables

The final flush command is `mysqladmin flush-tables`. This closes all open tables with the MySQL installation. MySQL is a multi-threaded environment and will open multiple copies of tables to serve different threads more efficiently. Running this command closes all tables associated with all threads. You can run this command from the command-line client by using `FLUSH TABLES`.

 You also use `mysqladmin` **to start and stop replication. More on replication in Session 26.**

Using mysqlshow

The `mysqlshow` utility outputs fairly generic information from a MySQL server. For starters, you can run this command without any extra flags to get a listing of databases. However, you can add the `-v` flag (on versions after 3.23.32) to get some extra information.

```
shell> ./mysqlshow -u root -pmypass -v
+-----------+--------+
| Databases | Tables |
+-----------+--------+
| mysql     |      6 |
| store     |      8 |
| test      |      0 |
+-----------+--------+
```

If you add a database name to this command, you get a listing of tables within the database. The simple command would be

```
shell> mysqlshow -u root -pmypass store
```

But you can also add a flag to this command to get more detailed information. For example, the following example adds the `-v` flag (for verbose) to the previous command.

```
shell> /mysqlshow -u root -pmypass -v store
Database: store
+----------------+---------+
|     Tables     | Columns |
+----------------+---------+
| addresses      |       9 |
| formats        |       1 |
| items_for_sale |       4 |
| order_items    |       5 |
| orders         |       4 |
| places         |       1 |
| products       |       3 |
| users          |       8 |
+----------------+---------+
```

And if you add the -i flag to mysqlshow, you get detailed information about the structure of a table. Further, you can get information on specific tables by adding a table name after the database name. Then by using combinations of -k, -v, and -i flags, you can get information on columns, keys and permissions. For example:

```
[osxbox:local/mysql/bin] jaygreen% ./mysqlshow -u root -pmypass -v store users
Database: store  Table: users  Rows: 5

+--------------+---------------+------+-----+------------+-------------------------------
+
| Field        | Type          | Null | Key| Extra      | Privileges                   |
+--------------+---------------+------+-----+------------+-------------------------------
+
| user_id      | int(11)       |      | PRI| auto_increment |
select,insert,update,references |
| fname        | varchar(25)   |      |     |            |
select,insert,update,references |
| lname        | varchar(25)   | YES  | MUL|            |
select,insert,update,references |
| email        | varchar(60)   | YES  | MUL|            |
select,insert,update,references |
| home_phone   | varchar(14)   | YES  |     |            |
select,insert,update,references |
| work_phone   | varchar(14)   | YES  |     |            |
select,insert,update,references |
| fax          | varchar(14)   | YES  |     |            |
select,insert,update,references |
| last_update  | timestamp(14) | YES  |     |            |
select,insert,update,references |
+--------------+---------------+------+-----+------------+-------------------------------
------+
```

mysqlshow can be run with other combinations of flags. Showing other possible combinations would take up several pages of this book, which is unnecessary. Instead, I encourage you to run the following commands on your system, changing the username and password as appropriate, and seeing what MySQL returns.

```
shell> mysqlshow -u root -pmypass -k store users
shell> mysqlshow -u root -pmypass -i store users
```

**10 Min.
To Go**

Putting the Clients to Work

If you are administering a MySQL installation, chances are you are going to want to add some automation to the process of creating new users and databases. For example, consider a situation that is common at ISPs. As new users are signed up, each is given a database of his or her own and will have access to only that database.

To ease this administration process, you may create (on Unix) a shell script that takes care of the entire process. The script would perform the following actions:

- Add a database to the MySQL installation.
- Add a user to the MySQL installation.

- Assign rights to the newly created database to the newly created user.
- Create a `.my.cnf` file in the new user's home directory.
- Give proper permissions to that file.

For starters, I'd create a simple `my.cnf` file that can be altered and copied to the home directory of each user (with the name `.my.cnf`). The most important item for this file is the password item for the `[client]` section. I don't need to supply a username because MySQL assumes that the MySQL username is the name as the system username if none is given. The file may look like this:

```
[client]
password        = PASSWORD
port            = 3306
socket          = /tmp/mysql.sock

[mysql]
safe-updates
```

I'm going to arrange the shell script so that it will read this file and change the string `PASSWORD` with the password entered by the user.

The shell script I've provided in Listing 23-1 is very simple. It should be run by the system's root user and requires three arguments. In order, these are the user's name, user's password, and the database name. So if the file were named `mysqlsetup`, you'd run it with the following command:

```
shell> mysqlsetup username password dbname
```

Listing 23-1   *Sample administrative shell script*

```
#!/bin/sh

#shell script to create new database and user for that database
#expects 3 variables, in order, username, password, and database name

#start by creating a new database and user
/usr/local/mysql/bin/mysqladmin -u root -pmypass create $3

# the -e flag runs the command and silently exits the client
/usr/local/mysql/bin/mysql -u root -pmypass -e "grant all on $3.* to
$1@localhost identified by '$2'"

#now copy a very generic version of the my.cnf file to the
#users home directory and at the same do a search and
#replace with SED looking for the string PASSWORD and
#replacing it with the supplied password. If you're new to SED, you can
#find documentation on your UNIX system (man sed).

sed 's/PASSWORD/$2/g' /home/jay/my.generic.cnf  > /home/$1/.my.cnf
```

```
#assigning proper rights to this new file
chown mysqlusr /home/$1/.my.cnf
chgrp mysqlusr /home/$1/.my.cnf
chmod 400 /home/$1/.my.cnf
```

Done!

REVIEW

This session introduced you to two of MySQL helpful clients: mysqladmin and mysqlshow. You saw how to apply each of the commands in a variety of ways. You saw that mysqladmin can be used for both basic administrative tasks and to receive detailed information on a MySQL installation. You also saw how mysqladmin can be used to flush tables, logs, and hosts. From there, you saw how to use mysqlshow to get various pieces of information about your server, including database names, table names, and column information. Finally, you saw how several clients could be combined into a single administrative script.

QUIZ YOURSELF

1. How do you force mysqladmin to drop a database without requesting confirmation? (See "Basic administrative commands.")
2. What common tool (other than mysqladmin) can you use to see if MySQL is working on a known port? (See "mysqladmin ping.")
3. What command can be run from the command-line client that is the equivalent of mysqladmin processlist? (See "See mysqladmin processlist.")
4. What mysqlshow flag gives "verbose" information? (See "Using mysqlshow.")
5. What mysqlshow flag gives information on keys? (See "See Using mysqlshow.")

Backing Up and Exporting MySQL Data

Session Checklist

✔ Using `mysqldump`

✔ Using `SELECT INTO OUTFILE`

✔ Using `BACKUP TABLE`

✔ Copying database files

✔ Using the binary log

✔ Instituting good backup practices

*30 Min.
To Go*

C hances are that after spending the time to normalize your data and write and deploy your application, there will be no more important information on your systems than that which is stored by MySQL. A good administrator (one who wants to retain employment) will take steps to make sure the data is backed up at regular intervals. Remember: Hard disks die, and you want to be ready when yours stops spinning. In addition to backups, this chapter shows you how to export data for other uses.

A few different utilities and techniques can be used for backing up and exporting data. Please read this entire session before deciding on the method you'll use for your own backups.

Using mysqldump

In Session 4, you loaded a set of data into you MySQL server. The file that holds all of that data is on the accompanying CD in a file named `table_1.sql` in the `/session4` directory. At this point, if you open that file in a text editor, you see a series of SQL statements that include both `CREATE` statements for tables and `INSERT` statements for table data. The commands look something like this:

```
# MySQL dump 8.14
#
# Host: localhost    Database: store
#-----------------------------------------------------------
# Server version   3.23.39

#
# Table structure for table 'addresses'
#
create database store;
use store;

CREATE TABLE addresses (
  address_id int(11) NOT NULL auto_increment,
  user_id int(11) default NULL,
  place varchar(25) NOT NULL default '',
  addr_1 varchar(255) NOT NULL default '',
  addr_2 varchar(255) default NULL,
  city varchar(50) NOT NULL default '',
  state char(2) NOT NULL default '',
  ZIP varchar(5) NOT NULL default '',
  country varchar(5) default NULL,
  PRIMARY KEY  (address_id)
) TYPE=MyISAM;

#
# Dumping data for table 'addresses'
#

INSERT INTO addresses VALUES (5,3,'home','1845 Fair Oaks','Apt 6','San
Francisco','CA','92147','USA');
INSERT INTO addresses VALUES (6,4,'home','30445 Haines St','Apt 8G','San
Francisco','CA','92149','USA');
INSERT INTO addresses VALUES (7,5,'home','8 Oak
Rd',NULL,'Atlanta','GA','14119','USA');
```

As you saw in Session 4, with a file like this, it becomes extremely easy to run all of these statements in a batch by directing this file into the command-line client.

```
shell> mysql -u root -pmypass < table_1.sql
```

The SQL statements in the store.sql file were created with the mysqldump utility. As you can see from the store.sql file, this utility exports both table structure information (CREATE TABLE statements) and table data (INSERT statements). By dumping the entirety of databases and tables into files, you create a backup of your data.

The mysqldump utility is very flexible and can take a variety of flags that return the exact MySQL data you need in a variety of formats. You can see the full set of mysqldump options by going to your mysql/bin directory and running mysqldump --help. In this session, I address only some of mysqldump's more commonly used options.

If you run `mysqldump` **without taking the precautions discussed later in this session, you will not have a reliable backup. When backing up, you want to make sure you have a snapshot of data at a specific point in time. If backing up on a live server, you need to make sure that all tables are *static* — that nobody can insert or alter table data — when you commence a backup. You see how to do this shortly.**

The basic format for a `mysqldump` command is

```
shell> mysqldump databasename
```

Or, optionally, you can add a table name after the database name to dump structure and data from a single table. And as you may expect, you need to have proper permissions to run `mysqldump`. Your `mysqldump` commands looks like one of the ones below; the first dumps the entire store database, and the second dumps only the `users` table. In the statements below, I've directed the output to files (`store.sql` and `users.sql`).

```
shell> mysqldump -u root -pmypass store > /usr/disk2/dbbackup/store.sql
shell> mysqldump -u root -pmypass store users >
/usr/disk2/dbbackup/users.sql
```

If you want to dump more than one database, you can include additional database names by including the `--databases` flag, or to dump all databases at once, you can use the `--all-databases` flag.

```
shell> mysqldump -u root -pmypass --databases store otherdb >
/usr/disk2/dbbackup/dbs.sql
shell> mysqldump -u root -pmypass --all-databases >
/usr/disk2/dbbackup/alldbs.sql
```

On Unix systems, you can use `mysqldump` with pipes to achieve some complex actions with a single command. The first command below takes the output of `mysqldump`, compresses it using `gzip`, and then outputs the compressed data to a file. The second transfers data from one MySQL installation to another. It connects the output of `mysqldump` on one server to the command-line client on another host

```
shell> mysqldump -u root -pmypass --all-databases | gzip > ~/dbs.sql.gz
shell> mysqldump -u root -pmypass store | mysql -u jay -pmypass -h
mysqlhost.mydomain.com
```

The MySQL manual recommends that when using `mysqldump` **on DOS, you should indicate the location of any output file using the** `--result-file` **flag instead of using the greater than sign (>). So a sample command looks like this:**

```
dos> mysqldump -u root -pmypass --result-file=c:\store.sql store
```

There are some other important flags you should be aware of. I cover some of these and their uses below:

- `-c` **or** `--complete-insert`: mysqldump outputs each row as an SQL INSERT statement. But the INSERT statements do not use complete column listings; instead, they list the values in the order the columns exists in the table. So, in a table that had the following structure:

  ```
  CREATE TABLE sample(
      id int not null primary key,
      fname char(15)
  )
  ```

  You'd have INSERT statements that looked like this:

  ```
  INSERT INTO sample VALUES (1, 'Jay Greenspan');
  ```

  This is potentially problematic if you're transferring data to a table that may be slightly different or is using a different SQL server. In these cases you'd want complete SQL statements like INSERT INTO sample (id, fname) VALUES (1, 'Jay Greenspan'). The `--complete-insert` flag gives INSERT statements in this form.

- `-e` **or** `--extended-insert`: Using this flag, each table's rows are inserted in a single statements, with row values surrounded by parenthesis and separated by commas. Without this flag, each row has its own INSERT statement. The first command below is what an INSERT STATEMENT looks like when run with `--extended-insert`. The second and third are statements that insert the same information and are created by mysqldump if this flag is not used.

  ```
  INSERT INTO SAMPLE VALUES (1, 'jay'), (2, 'john');
  INSERT INTO SAMPLE VALUES (1, 'jay');
  INSERT INTO SAMPLE VALUES (1, 'john')
  ```

- `--delayed`: In MySQL you can indicate to the MySQL engine that an INSERT statement is of a relatively low priority by using the syntax INSERT DELAYED. When MySQL sees one of these statements, it puts the statement in a queue rather than directly into the table if there are other INSERT or UPDATE statements coming from other clients. This is especially helpful if other clients are inserting rows that need to be available immediately. The DELAYed row waits for other updates to finish before data is written to the actual table. Using INSERT DELAYED is a good idea when doing bulk INSERTs as may be the case with rows taken from mysqldump.

- `--add-drop-table`: MySQL uses the command DROP TABLE IF EXISTS to remove a table if it exists in a database. If a table with the specified name does not exist, the command is ignored. When using the add-drop-table flag to mysqldump, a DROP TABLE IF EXISTS statement will be added before every CREATE TABLE statement. This way you can be sure that all your CREATE TABLE statements will run without conflict or errors.

- `-t` **or** `no-create-info`: Omits CREATE TABLE statements from the output.

- `-d` **or** `no-data`: Just dumps the CREATE TABLE statements with no row data.

- `--lock-tables`: Places a lock on all tables within a database before starting a dump.

- `--add-locks`: Adds a LOCK TABLES before and an UNLOCK TABLE command after each set of INSERTs. This allows the mysqldump thread to move with the greatest amount of speed because no other clients are able to write to the tables at the same time.

- `--flush-logs` **or** `(-f)`: Flushes the log files before starting a dump operation.
- `-q` **or** `--quick`: By default, `mysqldump` writes rows to memory before forcing the rows to standard output. This really isn't necessary. By using this flag, you force `mysqldump` to deliver its contents directly to standard output, thereby saving some memory and an immense amount of time.
- `-w` **or** `--where`: Allows you to put a `WHERE` condition on what is dumped. For example, from the `store users` table you can get a list of users with a `user_id` greater than five with the following. Note that each `WHERE` condition must be put in quotes.

```
mysqldump -u root -pmypass --add-locks "-wuser_id>5" store users
```

There are a couple of other `mysqldump` flags, which I discuss in the next section.

At the start of this session I mentioned that when you backup, you want to make sure you get a backup of the database as it exists at a particular moment in time. The easiest way to do that is to apply the `--opt flag`. This is the same as using `--quick`, `--add-drop-table`, `--add-locks`, `--extended-insert`, and `--lock-tables`. So for regular backups, add something like the following command to your cron tab:

```
./mysqldump -u root -pmypass --opt --all-databases >
/usr/disk2/dbbackup/mybackup.sql
```

**20 Min.
To Go**

Using SELECT INTO OUTFILE

So far you've seen how you can export single tables or entire databases. However, there may be times when you want to export results of a query. Imagine, for example, that you or someone from your company wants to do some detailed financial analysis of some database data. It's unfair to expect someone from the Finance department to know how to run SQL queries. Furthermore, there are things you can do in a spreadsheet that you can't accomplish with a query.

To write the results of a query to a file, all you need to do is a write a query and then follow the query text with the string `INTO OUTFILE` and follow that with a filename enclosed in quotes. For example:

```
SELECT orders.order_id, order_total, item_id, price
FROM orders, order_items
WHERE order_date > now() - INTERVAL 24 HOUR
INTO OUTFILE '/home/jay/order_stuff.txt'
```

If you don't include a location for the outfile, it will be written to the data directory.

If you were to run this command, tabs would separate the fields in the `order_stuff.txt` file. However, you can change the field delimiter by using the `FIELDS TERMINATED BY` clause and then specifying a delimiting character in quotes. For example, to create a comma-delimited file, you can use

```
SELECT orders.order_id, order_total, item_id, price
FROM orders, order_items
WHERE order_date > now() - INTERVAL 24 HOUR
INTO OUTFILE '/home/jay/order_stuff.txt'
FIELDS TERMINATED BY ','
```

In addition, you can specify the character that separates each line in the file. By default, a new line separates the line, but if by chance you need some other separator, use the LINES TERMINATED BY clause, and then put the separating character in quotes.

Finally, you can use the ENCLOSED BY and OPTIONALLY ENCLOSED BY clauses. These sets characters to surround field values. For example, if you wanted all fields to be separated by commas and surrounded by quotes, you can use

```
SELECT orders.order_id, order_total, item_id, price
FROM orders, order_items
WHERE order_date > now() - INTERVAL 24 HOUR
INTO OUTFILE '/home/jay/order_stuff.txt'
FIELDS TERMINATED BY ','
ENCLOSED BY '"'
```

The resulting file looks like this:

```
"2","19.95","1","25.00"
"2","19.95","2","12.99"
"2","19.95","2","14.99"
"2","19.95","3","25.99"
"2","19.95","2","14.99"
```

If you use OPTOINALLY ENCLOSED BY instead of ENCLOSED BY, only char and varchar columns will be surrounded by the indicated character (above, double quotes).

Each of these options can be applied to the mysqldump utility. You can't use mysqldump with a query, but you can export entire tables with the options seen for SELECT INTO OUTFILE. All you need to do is give the --tab flag, along with a directory for the resulting files, and then the other appropriate options. A sample dump command may look something like this:

```
/usr/local/mysql/bin/mysqldump -u root -pmypass --tab="/Users/jaygreen/"
--fields-terminated-by=',' --fields-optionally-enclosed-by='"' store
```

Note that when you run this command, mysqldump creates two files for each table. One, with an .sql extension, contains the CREATE TABLE statement. The other, with a .txt extension, contains the table data.

Data files created with either SELECT INTO OUTFILE **or** mysqldump --tab **can be imported back into a MySQL database. You need to use the** LOAD DATA INFILE **statement, which you learn about in Session 25.**

Using BACKUP TABLE

From the MySQL command-line client or another client you can use the BACKUP TABLE command. The basic syntax of the command is

```
BACKUP TABLE table1, table2, table3 TO /path/to/backup
```

Note that this command works on only MyISAM tables. It also issues locks on tables serially — first one table, then another, then another. So, in using this command, you don't get a view of these tables at a specific point in time unless you start by issuing a command that locks all of the tables before running BACKUP TABLE. Generally, I think you'll find one of the other methods for backing up easier and more complete.

Copying Database Files

**10 Min.
To Go**

As you've seen in various sessions in this book, MySQL stores database tables and indexes as files. The MyISAM tables use files with .frm and .myi extensions to store data and indexes. InnoDB tables use files that start with ibdata to store both table and index data. Gemini tables and indexes have .gmd and .gmi extensions. And bdb tables are stored with .db extensions. You can effectively back up all MySQL data by copying all files associated with MySQL data to a safe location.

But once again, when you do this, you're going to want to back up the data at a specific point in time. In order to make sure you get this temporal snapshot, you need to do one of two things: Shut down the MySQL server, or flush and lock all tables. After you have performed one of these two options, you can copy all relevant files to a safe place.

Another option for copying files is the mysqlhotcopy script — a Perl utility that is distributed with MySQL. In order to use mysqlhotcopy, you must have Perl's DBI module installed. For instructions on installation of DBI, see Session 17. You can see full documentation for mysqlhotcopy by using the PERLDOC utility on a Unix platform. However, mysqlhotcopy does not work on all table types — it won't work, for example, on InnoDB tables. I recommend writing your own script that freezes your tables (by either shutting down the server or issuing locks and flushing the tables) and copying the exact files you need to back up.

Using the Binary Log

Let's say that you've chosen a method of backup and you're regularly running mysqldump or copying the appropriate files to safe places. You may think that you're in pretty good shape. But you need to keep in mind that your database information is not like any other item on your server. If, for example, you're running daily backups on a word processing file and that file is destroyed in a disk failure, the most that you'll lose is a day's worth of work. Most companies can live with that sort of potential loss.

Databases, however, are an entirely different ball of wax. On most systems, losing a day's — or even an hour's — worth of data would be unthinkable. Imagine what would happen if an e-commerce site lost a couple of hour's worth of data. It's possible that users' credit cards would be charged but there'd be no way to determine who those users were or what they ordered. It could be a large-scale disaster.

So there needs to be a way to recover from failure. Even if the hard disk holding the tables and indexes dies, you need a way to recover all changes that took place between the time of the most recent backup and the time the disk failed.

This is where MySQL's binary log comes in. The binary log stores all queries that alter data — that is, all INSERTs, UPDATEs, CREATEs, DROPs, and DELETEs. Using this log, you can get the data back into the state it was in prior to a disk failure. Of course, the binary log will be of little use if it is on the same physical disk as the database tables and indexes. Store this log on a different disk — *please.*

To start the binary log, add the `--log-bin` flag when starting the MySQL daemon with `mysqld_safe` or add the item to the `my.cnf` file in the database's data directory. With this flag, you can supply a path or a path- and filename. When MySQL sees the following line in the `[mysqld]` portion of the `my.cnf` file, it creates a series of files associated with the binary logs.

```
log-bin    = /volume/otherdisk/logs/mylogs
```

With this flag, all files are kept in the `/volumn/otherdisk/logs` directory. The first file is `mylogs.index`. This file maintains a plain text listing of the log files in use. Then there are a series of files with the names `mylogs.001`, `mylogs.002`, and so on. These are the files that hold the actual statements that made changes to your databases. MySQL creates a new log file whenever you restart your server or run a FLUSH LOGS command (or `mysqladmin flush-logs`). It simply creates a new log file, incrementing the number in the file extension by 1.

The log files themselves are not human readable, nor can they be read in a text editor. But there is a tool that is delivered with MySQL that can be used to read and manipulate the binary log files: `mysqlbinlog`. This may be in the `/bin` directory of your installation, but on some installations you may have to hunt around for it in the source tree. I recommend copying it to the `mysql/bin` if it is not there to start with.

You can examine the contents of a log file by running `mysqlbinlog` against a log file. For example:

```
shell> /usr/local/mysql/bin/mysqlbinlog /volumne/otherdisk/logs/mylogs.001
# at 4
#011113 10:01:50 server id  1   Start: binlog v 2, server v 4.0.0-alpha-log created
011113 10:01:50
# at 79
#011113 10:03:11 server id  1   Query    thread_id=2      exec_time=1      error_code=0
use store;
SET TIMESTAMP=1005663791;
delete from formats where formats='Web Articles';
# at 163
#011113 10:03:49 server id  1   Query    thread_id=2      exec_time=0      error_code=0
SET TIMESTAMP=1005663829;
insert into formats values('Marketing Literature');
# at 249
#011113 10:04:00 server id  1   Query    thread_id=2      exec_time=0      error_code=0
SET TIMESTAMP=1005663840;
create database newstore;
```

As you can see here, in addition to the actual queries, the binary logs show the exact time of the statement and the thread that created the statement. The SET TIMESTAMP statements are very helpful; in any tables where you are using the TIMESTAMP column type, these statements ensure that when it comes time to restore data to the table, the TIMESTAMP reflects the moment the query was originally run — not the time the statement was restored from the log file. The time of the statement is also important because backup of MySQL data should correspond to a specific point in time. That is, you have a backup as of a specific second. When you know the exact moment of your backup, you can get every query that occurred following that moment by examining the binary log file.

Note that each of the SQL statements has a number associated with it. You can output statements starting with a certain number by applying the `-j` or `--position` flag. For example, the following gets all queries in the log, starting with number 163:

```
shell>  ./mysqlbinlog -j163 /volumne/otherdisk/logs/mylogs.001
# at 163
#011113 10:03:49 server id  1    Query    thread_id=2    exec_time=0    error_code=0
use store;
SET TIMESTAMP=1005663829;
insert into formats values('Marketing Literature');
# at 249
#011113 10:04:00 server id  1    Query    thread_id=2    exec_time=0    error_code=0
SET TIMESTAMP=1005663840;
create database newstore;
```

The output of a `mysqlbinlog` command can be directed to a file with the standard Unix `>` indicator, or on Windows, use the `--result-file` flag. For example:

```
shell>  ./mysqlbinlog -j163 /volumne/otherdisk/logs/mylogs.001 > /path/to/myfile.name
shell>  ./mysqlbinlog -j163 /volumne/otherdisk/logs/mylogs.001 --result-
file=/path/to/myfile.name
```

Or, on UNIX, you can pipe the output of `mysqlbinlog` to the MySQL command-line client.

```
shell>  ./mysqlbinlog -j163 /volumne/otherdisk/logs/mylogs.001 | mysql -u root -pmypass
```

There a few other flags that can be used with `mysqlbinlog`. Run `mysqlbinlog --help` to see a full listing.

The binary log is a key part to MySQL's replication features. You learn more about replication in Session 26.

Instituting Good Backup Practices

Now that you know the methods you can use for backing up MySQL, you need to spend some time instituting practices that ensure your data is available when you need it. My recommendation is this: Set up script that runs `mysqldump` with the following flags.

```
mysqldump --opt --all-databases --flush-logs
```

Note that `--flush-logs` starts a clean log file. It should run daily via a cron job at a time when you know the database is not handling a lot of traffic. The result of this command should be output to a file with a unique name, perhaps with the date as an extension.

If you run this command on a daily basis, you also have binary log files that correspond to a day's worth of data. Therefore, when it comes time to restore lost data, it should be pretty easy to find the exact log files you need to use.

Done!

REVIEW

In this session, you learned how to back up and export MySQL data. This is one of the most important administrative tasks for any database installation, and it's vital that you institute and test backup procedures. You saw several methods for backing up data: mysqldump, the BACKUP TABLE command, the SELECT INTO OUTFILE command, and copying of files containing database data. Further, you learned that despite your best efforts at backing up, it's possible that a hard disk failure can cause a data loss if you don't take proper precautions. This is where the binary log comes in. You saw the purpose of the log and how it can be used to restore data not caught in a backup. You also learned that you must use the mysqlbinlog utility to read binary log.

QUIZ YOURSELF

1. What mysqldump flag specifies that a list of column names should be included with INSERT statements? (See "Using mysqldump.")

2. What mysqldump flag allows you to use a WHERE clause? (See "Using mysqldump.")

3. How would you create a comma-delimited set of fields from SELECT INTO OUTFILE? (See "Using SELECT INTO OUTFILE.")

4. Why should the binary log be stored on a separate physical disk? (See "Using the Binary Log.")

5. What is the purpose of the binary log's SET TIMESTAMP statements? (See "Using the Binary Log.")

Transferring and Importing Data into MySQL

Session Checklist

✔ Using LOAD DATA INFILE

✔ Using mysqlimport

✔ Transferring applications data to MySQL

✔ Importing Apache log files

**30 Min.
To Go**

I n the previous session, you saw that MySQL offers many ways to export and back up data. But many people come to MySQL after using other programs or other relational databases. If you happen to have data that is in a program like Microsoft Excel or Microsoft Access, this session shows you how you can transfer that information into MySQL.

Among developers, MySQL is often used for examining log files. Every Web server, including Apache, writes a log file, which records every hit to that Web server. Though there are programs that can be used to get statistical information directly from these log files, it is often more convenient to use a database to examine these logs. In this session, I show you how you may go about doing that.

Using LOAD DATA INFILE

To import data into MySQL, you must use the LOAD DATA INFILE statement or its command-line equivalent, mysqlimport. For the most part, LOAD DATA INFILE should look familiar, as it takes many of the same clauses as SELECT INTO OUTFILE. The FIELDS TERMINATED BY, FIELDS ENCLOSED BY, OPTIONALLY ENCLOSED BY, and LINES TERMINATED BY clauses have the same meaning for LOAD DATA INFILE as they do for SELECT INTO OUTFILE. Check Session 24 if you need to re-familiarize yourself with these meanings.

Here's a basic example of LOAD DATA INFILE. Imagine that the following plain-text file was placed in MySQL's data directory and named infile.txt:

```
1,foo
2,var
3,foobar
```

Then from the command-line client, you can create a simple table in the test database.

```
mysql> create table loader (
    -> id int not null,
    -> txt char(15));
```

Now from the command-line client, you can run the following command to import the text file into the table. Each line in the text file becomes a row in the newly created table.

```
mysql> LOAD DATA INFILE '/usr/local/mysql/var/infile.txt'
    -> INTO TABLE test.loader
    -> FIELDS TERMINATED BY ','
    -> (id, txt);
```

Note that if the file resides on the machine hosting the MySQL database server, it must either be located in the MySQL data directory or have permissions that make the file readable to all (chmod +r). Otherwise, for security purposes, LOAD DATA INFILE will not be able to process the file. If you need to load data from a text file located on an external host, you must use the LOCAL keyword, which is described below.

LOAD DATA INFILE also includes many optional keywords that you can use for specific purposes. The meanings of the keywords are given below. The following snippet shows where these keywords will show up within the LOAD DATA INFILE statement.

```
LOAD DATA [LOW_PRIORITY | CONCURRENT] [LOCAL] INFILE 'file_name.txt'
    [REPLACE | IGNORE]
    INTO TABLE tbl_name
    [FIELDS
        [TERMINATED BY '\t']
        [[OPTIONALLY] ENCLOSED BY '']
        [ESCAPED BY '\\' ]
    ]
    [LINES TERMINATED BY '\n']
    [IGNORE number LINES]
    [(col_name,...)]
```

- LOW_PRIORITY: Delays the execution of the load operation until no other threads are using the indicated table.
- CONCURRENT: Other threads will be able to read from the table (if it's a MyISAM table) while the load is ongoing.
- LOCAL: Normally, the load operation looks for the file on the machine hosting the MySQL server. However, if you are working from a client on an external host, you can use the LOCAL keyword to let LOAD DATA INFILE know it needs to look on the client's machine for file rather than on the server's.

- REPLACE and IGNORE: The REPLACE and IGNORE keywords come into play when a line from the loaded file has a value that conflicts with a primary key or unique index of the table. If you include REPLACE, the lines in the text file overwrite the rows in the database. If you use INGNORE, the rows in the text file are skipped over and the rows already in the table are maintained.

- IGNORE <number> LINES: The clause indicates that a line number in the file should be ignored. You may use this to skip over a list of column headings that are in the first line of a file with IGNORE 1 LINES.

If you want to use LOAD DATA INFILE, **you must have the** FILE **privilege in the** GRANT **tables. See Session 20 for more information on the** GRANT **tables.**

Using mysqlimport

The mysqlimport utility does exactly the same thing as LOAD DATA INFILE. It takes a series of flags that replace the various clauses you saw above. An example a mysqlimport command similar to the previous LOAD DATA INFILE example given above looks like this:

```
shell> ./mysqlimport --u root -pmypass --columns=id,txt --fields-terminated-by="," test
/usr/local/mysql/var/loader.txt
```

The first thing to note is that this statement does not take a table name. The database name is provided (above, test), but the utility determines the table name by stripping the extension from the filename. So in the above statement, rows will be inserted in a database named loader in the test database. Table 25-1 shows some the other flags for the mysqlimport file. You should be able to match these flags to clauses from LOAD DATA INFILE and other client applications.

Table 25-1 *Other mysqlimport Flags*

Flag	LOAD DATA INFILE Equivalent	If No Equivalent Other Meaning
--fields-terminated-by	FIELDS TERMINATED BY	
--fields-enclosed-by	FIELDS ENCLOSED BY	
--lines-terminated-by	LINES TERMINATED BY	
--ignore	IGNORE	
--replace	REPLACE	
--local	LOCAL	
--force		Ignore errors and continue
--lock-tables		lock tables before loading
--host		host name

**20 Min.
To Go**

Transferring Applications Data to MySQL

Many companies start by using programs like Excel or Access for data manipulation. If you happened to start with Excel, you can quickly grow frustrated with its lack of relational properties.

Access, on the other hand, is a relational database. It stores data in multiple tables like all other RDBMSs. While Access has its place, it's not great for high-volume environments. If many clients try obtaining data at the same time, you quickly see Access slows to a near halt. A lot of people come to MySQL after discovering that Access no longer suits their needs. Happily, the MySQL commands and utilities that you've seen so far make transferring data to MySQL a very easy task.

Moving from Excel to MySQL

From Excel, save a worksheet in CSV (comma-separated values) format. I had better luck using the CSV Windows format from my Mac. You can select the format after choosing Save As from the File menu, as shown in Figure 25-1.

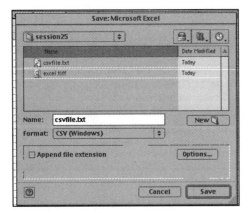

Figure 25-1   *Choosing CSV format for Excel*

A spreadsheet program like Excel is not going to give you table creation information. So, you'll have to spend some time looking over your spreadsheet data and deciding on a table structure and column types. After you've created your tables, you can use LOAD DATA INFILE or mysqlimport, as you've seen in the previous pages.

Moving from Access to MySQL

Chances are that if you're moving from Access, you've got complex table structures to deal with. While Access does offer the option of exporting to a text file, a little more functionality saves you time. Unfortunately, Access doesn't have a built-in tool that dumps both table and structure information like mysqldump. But the good news is that several people have written applications that mimic mysqldump perfectly. There are several of these tools, and you can find a listing of these at www.mysql.com/doc/S/E/SEC627.html. I'm going to show how to use just one of these tools, which works very well. The name of the tool is access_to_mysql.txt and you can find a copy of it at http://mysql.mirrors.netnumina.com/Downloads/Contrib/access_to_mysql.txt.

To use this script, all you have to do is go to the database you want to export and open up the Modules tab. Then click the button to create a new module. Copy the contents of the access_to_mysql.txt file into this module (see Figure 25-2).

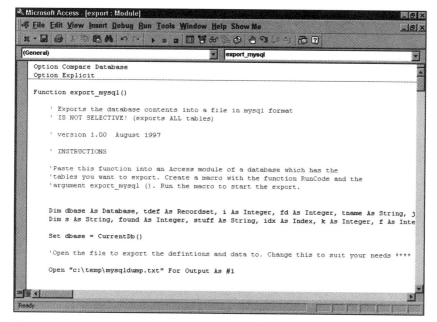

Figure 25-2   *The* access_to_mysql *module window*

When you close the module window, you are asked to name the module. Choose something like "export."

Now you can move to the Macro tab and create a new Macro. In the Macro, you want to choose RunCode for the Action and export_mysql () for the function name. The window should look as it does in Figure 25-3.

You can then close this window and run the macro, which creates a file in the c:\temp directory name mysqldump.txt. If the c:\temp directory doesn't exist, you have to create it. Or, if you want to create this file in a different directory or give it a different name, you can change the following line:

```
Open "c:\temp\mysqldump.txt" For Output As #1
```

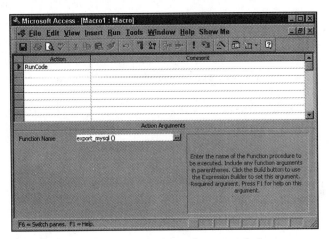

Figure 25-3 *The access_to_mysql macro window*

When you have this file, you can treat it as you would any file created by `mysqldump`. You'd direct the file into the command-line client for processing:

```
shell> mysql -u root -pmypass < c:\\temp\\mysqldump.txt
```

If you're coming to MySQL from FoxPro, Oracle, or about any application commonly used for data storage, chances are someone has built a MySQL converter. Check section B.6 of the MySQL manual for a converter that may work for you. Go to www.mysql.com/doc/S/E/SEC627.html.

Importing Apache Log Files

**10 Min.
To Go**

When using the MyISAM table type, MySQL is very well suited for log analysis. This table was designed to process SELECTs as quickly as possible. For a task like log analysis, you're not going to need features like transactions or row-level locking (all you need is speed. Chances are you're going to need only SELECT statements with GROUP BY clauses.

Apache and other Web servers' log formats are configurable. In the case of Apache, the format of the log is set in the `httpd.conf` file. On a standard installation, you're likely to find entries like these in your `httpd.conf` file:

```
LogFormat "%h %l %u %t \"%r\" %>s %b" common
CustomLog "/volume/httpd/logs/access_log" common
```

You can check Apache documentation (http://httpd.apache.org/docs/logs.html#accesslog) for the meaning of each of the specifiers in the LogFormat line. In the actual log file, you'd see an entry like this for each hit on the Web server:

```
162.83.203.83 - - [15/Nov/2001:08:55:44 -0500] "GET /images/nav_about_on.
gif HTTP/1.1" 200 310
```

This log entry contains some good information, including the URL requested, date and time of the hit, status of the request (200 means it was successful), and the bytes served (here 300). But this log can be improved so that it is easier to analyze with MySQL. I suggest commenting out the other log files and going with the following lines in the httpd.conf file.

```
LogFormat \
    "\"%h\",%{%Y%m%d%H%M%S}t,%>s,%b,\"%{Content-
Type}o\",\"%U\",\"%{Referer}i\",\"%{User-Agent}i\"" combined


CustomLog "/volume/httpd/logs/access_log" combined
```

Then in your access_log, you will see entries such as this:

```
"10.0.1.12",20011115091919,200,1326,"text/html",
"/~jaygreen/test1.php","http://localhost/~jaygreen/test11.php","Mozilla/4.
0 (compatible; MSIE 5.12; Mac_PowerPC)"
```

This entry is a bit more informative. It includes, in comma-delimited format, the following entries: host making the request, time of the request in MySQL's TIMESTAMP(14) format, status of the request, bytes sent, MIME type of the request, URL requested, referrer, and user agent. This format, as you may have guessed, is designed to work with the LOAD DATA INFILE statement.

To use these logs in MySQL, you first need to create a database and table for these logs:

```
mysql> CREATE DATABASE apache_logs;
mysql> CREATE TABLE hits (
    -> host_name char(40),
    -> hit_time TIMESTAMP,
    -> status int,
    -> bytes int,
    -> hit_format char(40),
    -> url char (255),
    -> referrer char(255)
    -> user_agent char(100),
-> );
```

Note that depending on the queries you run, you'll want to add indexes to table. On a busy Web server, you can have hundreds of thousands of hits a day, so indexes on the proper fields are vital. When you're ready to import the log file on Unix, you'll need to make the file universally readable.

```
shell> chmod +r /path/to/access_log
```

You can then import the logs directly into the database table with the following command:

```
mysql> LOAD DATA INFILE '/path/to/logfile'
    -> INTO TABLE apache_logs.hits
    -> FIELDS TERMINATED BY ','
    -> OPTIONALLY ENCLOSED BY '"';
```

With this data in MySQL, you can run all kinds of reports. For example, if you want to get the number of hits on a given day for each file in text/html format, you can run the following query. I've limited the format to text/html because I'm not interested in hits logged by gif or jpeg images.

```
SELECT url, count(*) as pageviews
FROM hits
WHERE hit_format='text/html'
AND hit_time BETWEEN 20011115000000 and 20011115235959
GROUP BY url
```

This query returned all pageviews for November 15, 2001. If you want to get a bit more complex, you can run a query to get the total views for each page on each day of the month.

```
SELECT url, dayofmonth(hit_time) as 'Day', count(url) as 'Daily Total'
FROM hits
WHERE hit_format='text/html'
AND month(hit_time)=11
GROUP BY
url, dayofmonth(hit_time)
```

This gives you a listing like this:

```
+----------------------+------+-------------+
| url                  | Day  | Daily Total |
+----------------------+------+-------------+
| /~jaygreen/test8.php |  14  |           1 |
| /~jaygreen/test1.php |  15  |           5 |
| /~jaygreen/test11.php|  15  |           4 |
| /~jaygreen/test2.php |  14  |           1 |
| /~jaygreen/test2.php |  15  |           1 |
+----------------------+------+-------------+
```

There are some alternate methods for working with Apache log files that you should be aware of. If you don't want to go through the process of altering and then importing log files to MySQL, you can log pageview data directly into a MySQL database. This is often an easier way to go. For example, on one of my sites, I created a simple database table like this:

```
create table counter (
    counter_id int not null primary key,
    url varchar(255),
    referrer, varchar(255),
    time_of_hit timestamp(14)
)
```

Then I make sure that the following script is included in each PHP page on my site:

```
$conn=@mysql_connect("localhost", "jay", "pword");
@mysql_select_db("counter");
$query="INSERT INTO counter(url, referrer)
VALUES('$PHP_SELF','$HTTP_REFERER');
@mysql_query($query);
```

I can then do the analysis I need from this table data.

Another method, if you have control of your Apache installation, is to use mod_log_mysql, an Apache module that can be used to log directly to MySQL without any additional middleware or data loads. In order to use this, you'll need to have authority to re-compile your Apache installation. See www.mysql.com/downloads/contrib.html#SEC624 and the source file of this module for information on use and installation.

Done!

REVIEW

In this session, you learned how to import data into MySQL using the LOAD DATA INFILE statement and mysqlimport. You learned the various clauses you can use with LOAD DATA INFILE and the corresponding flags for mysqlimport. Following this overview, you saw how these statements can be used to import data from Microsoft Excel, Microsoft Access, and Apache log file. Further, you saw how the information from the Apache logs can be manipulate to provide valuable data.

QUIZ YOURSELF

1. On Unix systems, the LOAD DATA INFILE statement will only work if the file has what permissions? (See "Using LOAD DATA INFILE.")

2. What LOAD DATA INFILE clause indicates that the file to be loaded is located on the client machine? (See "Using LOAD DATA INFILE.")

3. How does mysqlimport determine the table name into which the data will be loaded? (See "Using mysqlimport.")

4. What utility can be used to mimic mysqldump? (See "Moving from Access to MySQL.")

5. Other than importing log files, what two methods can be used to log hits? (See "Importing Apache Log Files.")

Replication

Session Checklist

✔ Understanding replication

✔ Setting up replication

✔ Replication commands

I n the previous few sessions, I have covered aspects that an administrator of MySQL needs to be aware of. Issues like security, backup, and use of the my.cnf files normally fall under the purview of the database administrator (DBA), not the applications developer. Although in many cases, the DBA and developer are the same person. (This is especially true of a package like MySQL, which is fairly small and not terribly difficult. A large Oracle installation usually requires a full-time DBA in addition to developers.)

This session deals with a fairly advanced database concept called *replication*. Before you decide on an environment that replicates MySQL, both the DBA and developer need to be in on the planning and implementation of the system. Why do you need this kind of planning? The reason why becomes clear after you read the description of replication that follows.

Understanding Replication

30 Min.
To Go

To describe replication, I return to the example of the store database that I've used throughout most of this book. Imagine that after creating and deploying an application, my online store gets picked up by major media outlets and becomes more popular than

I ever imagined. It could get to the point where my systems are serving many hundreds of thousands of Web pages a day. MySQL is fast, but in a very intense environment, it's possible to run up against the application's limitations.

In a case like this, when you're getting everything you can out of a single MySQL server, where do you go for that extra performance? (As Spinal Tap might ask, how do you turn that server up to 11?) You can optimize queries, get a faster server, get more RAM, or try to install some caching system, but all of these approaches have limitation. Severs only go so fast, you can max out on RAM, and caching is not always viable.

Often your best course of action is to create multiple copies of your database on multiple servers. The idea of having the same data mimicked under another server daemon on another host is the concept behind replication. If the stress on one server is too great, simply load up another server with MySQL, replicate the data on that server, and then make sure client applications interact with both servers as appropriate.

Some database servers, like Oracle, make use of extremely sophisticated replication models. MySQL's replication scheme is by comparison a bit limited, but it is still quite effective. MySQL makes use of a *master-slave replication system*. Essentially, one server is the master. All other servers that replicate look to the master and do their best to replicate exactly what is in the master's databases and tables.

The application developer and DBA must keep the master-slave model in mind when deploying applications. Because all replicated copies of the database look to a single master, all changes to the data — all INSERTs, DELETEs, UPDATEs, and DROPs — must be made to the master database. The changes to the master are then replicated in the slaves. If you, for example, ran an UPDATE against a slave's copy of the database, those changes don't make it to the master. The slaves, however, are perfectly suited for running SELECT statements. Running SELECT statements against a slave can greatly reduce the load on a master.

Using the store database and application as an example, there are certain parts of the application that you can quite safely move to a slave in a replicated environment. A good portion of any user's time at an e-commerce site will be spent browsing through a catalogue, looking at the items available and their prices and descriptions. This kind of information, which is gathered entirely through SELECT statements, can be taken from a slave. However, when the user wants to complete a sale and process an order, INSERT and UPDATE statements are required as new information makes its way into several tables. These actions need to be performed against the master. Figure 26-1 illustrates how the master-slave environment would be applied to an online store.

Note that administration of the application — updating prices, adding and deleting items, and so forth — must be conducted on the master.

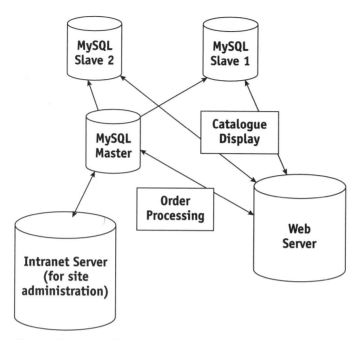

Figure 26-1 *Applying replication to an online store*

Setting Up Replication

It probably goes without saying that in order to use replication in MySQL, you're going to need a couple of different servers with MySQL installed. Beyond that, you're going to need to make sure that specific changes are made to both the master and the slaves.

Setting up the master

The general set up works like this: You add a user to the MySQL GRANT tables that slave servers use to log in to the master; then you make a copy of your data at a specific point in time. When running, the slave servers read from the binary log. In order to read from the binary log, the slave needs to have the File privilege in the GRANT tables. In fact, this is the only privilege the slave needs. Chances are, you don't want to specify a host for the slave as the name or the IP address of the slave server may change, or you may have a need for more than one slave. But there's really no need to have two users who do exactly the same things. So, to create a new user with File privileges from any host, you can run the following command from the command-line client.

```
GRANT FILE ON *.* TO repuser@"%" IDENTIFIED BY 'pword'
```

Note that by using the wildcard character % in the statement, you make these permissions available on any host.

Following this command, you want to shut down the your MySQL daemon (mysqladmin shutdown) and copy the database files from your master to your slave. The data on each of these servers needs to be identical. Doing a copy from one server to another is the easiest way to ensure that each server contains the same information. On Unix, you'll probably want to run the tar utility to make the transfer from one server to another easier; on Windows, a utility like WinZip serves the same purpose.

Before you restart the master, you need to make sure it is set up to use the binary log. This requires only one line in the my.cnf. file (the one in the data directory). In addition, you need to make sure that your server is set up with a server_id of 1. Also make sure that your my.cnf file contains the following two lines.

```
log-bin
server-id      = 1
```

Keep in mind that any changes made to the binary log, such as restricting the databases for which changes are logged, affect replication.

For information on setting up and using the binary log, see Session 24. For a full explanation of the MySQL GRANT tables, see Session 20.

Setting up the slave

In order to set up the slave, you need to shut down the slave's server and install the data files taken from the master. Before you restart the slave server, you must add a series of lines to the slave's my.cnf file.

```
master-host=
master-user=
master-password=
master-port=
server-id=
```

For the master_host item, you can use either the IP address of the master server or the full domain name. The master_user and master_password items are the same as those used for the GRANT statement run on the server. The server_id must be a number other than 1. If you're working in an environment where there are many slaves, each sever must have a unique server_id. It's probably best to keep the numbering scheme simple and number the slave servers 2, 3, and so forth.

At this point, to start replication, all you need to do start the servers. First the master, then the slaves. When you make changes to the master, you'll soon see them mirrored in the slave.

In addition to the flags previously shown, Table 26-1 shows other flags that can be used to configure replication on the slaves.

Table 26-1 *Slave Configuration Options*

Flag	Description
`master-connect-retry`	The number of seconds the slave thread will sleep before retrying to connect to the master in case the master goes down or the connection is lost. Default is 60. Example: `master-connect-retry=60`.
`master-info-file`	The location of the file that remembers where replication left off. The default is `master.info` in the data directory. There's really no reason ever to change this option.
`replicate-do-table=db_name.table_name`	Tells the slave thread to restrict replication to the specified table. To specify more than one table, use the directive multiple times, once for each table. This will work for cross-database updates, in contrast to replicate-do-db. Example: `replicate-do-table=some_db.some_table`.
`replicate-ignore-table=db_name.table_name`	Tells the slave thread to not replicate the specified table. To specify more than one table to ignore, use the directive multiple times, once for each table. This will work for cross-datbase updates, in contrast to `replicate-ignore-db`. Example: `replicate-ignore-table=db_name.some_table`.

Continued

Table 26-1 *Continued*

Flag	Description
`replicate-wild-do-table=db_name.table_name`	Tells the slave thread to restrict replication to the tables that match the specified wildcard pattern. To specify more than one pattern, use the directive multiple times, once for each table.
	This works for cross-database updates. Example: `replicate-wild-do-table=foo%.bar%` replicates only updates to tables in all databases that start with `foo` and whose table names start with `bar`.
`replicate-wild-ignore-table=db_name.table_name`	Tells the slave thread to not replicate to the tables that match the given wildcard pattern. To specify more than one pattern to ignore, use the directive multiple times, once for each table.
	This works for cross-database updates. Example: `replicate-wild-ignore-table=test%.user%` will not do updates to tables in databases that start with `test` and whose table names start with `user`.
`replicate-ignore-db=database_name`	Tells the slave thread to not replicate to the specified database. To specify more than one database to ignore, use the directive multiple times, once for each database. This option will not work if you use cross database updates. Example: `replicate-ignore-db=db_name`.

Flag	Description
replicate-do-db=database_name	Tells the slave thread to restrict replication to the specified database. To specify more than one database, use the directive multiple times, once for each database. Note that this works only if you do not use cross-database queries such as UPDATE dbname.tablename SET foo='bar' while having selected a different or no database.
log-slave-updates	Tells the slave to log the updates from the slave thread to the binary log. You need to turn this on if you plan to daisy-chain the slaves.
replicate-rewrite-db=from_name->to_name	Updates to a database with a different name than the original Example: replicate-rewrite-db=master_db_name->slave_db_name.
skip-slave-start	Tells the slave server not to start the slave on the startup. The user can start it later with SLAVE START.
slave_read_timeout=#	Number of seconds to wait for more data from the master before aborting the read.

Replication Commands

10 Min. To Go

There are some commands related to replication that can be sent to the server engine from a client. Using these commands, you can see how replication is working on your servers and manipulate replication parameters. Table 26-2 shows commands that work on the master, and Table 26-3 shows commands that work on the slave.

Table 26-2 *Replication Commands for the Master*

Command	Description
SET SQL_LOG_BIN=0	Disables update logging if the user has process privilege. Ignored otherwise.
SET SQL_LOG_BIN=1	Re-enables update logging if the user has process privilege. Ignored otherwise.
RESET MASTER	Deletes all binary logs listed in the index file, resetting the binary log index file to be empty.
SHOW MASTER STATUS	Provides status information on the binary log of the master.
SHOW MASTER LOGS	Lists the binary logs on the master. You should use this command prior to PURGE MASTER LOGS to find out how far you should go.
PURGE MASTER LOGS TO 'logname'	Deletes all the replication logs that are listed in the log index as being prior to the specified log, and removes them from the log index, so that the given log now becomes first. Example:
	PURGE MASTER LOGS TO 'mysql-bin.010'
	This command will do nothing and fail with an error if you have an active slave that is currently reading one of the logs you are trying to delete. However, if you have a dormant slave, and happen to purge one of the logs it wants to read, the slave will be unable to replicate once it comes up. The command is safe to run while slaves are replicating; you do not need to stop them. You must first check all the slaves with SHOW SLAVE STATUS to see which log they are on, then do a listing of the logs on the master with SHOW MASTER LOGS, find the earliest log among all the slaves (if all the slaves are up-to-date, this will be the last log on the list), back up all the logs you are about to delete (optional).

Table 26-3 *Replication Commands for the Slave*

Command	Description
SLAVE START	Starts the slave thread.
SLAVE STOP	Stops the slave thread.
SET SQL_SLAVE_SKIP_COUNTER=n	Skip the next n events from the master. Only valid when the slave thread is not running; otherwise, gives an error. Useful for recovering from replication glitches.
RESET SLAVE	Makes the slave forget its replication position in the master logs.
LOAD TABLE tblname FROM MASTER	Downloads a copy of the table from master to the slave.
SHOW SLAVE STATUS	Provides status information on essential parameters of the slave thread.

CHANGE MASTER TO ...	Changes the master parameters to the values specified in the command and restarts the slave thread. You may run the command like so:
	
	CHANGE MASTER TO
	  MASTER_HOST='myserver.myco.com',
	  MASTER_USER='repuser',
	  MASTER_PASSWORD='mypass2',
	  MASTER_PORT=3306,
	
	You only need to specify the values that need to be changed. The values that you omit will stay the same with the exception of when you change the host or the port. In that case, the slave will assume that since you are connecting to a different host or a different port, the master is different. Therefore, the old values of log and position are not applicable anymore, and will automatically be reset to an empty string and 0, respectively (the start values). Note that if you restart the slave, it will remember its last master. If this is not desirable, you should delete the master.info file before restarting, and the slave will read its master from my.cnf or the command line.

On a slave that is running properly, the SHOW SLAVE STATUS command looks something like this:

```
mysql> show slave status \G
*************************** 1. row ***************************
        Master_Host: 10.0.1.8
        Master_User: repuser
        Master_Port: 3306
      Connect_retry: 60
           Log_File: master-servername-bin.001
                Pos: 294
      Slave_Running: Yes
     Replicate_do_db:
 Replicate_ignore_db:
          Last_errno: 0
          Last_error:
        Skip_counter: 0
1 row in set (0.00 sec)
```

Done!

REVIEW

In this session, you learned how you can apply replication to your MySQL servers. You started by learning where replication can be helpful and how replication needs to be handled in deployed applications. Then you saw how to set up both the master and slave servers. You learned that you must shut down the servers, copy data, and make specific changes to the my.cnf file. Finally, you saw the commands and configurable options you can use when arranging your MySQL servers.

QUIZ YOURSELF

1. Why must all UPDATE statements be run on the master? (See "Understanding Replication.")

2. How do slaves read changes to the master? (See "Setting Up Replication.")

3. What is the required server_id of the master.? (See "Setting Up Replication.")

4. What command can change the parameters a slave uses to connect to a master? (See "Replication Commands.")

5. What command shows details of the slave's connection status? (See "Replication Commands.")

PART

V

Sunday Morning Part Review

1. What command shuts down the MySQL server daemon?
2. Why should the MySQL server not be run as the system root user?
3. When starting the MySQL server daemon, what flag indicates the user you would like the server to run as?
4. How can you make sure that the security of your Linux system is up-to-date?
5. What are the three possible locations for the my.cnf file on a Linux/Unix system?
6. What variable determines the data directory used by MySQL?
7. If you put a copy of the my.cnf file in a user's home directory that contains the user's password, who should be assigned ownership of the file (with chown)?
8. How can you use mysqladmin to see if a MySQL is running on a specific host?
9. How can you view the processes running on a MySQL sever?
10. How can you use mysqladmin to end a specific process?
11. What mysqladmin command will reveal the number of queries MySQL has executed, the number of queries it processes per second, and other information?
12. What MySQL utility will show basic information about databases, tables, and columns?
13. What MySQL utility exports MySQL data into a text file?
14. What mysqldump flag specifies that all databases should be exported?
15. What command executed from a client exports data to a file?
16. Which log maintains a record of all SQL statements that have in any way altered data?
17. Why should the binary log be kept on a disk that does not store the databases and indexes?
18. What utility is used to read the binary log?

19. What statement can be used to load data into a table from a file?
20. Name a utility that can be used to transfer data from Access to MySQL?
21. What type of replication process does MySQL use?
22. What file do slave servers use to read changes from the master?
23. What is the required server-ID of the master?
24. What command can show how a slave is performing?

PART

VI

Sunday Afternoon

Session 27
Diagnosing and Repairing Table Problems

Session 28
MySQL GUI Clients

Session 29
Optimizing MySQL

Session 30
Answering Remaining Questions

Diagnosing and Repairing Table Problems

Session Checklist

✔ Using SQL Commands for checking and repairing tables

✔ Using utility programs for checking and repairing tables

MyISAM tables, which you will likely use frequently — if not exclusively — in your applications, require a bit of looking after. Under heavy load or in some difficult circumstances, tables become corrupted. This won't happen too often, but when it does, you need to find a way to repair the broken tables. MySQL does ship with utilities that can help you look after your tables and make sure they are in the best possible condition. When you are setting up your sever that will host MySQL, make sure that some of these utilities are run on a regular basis.

Using SQL Commands for Checking and Reparing Tables

**30 Min.
To Go**
When it comes time to examine and repair and damaged tables or indexes, you have two choices: You can either run commands from a client, such as the command-line client, or you can use utilities from the shell or DOS prompt. The sections below describe the SQL commands you can issue from the clients.

Using the CHECK TABLE command

There are a couple of ways to check the status of MyISAM tables. The easiest method uses the CHECK TABLE command from a MySQL client. At its simplest form, you can check a table by entering CHECK TABLE table_name from the command-line client. You get a response like the one below:

```
mysql> CHECK TABLE store.users;
+-------------+-------+----------+----------+
| Table       | Op    | Msg_type | Msg_text |
+-------------+-------+----------+----------+
| store.users | check | status   | OK       |
+-------------+-------+----------+----------+
```

The first two columns in the table returned by CHECK TABLE show, respectively, the name of the table checked and the operation being performed, which will always be check. The last two columns give the information you want to examine. The Msg type column shows one of the following values: status, error, info, or warning. If you get a response of error or warning, you have to carry out further actions to get your tables and indexes into shape. If a table has a problem, the Msg text column gives more details on the error within the tables or indexes.

The majority of errors that occur within MyISAM tables involve indexes. If, for example, the daemon or a client crashes during an update operation, it's possible that the table has been updated but the indexes do not accurately reflect the most recent additions to the tables.

There are five options you can use with the CHECK TABLE that give varying degrees of detail in the examination of the tables and indexes. The options are

- QUICK: Takes a short look at the table but does not check links between index items and table rows.
- FAST: Reviews only tables that had not been closed properly.
- CHANGED: Reviews only tables that had not changed since the last time CHECK TABLE was run.
- MEDIUM: Verifies that the links between tables and indexes are accurate. CHECK TABLE defaults to MEDIUM if no options are given in the command.
- EXTENDED: Does a full check between each row and each index. This is extremely complete, but can take quite a long time. Usually, unless you suspect that there are serious problems that are not being found by MEDIUM, you shouldn't bother with this.

For example, if you want to run an EXTENDED check on only tables that had not been closed properly, you can run the following command:

```
mysql> CHECK TABLE store.users, store.products CHANGED EXTENDED
```

If a CHECK TABLE command shows that a table has problems, you need to run a command to repair the table.

The CHECK TABLE command works well when there is a specific table or two you want to examine. If, for example, a query is not returning accurate results or the table is obviously corrupted, you may log in to the command-line client and run this command. However, if you want to check all tables in a MySQL installation, perhaps as part of regularly scheduled maintenance routine, you're better off using the mysqlchk or mysqlcheck utilities, whose usage is described later in this session.

Using REPAIR TABLE

One way to repair a damaged table or index is with the REPAIR TABLE command. You'd only want to run this command if your examination of the table reveals that a table or index has problems. To use this command, you can log into the command-line client and run REPAIR TABLE table_name with one of the following keywords, QUICK or EXTENDED.

If you use the keyword QUICK, the repair process only reworks the index tree. If you use EXTENDED, MySQL rebuilds the indexes, row by row. This can be a very time-consuming process and often is not necessary. Usually QUICK fixes all the errors present in the table.

 If a table is in really bad shape you may be better off using the myisamchk **utility, which is described later. You will want to copy the damaged table to a different directory and run** myisamchk **with the flags that force the repair of the table.**

Using ANALYZE TABLE

The ANALYZE TABLE command looks at the keys on a given table. If a table has gone through a lot of changes (multiple INSERTs and DELETEs), it is possible that the index will not be in the most advantageous format. If you are optimizing a SELECT query and your EXPLAIN statement is returning unexpected results, it may be because an index needs work.

In a case like this, you can run ANALYZE TABLE. This command examines the indexes on a table and gets them into the best possible shape. The command takes no special keywords. From a client, you can simply run something like

```
ANALYZE TABLE store.users
```

Using OPTIMIZE TABLE

Use the OPTIMIZE TABLE command after running extensive deletes on tables. MySQL won't automatically make use of the room vacated by deleted records. Running this command allows MySQL to reclaim empty space.

```
OPTIMIZE TABLE store.users
```

Using Utility Programs for Checking and Repairing Tables

20 Min. To Go

There are two utilities that you can operate from a Unix shell or DOS prompt that keep your tables in shape. They are mysqlcheck and myisamchk. Why are there two? They have slightly different uses. In order to run any of these checking or repair operations, you need to be sure that the tables are not in use by other clients. In older versions of MySQL, when myisamchk was the only available utility, the user of the utility needed to make sure that the server daemon was taken down or that locks were placed on all tables going through analysis. This can be a somewhat lengthy and unpleasant process. Now, with mysqlcheck, you can run these utilities while the server daemon is running and without worrying about locking; the utility takes care of that process for you.

**10 Min.
To Go**

Using mysqlcheck

To conduct regularly scheduled checks and repairs on databases and tables, you can make use of the mysqlcheck utility. This is a pretty interesting utility that you can use for a variety of tasks. In fact, mysqlcheck can do everything that the CHECK TABLE, REPAIR TABLE, ANALYZE TABLE, and OPTIMIZE TABLE commands do. All you need to do is invoke the correct flags to make use of the different levels of functionality. Table 27-1 shows some of mysqlcheck's flags and shows how they correspond the MySQL commands you saw earlier in this session.

Table 27-1 *mysqlcheck Flags and Their Corresponding Commands*

Flag	Alternate Flag	Corresponding Command
-a	--analyze	ANALYZE TABLE
-c	--check	CHECK TABLE
-r	--repair	REPAIR TABLE
-o	--optimize	OPTIMIZE TABLE

So to run a check on all tables in the store database from a shell or DOS prompt, run a command like this:

```
shell>% ./mysqlcheck -u root -pmypass ----check store
store.addresses                                       OK
store.formats                                         OK
store.items_for_sale                                  OK
store.order_items                                     OK
store.orders                                          OK
store.places                                          OK
store.products                                        OK
store.users                                           OK
```

Notice that the command takes the typical -u and -p flags you have seen in all other clients.

In addition, you can run mysqlcheck against specific tables, specific tables, or against all databases with commands like the following:

```
shell> ./mysqlcheck database_name.table_name_1, database_name.table_name_2
shell> ./mysqlcheck --databases database_name_1 databases_name_2
shell> ./mysqlcheck --all-databases
```

This command has an interesting feature you can use on Unix systems. Instead of using the -r, -a, and -o flags, you can make a copy of mysqlcheck and rename it. Depending on the name you give the copy mysqlcheck, the copy performs a specific function. You make copies of mysqlcheck and rename the copies mysqlrepair, mysqlanalyze, and mysqloptimize and run those in place of mysqlcheck with the -r -a and -o flags, respectively.

In addition to the flags you have seen so far, there are a few other options for mysqlcheck to know about. These are listed in Table 27-2.

Table 27-2 *Other mysqlcheck Options*

Flag	Alternate Flag	Meaning
--auto-repair		Use with the --analyze flag; if table is damaged automatically repair it.
-C	--check-only-changed	Check only tables that have changed since last checked.
-f	--force	Continue even if an SQL error is encountered.
-e	--extended	Same as the EXTENDED keyword in the CHECK and REPAIR statements.
-m	--medium-check	Same as the MEDIUM keyword in both CHECK and REPAIR.
-q	--quick	Same as QUICK in both CHECK and REPAIR statements.
-s	--silent	Print only error messages.

If you are running your own MySQL installation, you may want to add a mysqlcheck command to your cron tab. You may want to check and automatically repair any errors to your tables on a daily basis at a time when the load on your server is at its lowest. The command for check and repairing may look something like this:

```
/usr/local/mysql/bin/mysqlcheck --check --quick --auto-repair --all-
databases -u root -pmypass --silent
```

Using myisamchk

You'll use myisamchk while the server is down. If you've encountered a crash and have found that your tables are clearly corrupted, you can run myisamchk for all of your diagnosis and repair needs. Almost all of the functionality for myisamchk has been covered in the previous portions of this session. You'll just need to be made aware of the flags specific to myisamchk. You can find the flags and their meanings in Table 27-3.

The basic format for the myisamchk command is

```
shell> ./myisamchk /path/to/tables/table_name.MYI
```

You can run the command against all MyISAM tables in a directory using the following:

```
shell> ./myisamchk /path/to/tables/*.MYI
```

Or, to run against all MyISAM tables in the data directly, you'd run a command like this:

```
shell> ./myisamchk /path/to/data/dir/*/*.MYI
```

Table 27-3 *myisamchk Flags*

Flag	Alternate Flag	Meaning
-s	--silent	Prints errors only. One can use two -s to make myisamchk very silent.
-v	--verbose	Prints more information. This can be used with --describe and --check. Use many -v for more verbosity!
-V	--version	Prints version and exit.
-w	--wait	Holds off on operations if table is locked.
CHECK options. Analogous to the CHECK TABLE command. (Check is the default action for myisamchk.)		
-c	--check	Checks table for errors.
-e	--extend-check	Checks the table *very* thoroughly. Use this only in extreme cases as myisamchk should normally be able to find out if the table is okay even without this switch.
-F	--fast	Checks only tables that haven't been closed properly.
-C	--check-only-changed	Checks only tables that have changed since last check.
-f	--force	Restarts with -r if there are any errors in the table. States will be updated as with --update-state.
-I	--information	Prints statistics information about table that is checked.
-m	--medium-check	Checks table for errors. This is faster than extended-check, but only finds 99.99 percent of all errors. Should be good enough for most cases.
-U	--update-state	Marks tables as crashed if you find any errors.
-T	--read-only	Doesn't mark table as checked.
Repair options. Analogous to using REPAIR TABLE (When using -r or -o)		
-B	--backup	Makes a backup of the .MYD file as "filename-time.BAK."

Flag	Alternate Flag	Meaning
`--correct-checksum`		Provides `correct` `checksum` information for table.
`-D`	`--data-file-length=#`	Specifies max length of data file (when re-creating data file when it's full).
`-e`	`--extend-check`	Attempts to recover every possible row from the data file. Normally this also finds a lot of garbage rows. Don't use this option unless you are totally desperate.
`-f`	`--force`	Overwrites old temporary files.
`-k`	`--keys-used=`	Tells MyISAM to update only some specific keys. # is a bit mask of which keys to use. This can be used to get faster inserts!
`-r`	`@ recover`	Fixes almost anything except unique keys that aren't unique.
`-n`	`--sort-recover`	Forces recovering with sorting even if the temporary file would be very big.
`-o`	`--safe-recover`	Uses old recovery method. Slower than `-r` but can handle a couple of cases where `-r` reports that it can't fix the data file.
`-t`	`--tmpdir=path`	Serves as a path for temporary files.
`-q`	`--`	Results in faster repair by not modifying the data file. Once can give a second `'-q'` to force myisamchk to modify the original datafile in case of duplicate keys.
`-u`	`--unpack`	Unpacks file packed with `myisampack`.
Other actions:		
`-a`	`--analyze`	Analyzes distribution of keys (analogous to ANALYZE TABLE.). Will make some joins in MySQL faster. You can check the calculated distribution by using `--describe` `--verbose table_name`.
`-d`	`--description`	Prints some information about table.

Continued

Table 27-3   *Continued*

Flag	Alternate Flag	Meaning
-A	--set-auto-increment [=value]	Forces auto_increment to start at this or higher value. If no value is given, then sets the next auto_increment value to the highest used value for the auto key + 1.
-S	--sort-index	Sorts index blocks. This speeds up read-next in applications.
-R	--sort-records=#	Sorts records according to an index. This makes your data much more localized and may speed up things. (It may be *very* slow to do a sort the first time!)

The commands and utilities you've seen in the chapter are helpful, and they can definitely help you recover tables that have sustained damage. However, nothing can protect you from a catastrophic crash. You must take your backup seriously. Maintaining quality backup is the only way to be sure your data will available after a crash.

Done!

REVIEW

In this session you saw the utilities and commands that help you maintain and repair your MyISAM tables. The session started by showing several commands — ANALYZE TABLE, REPAIR TABLE, OPTIMIZE TABLE, and CHECK TABLE — that can be used from a MySQL client. The session then went on to show the utilities that can be used from the DOS prompt or Unix shell to check and repair tables. Along the way you saw how these commands and utilities can be used for both preventive maintenance and to speed joins in SELECT statements.

QUIZ YOURSELF

1. Which keyword in the CHECK TABLE command forces a full check of every entry in each index? (See "Using the CHECK TABLE command.")
2. How can running ANALYZE TABLE affect SELECT statements? (See "Using ANALYZE TABLE.")
3. Which of the utilities discussed in this session should be run while the server is running? (See "Using Utility Programs for Checking and Repairing Tables.")
4. What mysqlcheck flag is equivalent to running CHECK TABLE? (See "Using mysqlcheck.")
5. What mysqlcheck flag automatically repairs tables as errors are found? (See "Using mysqlcheck.")

MySQL GUI Clients

Session Checklist

✔ phpMyAdmin

✔ mySQLfront

✔ MysqlGUI

✔ Using MySQL with ODBC

✔ Using MacSQL

30 Min.
To Go

So far in this book, I've shown you how to run MySQL queries, commands, and utilities. Everything you've learned so far has been important: you will be using all of these methods as you work with MySQL. However, sometimes SQL syntax can be a bit cumbersome — it can be annoying to have to refer back to a book or a manual when you need to remember the exact wording of a particular command. When the time comes, are you going to remember how to put together an ALTER TABLE statement that adds a two-column unique index to a table? Maybe not.

Happily, there are several graphical clients that can use to perform most of your administrative tasks with MySQL. If you'd rather not type in full CREATE and ALTER statements when working with tables, or if you'd like a more attractive interface from which you can view databases, tables, and data, you'll probably want to make use of one of the clients I describe in this session.

phpMyAdmin

The folks at phpWizard.net (www.phpwizard.net) have created what is probably the most widely used and fully featured MySQL GUI administrative client. Their software, called phpMyAdmin, is free and portable. It runs off any PHP-enabled Web server that has access to a MySQL installation. If you followed the instructions in Session 14 for installing PHP with MySQL support, you should be able to run phpMyAdmin without difficulty.

To install phpMyAdmin, all you need to do is go to the phpMyAdmin download page (`http://phpmyadmin.sourceforge.net/download.html`) and get the latest source files. If you're working off a Windows platform, you'll want to download the file with a `.zip` extension — something like `phpMyAdmin-2.2.2-rc1-php.zip`. On Unix and Mac OS X systems, you can download a file with a `.tar.gz` extension — something like `phpMyAdmin-2.2.2-rc1-php.tar.gz`. Then you need to extract the file to a location where it is available to your Web server. Assuming you are using Apache, this is normally in the `/htdocs` folder. Depending on the location of your Apache installation, on Unix, the command to extract looks something like this:

```
shell> cp phpmyadmin-2.2.2.-rc1-php.tar.gz /Apache-install/htdocs
shell> tar xzf phpmyadmin-2.2.2.-rc1-php.tar.gz
```

You should now have a new folder named `phpmyadmin-2.2.2-rc1`, which contains a series of PHP files.

On Windows, use WinZip or a similar utility to extract the contents of the zip file to your Apache installation's `\htdocs` folder.

If you used the NuSphere installation, you already have a copy of phpMyAdmin available. All you need to do is start the "Start MySQL Admin Web Site Item" from the Start menu.

Your first stop after unzipping this file should be the `Documentation.html` page (if you followed the instructions above, it should be in a location like `http://localhost/phpmyadmin-2.2.2.-rc1/Documentation.html`. phpMyAdmin is a flexible tool that can be used to administer multiple MySQL installations with a variety of options. Make sure you read through this file before making phpMyAdmin accessible on your Web server — especially if the server is available to the world at large. You can open a huge security hole if you're not careful.

The `Documentation.html` file contains clear instructions on how you should set up users with `GRANT` statements so you can get the most out of phpMyAdmin. I won't attempt to reconstruct those instructions here.

Figures 28-1 and 28-2 show two views of the `store` database from phpMyAdmn.

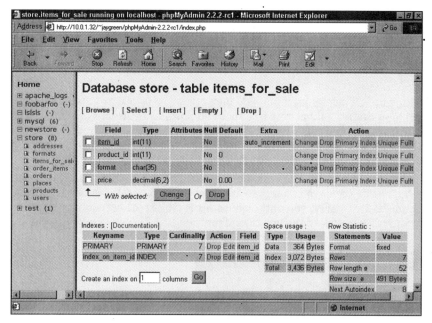

Figure 28-1   *View of the* store *database from phpMyAdmin*

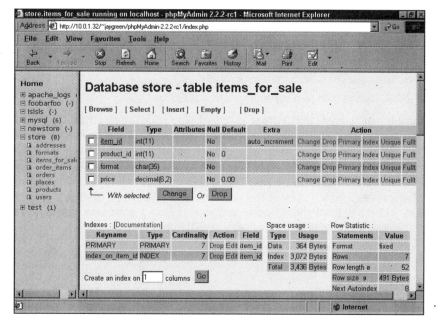

Figure 28-2   *View of the* items_for_sale *table from phpMyAdmin*

Note that there is a lot more information available from phpMyAdmin, and I encourage you to download the tool and see what it has to offer.

mysqlFront

**20 Min.
To Go**

If you're working on a Windows machine, you may enjoy the mySQLfront tool created by Ansgar Becker. You can read about this free tool and download it from `http://anse.de/mysqlfront/index.php`. For most, to install MySQLfront, all you need to do is download the latest `.zip` file from `www.anse.de/mysqlfront.zip`, unzip the file, and then double-click on the `mysqlfornt.exe` file that was extracted from the zip file.

When you double-click on the file, you are presented with a window into which you need to enter the host name (you can connect to any host or IP address), username, and password (see Figure 28-3). Usually, you enter values for MySQL's root user so that you can fully administer your MySQL installation from mysqlFront.

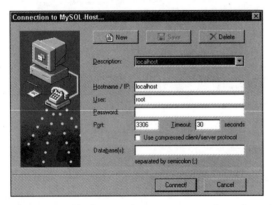

Figure 28-3　*Connecting to a server through mySQLfront*

The best way to get to know mySQLfront is to just play with the interface. There is not a whole lot of documentation that comes with the program, but with the knowledge you already have of MySQL, you should have little trouble figuring out what the various commands do. About every server, database, and table attribute is easily configured with this tool. You just need to click the correct buttons.

Figures 28-4 and 28-5 show a view of the order_items table and a view of a specific column within that table. From these figures you should have a good idea of how you can easily change tables and column attributes with mySQLfront.

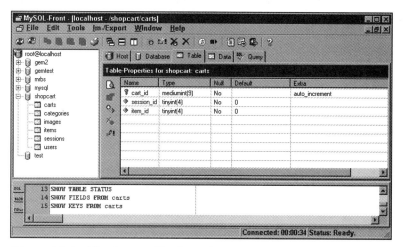

Figure 28-4   *Viewing a table through mySQLfront*

Figure 28-5   *Viewing a table column mySQLfront*

With mysqlFront, phpMyAdmin, and MysqlGUI, you're not going to be able to get commercial support. If, for example, you have difficulty installing mySQLfront, you're not going to be able to make a phone call and find someone who will help you. However, all of these products have Web sites with discussion forums where you can post problems. In most cases, you'll be able to find someone who can quickly answer your questions.

MysqlGUI

This program is an offering from MySQL AB, the company that does most of the work on the MySQL server daemon and maintains mysql.com. The graphical client, called MysqlGUI, has the advantage of working on a wide variety of systems, including FreeBSD, OpenBSD,

Solaris, and Linux. If you want a graphic administrative client that doesn't use HTTP, like phpMyAdmin, this will be one of your better choices.

At the time of this writing, the Windows version of this client was a bit underpowered — especially when compared to mySQLfront. But if you work on some other operating system, this may be worth a look.

To give MysqlGUI a spin, you can download it from `www.mysql.com/downloads/gui-mysqlgui.html` and follow the installation instructions. Figure 28-6 shows what you can expect from MysqlGUI.

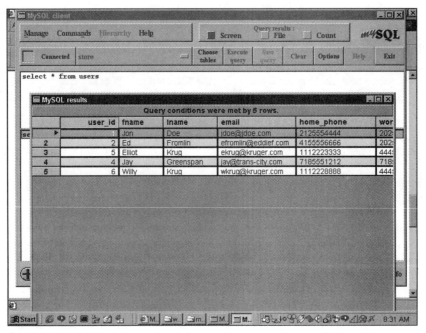

Figure 28-6   *A view of MysqlGUI*

**10 Min.
To Go**

Using MySQL with ODBC

For the most part, if you're using MySQL with a Web site, you can use the MySQL client libraries and languages like PHP and Perl to connect directly to the MySQL database engine. However, if you'd like to use another type of client, perhaps something native to Windows, you use ODBC. Standing for *Open Database Connectivity*, ODBC is a standard used for connecting to database servers. Through ODBC, you can use Windows to connect a database server to a client application. The client may be VisualBasic, Access, Excel, or some other front end. In a moment, I show how you can use ODBC and Access to create a graphic interface to MySQL data.

The first step in using ODBC is downloading and installing the MyODBC application. You can get it from `www.mysql.com/downloads/api-myodbc.html`. All you need to do is unzip this file and double-click on the `setup.exe` file, and MyODBC will be installed.

After MyODBC is installed, you need to setup a Data Source. In Windows Control Panel, open the 32-bit ODBC item. At this point, click on the System DSN tab and the hit the Add button. You should see a screen like that in Figure 28-7.

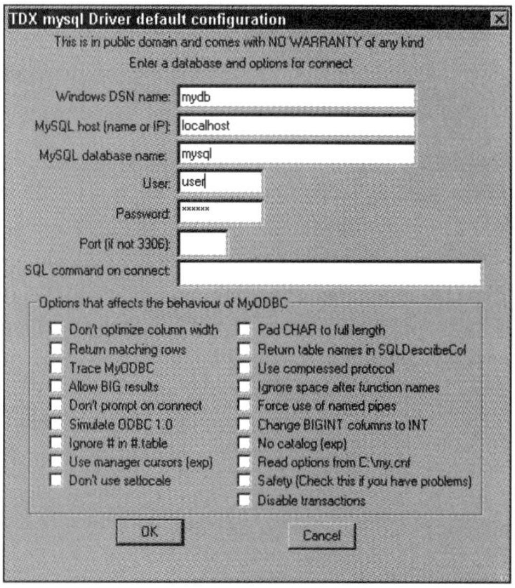

Figure 28-7 *Adding a System DSN on Windows*

When you accept these changes, your system has a System DSN that is available to all clients that can use ODBC. If you wanted to use the data source in Access, you would create a new database (choose File ⇨ New) and then import the tables (File ⇨ Get External Data ⇨ Link Tables). When the Link Tables dialogue box comes up, move to the Files of Type box and choose ODBC Databases. If you click the Machine Data Source tab, you see the DSN you just created. In Figure 28-8, you can see the mydb item, which links to the store database.

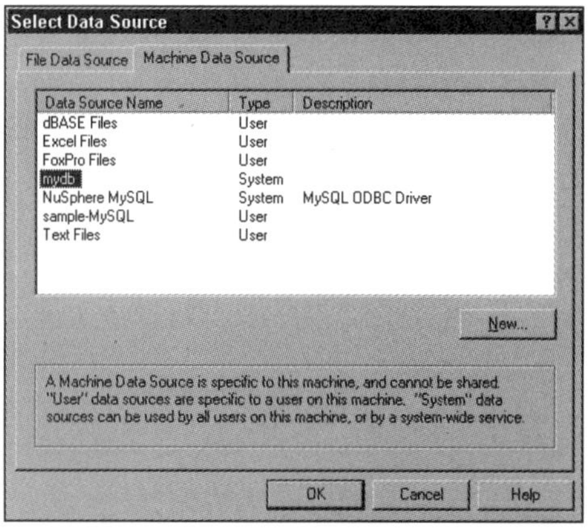

Figure 28-8 *Linking to a System DSN from Access*

You are then presented with a window that allows you to select the tables you need in your Access application. You can then use the data from MySQL to create Windows client applications in Access, using all of the form builders and wizards available in that program.

If you wish to link to MySQL through ODBC from Visual Basic or another application, check the application's Help files for proper linking mechanism. It shouldn't be very difficult.

Using MacSQL

The people at Runtime Labs have created a very nice, sophisticated GUI front for MacOS X that connects to a variety of SQL Servers, MySQL included. You can get a copy of this software, called MacSQL, from the rtlabs.com Web site. There is a free demo that you can take for a test run.

After you download and install MacSQL, you can start the application by double-clicking the MacSQL icon. At that point MacSQL will detect that you have MySQL installed and will offer you a screen like that shown in Figure 28-9.

Figure 28-9   *Connections screen for MacSQL*

To make a connection to MySQL on the local machine, make sure the Port item is blank and that the username, host (localhost), and password are appropriate. At this point you'll be presented with a screen, like that in Figure 28-10, that offers several options.

If you're using OS X, I recommend you download the free demo and work through each of the options on this screen. You'll find that most anything you want to do with MySQL, you can accomplish with this software. At that point you may decide that it's time for the $99 version of MacSQL Lite.

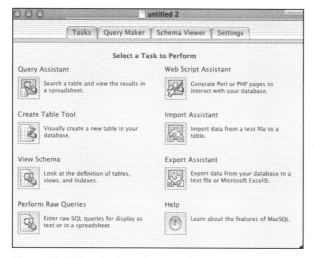

Figure 28-10   *Options for MacSQL*

Done!

REVIEW

In this session, you saw several ways to connect to MySQL from a variety of GUI clients. You saw that most of the clients, like phpMyAdmin, MysqlGUI, and mySQLfront, can be used to administer MySQL and ease the process of creating and altering databases, tables, columns, and indexes. Finally, you saw how ODBC can be helpful for connecting MySQL to Windows Clients like Access and VisualBasic. You saw how to configure ODBC and use MySQL data in an Access application.

QUIZ YOURSELF

1. True or False: phpMyAdmin should immediately be put on a live server? (See "phpMyAdmin.")
2. True or False: mySQLfront can only administer a database installed on the same machine? (See "mySQLFront.")
3. What platforms can run MysqlGUI? (See "MysqlGUI.")
4. What Control Panel item is used to add a DSN to a Windows system? (See "Using MySQL with ODBC.")
5. Name three clients that can use MySQL data through ODBC? (See "Using MySQL with ODBC.")

Optimizing MySQL

Session Checklist

✔ Creating a cache

✔ Un-normalizing data

✔ Examining your configuration

✔ Upgrading hardware

✔ Packing tables

30 Min.
To Go

A t this point, as you near the end of this book, you should have a fairly good idea of how MySQL works and how you can make use of the database server in your applications. Further, you should have a reasonable understanding of how you can administer a MySQL server. Using this book, the online manual, and your own smarts, you should be able handle most any MySQL-related tasks that come your way. However, along the way there are bound to be some difficulties.

Imagine that you've created and deployed a Web application, something like the shopping cart discussed throughout this book. After some time on the Web, as the number of hits on your server steadily increases, you've started to receive complaints from users that your pages are loading very, very slowly. You first want to make sure that MySQL is the cause of the slowdown. If, after you examine the time it takes MySQL-driven pages to render versus those that have no database content, you notice a significant difference, you know MySQL is the problem. After reading Session 19, you know to check the slow query log and look at potentially slow joins. But if these queries are performing adequately, you know there's another problem.

So what are you going to do about it? How are you going to speed up you application? In the broadest sense, there are two avenues you can go to speed things up. First, you can modify the design of your code and database so that you reduce the load on your database. Or, secondly, you can try to speed up you MySQL server so that it responds faster.

I've said it before and I'll say it again: The easiest and best way to speed up MySQL is to use indexes properly. Look over Session 19 again if you need a refresher.

Creating a Cache

Often, Web applications are designed in a way that serves content that is generally static dynamically. For example, in a Web application that works with the store database, many — and perhaps a great majority — of page views are created by hits to the product catalogue. There may be a page that gives product details that accounts for a great percentage of hits to your server. This page gives product price, description, a picture, and other information. If written in PHP, the basics of the page may look like Listing 29-1. Note that the page is expecting a value for item_id to be passed via the URL. So imagine this page is called with a URL like http://example.com/prod_details?item_id=44.

Listing 29-1   *Page to view product details*

```php
<php
include "header.php";

//connect to database
$conn = mysql_pconnect("localhost", "webuser", "password");
$db = mysql_select_db("store");

//get all information related to this product
$query = "SELECT items_for_sale.product_id, format, price,
            product_name, product_description, image_location
        FROM items_for_sale, products, images
        WHERE items_for_sale.product_id=products.product_id and
            items_for_sale.item_id=images.item_id and
            items_for_sale.item_id=$item_id
    ";
$result = mysql_query($query);
?>

<!-- Print out all product info ‡

<h1>View of <? echo $result["product_name"]; ?> </h1>
<p><? echo $result["product_description"]; ?></p>
<p>Now only <? echo $result["price"]; ?></p>
<p><img src="<? echo $result["price"]; ?>">


<?php
include "footer.php";
?>
```

As the `item_id` passed in the URL changes, the contents of the page change. For many applications, a page like this works just fine. Using some fancier HTML, this page can serve as a nice template. It requires very little maintenance and is always up to date — as soon as an administrator changes items in the database. That is, as soon as the database changes, the live catalogue changes.

But the fact of the matter is that pages like this dynamically serve content that is by and large static. In most applications, this type of data just won't change that frequently. Maybe it will change once a week, once a month, or once every few months. For the vast majority of the time, there's no really good reason for this page to be seeking data from the database in real time. There's no need for up-to-the-second information.

On a server that is bucking under heavy load, you can reduce some strain by creating a *cache,* which is a location where the files presenting this information are stored statically. You can then have your Web server access these static files. You will, of course, need to update the static files when a change occurs in the database. You can add code to your application that updates the static files as soon as a change occurs to a related row in the database.

There are many ways you can go about creating a cache. You can have a series of fragments with name like `220.frag`, `221.frag`, and so on. These files contain the product details laid out in HTML format. Then as `item_id`s are indicated in the query string of a URL, you can serve up the correct fragment. Again, this page is expecting a URL like `http://example.com/prod_details?item_id=44`.

```php
<?php

include "header.php";
include "$item_id.frag";
include "footer.php";

?>
```

But there is another method that I feel is superior. I suggest creating an entirely separate page for each item that contains as little dynamic content as is possible. So for each item in your catalogue, you create a static HTML file with no dynamic content sitting on your file system that is served out when requested. This way, no database access and very little scripting is necessary.

One way to arrange this is so that each file has the name of the `item_id` or some other unique identification that can by used for file naming, plus an `.html` extension. You may put these all in a folder called `/products` so the filenames are accessed by a name like `www.mydomain.com/products/223.html`.

This type of file-naming convention has one major advantage over using query string values — these URLs are search-engine friendly. Most search engine crawlers don't recognize that query strings may substantially alter page contents. So if using the query string approach, it's quite possible that the bulk of your catalogue will be inaccessible to Google, HotBot, and others search engines.

Building and maintaining this type of cache takes some work. You need to write scripts to generate and update the cache when necessary, and you also have to put procedures in place that ensure your cache is updated when the database data is changed. You can write these scripts in any language that can access MySQL. In pseudo-code, the scripts operate something like this:

```
connect to database
get listing of all items along with relevant item data, order by item_id
for each item
    import html page header text
    create page body by inserting proper item data
    import html page footer text
    create file named /products/$item_id.html #item_id is a variable
    export header, body, and footer to new file
exit
```

The exact contents of any script that creates a cache largely depend on the specifics of your application and system. For many applications, there is a lot to be gained by implementing some sort of caching system.

Un-Normalizing Data

Whereas a cache is frequently a very good idea and is seldom a bad idea, un-normalizing data is seldom a good idea and is quite often a very bad idea. Before I explain the dangers of un-normalized data, I should explain what un-normalized means.

Early in this book, I spent an entire session explaining the need for normalization and the processes needed to get data into 3rd normal form. In general, if your data is not in 3rd normal form, you can have all kinds of problems with repeating and redundant data that can become a major hassle as you try to keep your data in a usable condition.

But, when your data gets divided into multiple tables, the database server engine has to work to put the data back together. Put simply, joins take time. Large joins, those involving multiple tables and thousands of rows, can be slow — even when indexes are properly applied. In the process of un-normalizing data, one takes data that has been divided into two or more tables and puts the data back into one.

For example, in the store database, moving the fields in the addresses table back into the users table would un-normalize the database. If you were to do this, you'd gain the advantage of not having to join those tables with SELECTs; however, on the negative side — and this is a really big negative — you'd have repetitive data as users' names would be repeated in multiple rows, once for each address.

With one exception, which I cover in a moment, I recommend doing about anything before un-normalizing data. Create a cache, upgrade your server, but don't put your data in a state where it's difficult to maintain.

Now that you have all these caveats, there is one case where I think un-normalized data can be quite helpful. I don't suggest you spend time revising tables; rather, I think there are times when a type of cache within the database can be helpful. Here's an example:

Imagine a shopping cart that has a dynamic product catalogue. Think of something like eBay, where users can enter products. Each product belongs to a specific category. You may have tables like these:

```
categories
+-------------+---------------+
|category_id  |  product_name |
+-------------+---------------+
|      1      |     toys      |
|      2      |   electronics |
+-------------=-+---------------+
```

```
items
+-----------+---------------+----------------+--------+_
|  item_id  |  category_id  |  description   |  cost  |
+-----------+---------------+----------------+--------+_
|     1     |      1        |  good stuff    | 44.43  |
+-----------+---------------+----------------+--------+_
|     2     |      1        |  better stuff  | 55.55  |
+-----------+---------------+----------------+--------+
```

In the second table, there could be hundreds of thousands of rows, one row for each item. To entice potential buyers on the front page of your Web site, you may want to show many items you have available for each category. For example, "Toys — 155 available now." With these properly normalized tables, you can easily get this type of information using a SELECT with a GROUP BY clause:

```
SELECT category_id, count(*) FROM items GROUP BY category_id;
+-------------+----------+
| category_id | count(*) |
+-------------+----------+
|           1 |      223 |
|           2 |      118 |
|           3 |      145 |
|           4 |      864 |
|           5 |     1028 |
+-------------+----------+
```

If you have a busy site, you can be running this query thousands of times an hour as users come to the front page of your site. But this information doesn't really need up-to-the-second accuracy. All you really want to do is give the user a good estimate of the number of products for each category. In a case like this, you can create another table in your database in which you can store the results of the GROUP BY statement. You'd need just a very simple table:

```
CREATE TABLE count_holder
(
    category_id int not null primary key,
    total int not null
)
```

Then, whenever you needed to update the table, you can run the following query:

```
REPLACE INTO count_holder SELECT category_id, count(*) from items GROUP BY
category_id;
```

Probably the easiest way to run this command is from the shell, using the command-line client with the -e flag and adding this command to the cron tab so that it runs on a regularly scheduled basis.

```
/usr/local/mysql/binmysql -u root -pmypass --database=test -e"REPLACE INTO
count_holder SELECT category_id, count(*) from items GROUP BY category_id"
```

The count_holder table contains data that is redundant — and therefore isn't properly normalized — but it's unlikely to cause any real problems and can, in fact, save some stress on your server.

Examining Your Configuration

If you're experiencing slowdowns in you MySQL server, take some time examining your server configuration, making sure you're getting the most out of the hardware you have available. In general, you want to make sure that your server is using as much RAM for tables and indexes as possible. You may remember that one reason indexes are so fast is that they reside in RAM and it's much faster to search through memory-resident information than to read from disk.

You can get information on how indexes are using RAM by running the SHOW STATUS command (or mysqladmin extended-status from the shell). This returns a few dozen parameters. Below I've pulled out some of the more important items.

```
mysql> show status;
+-----------------------------+------------+
| Variable_name               | Value      |
+-----------------------------+------------+
| Handler_delete              | 120730     |
| Handler_read_first          | 1737423    |
| Handler_read_key            | 134763457  |
| Handler_read_next           | 3152704506 |
| Handler_read_prev           | 681013     |
| Handler_read_rnd            | 57055446   |
| Handler_read_rnd_next       | 4267358206 |
| Handler_update              | 7199226    |
| Handler_write               | 11351202   |
| Key_blocks_used             | 17815      |
| Key_read_requests           | 866414419  |
| Key_reads                   | 15310      |
| Key_write_requests          | 887667     |
| Key_writes                  | 628175     |
| Opened_tables               | 563        |
+-----------------------------+------------+
```

Every MySQL installation comes with sample .cnf **files. You can use these to get some good baseline setting for your MySQL installation. The files are named** my-small.cnf, my-medium.cnf, my-large.cnf, **and** my-huge.cnf. **The comments in each of these files tell you which files are appropriate for specific hardware configurations (RAM, disk size, and so on). Use these settings as a baseline and make changes only when you are experiencing problems.**

To start with, look at the Key_read_requests and Key_reads values. The former variable shows the total number of times an index was used for resolving a query. The latter shows the number of times the key needed to be read from the hard disk and placed into memory. If you don't have enough RAM available for keys, MySQL has to read keys from disk, put them in memory, and then clear up the RAM for other uses.

The value of Key_reads should be less than 1 percent of value of the Key_read_requests. In the above listing, the Key_reads value is far less than 1 percent of the value of Key_read_requests. If this is not the case on your server, restart your MySQL server daemon, increasing the value of key_buffer_size parameter.

You can find the value of key_buffer_size by running the SHOW VARIABLES command:

```
mysql> SHOW VARIABLES LIKE '%key%';
+-----------------+----------+
| Variable_name   | Value    |
+-----------------+----------+
| delay_key_write | ON       |
| key_buffer_size | 16773120 |
+-----------------+----------+
```

You can consider changing the value of this variable to one quarter of the total RAM available on your machine. So, for example, if your server has 256 MB of RAM, you may want to give 64 MB to your key_buffer by including the following in your my.cnf file.

```
set-variable    = key_buffer=64M
```

You should also look for at the value of the Opened_tables variable in the SHOW STATUS listing. This shows the number of times tables have been opened by your server. If there's not enough cache available to keep tables opened and in memory, MySQL will have to continually open and close tables for many operations. The table_cache variable controls the amount of RAM used to store open tables.

```
mysql> show variables like '%table_cache%';
+---------------+-------+
| Variable_name | Value |
+---------------+-------+
| table_cache   | 512   |
+---------------+-------+
```

You can change the value of this variable in the my.cnf file by altering the following line:

```
set-variable    = table_cache=64M
```

There are other configurable parameters that can affect the performance of your server, but these are by far the two most important items.

Upgrading Hardware

If, after taking the steps discussed so far, you still find that you're having performance problems, you may want to consider upgrading your hardware. As you may guess from the previous sections, the most important upgrade you can make is to RAM. The more RAM you have in your machine, the more you can dedicate to your index and table caches. As cheap as RAM is these days, this should be an easy upgrade to make.

The second most important upgrade is to your hard disk. MySQL does have to read frequently from the hard disk, and you can gain substantial time savings by installing faster disks or some sort of RAID system. Also keep in mind that having at least two physical disks is highly recommended. In fact, it's nearly vital. As discussed in Session 24, you should be logging changes in the binary log. In the event that you have a catastrophic disk failure, you want to make sure that the binary log sits on a different physical disk than the one that holds the tables and indexes.

If you're looking to upgrade your hardware setup, the best single thing you can do is transfer MySQL to its own server. If, for example, you're running Apache, Perl, and MySQL off of the same box, you're likely to run into problems with load as your traffic increases. You're likely to find that Apache/Perl is fighting for disk and processor access with MySQL. Moving MySQL to its own server can really speed things up.

If all the hardware and software changes discussed here have no effect, it may be time to try replication. See Session 26 for a description of replication and instructions on how to implement replication in your system.

Packing Tables

When I discussed the LOAD DATA INFILE statement, I showed how MySQL can be helpful with the task of log analysis. On a busy machine, Apache or another Web server can log hundreds of thousands of hits a day — or more. After you load these files in to MySQL after several days or weeks or months, you may have some massive tables with millions of rows. The interesting thing about these tables is that you can be sure that row contents are never going to change. This is totally static data.

From what you've learned already, you know that MyISAM tables are a superior choice for this type of data. You can make these MyISAM tables even faster by compressing them with the myisampack utility. After a table is packed, you will no longer be able to insert or alter any data in the table. But you do gain some disk space and get faster response times from the table.

Before running myisampack, **make sure to make a backup of your table. When running any type of compression software, there is a possibility that data will be corrupted.**

The process is fairly simple. First, you need to locate the myisampack utility in the /bin directory of your MySQL installation. You need to supply the location of the table you want to pack and its name. For example, to pack the hits table in the /apache_logs directory, you can run the following:

```
shell> jaygreen% ./myisampack  ../var/apache_logs/hits
Compressing ../var/apache_logs/hits.MYD: (87241 records)
- Calculating statistics
- Compressing file
70.83%
```

Then, to check that the table is still functioning, you can use the `mysqlchk` utility:

```
shell> ./myisamchk -dv ../var/apache_logs/hits
MyISAM file:          ../var/apache_logs/hits
Record format:        Compressed
Character set:        latin1 (8)
File-version:         1
Creation time:        2001-11-15 10:08:10
Recover time:         2001-11-27  9:45:46
Status:               checked,analyzed
Checksum:                 795486116
Data records:                    13  Deleted blocks:              0
Datafile parts:                  13  Deleted data:                0
Datafile pointer (bytes):         2  Keyfile pointer (bytes):     3
Datafile length:                719  Keyfile length:           1024
Max datafile length:     4294967294  Max keyfile length: 17179868159
Recordlength:                   603
```

Done!

REVIEW

In this session, you learned several methods for improving the performance of MySQL. First, you saw how creating a cache can save significant load on your server. Next you saw both the dangers and advantages of un-normalized data. You saw an example of where un-normalized data is relatively danger free and quite capable of saving load on your server. Then, you reviewed some server parameters to check so that you can be sure MySQL is getting the most of the RAM available on your machine. The session went on to discuss potential hardware improvements and the advantages of compressing tables with `myisampack`.

QUIZ YOURSELF

1. What is the disadvantage of specifying page contents via a parameter in a URL? (See "Creating a Cache.")

2. Why should you be reticent to un-normalize data? (See "Un-Normalizing Data.")

3. What server parameter controls the amount of RAM available to index caches? (See "Examining Your Configuration.")

4. What server parameter controls the amount of RAM available to table caches? (See "Examining Your Configuration.")

5. What type of tables should you consider compressing with `myisampack`? (See "Packing Tables.")

Answering Remaining Questions

Session Checklist

✔ RTFM

✔ Using files included with MySQL installation

✔ MySQL mailing lists

✔ Web sites

✔ Buying commercial support

*30 Min.
To Go*

As stated in the Preface of this book, MySQL Weekend Crash Course was not written to be a complete reference to all MySQL-related topics. Instead, it was written in a way that hopefully gave you all the information you need to carry out the greatest majority of your tasks And hopefully, on the items that weren't covered in great detail, you at least have been pointed in the right direction.

Because we both know that the book doesn't cover everything, this last chapter gives you some hints into how you can go about the approaching problems that you will inevitably encounter for which this book does not provide answers.

RTFM

If you've been around software for a while, you've probably heard of this abbreviation, which is short for *Read the Fine Manual*. (In less delicate circles, you may see another word substituted for *Fine*). The entire manual can be found on the MySQL Web site at www.mysql.com/doc. In general, the manual is well-written and very complete. It is also searchable, so if you have a question regarding any specific function or command, you can just enter the term in the search box, and you'll quickly see the relevant pages. For quick reference, you can also find an index of all of MySQL's functions, operators, and commands at www.mysql.com/doc/functions.html.

Some packaged installations, including the NuSphere install, include an HMTL copy of the manual with the installation. If you don't have a copy of the manual handy, I hardily recommend downloading a complete copy, which you can install locally. Then you can look at specific sections without connecting to the Internet. From `www.mysql.com/documentation/mysql/alternate.html`, you can download the manual in both HTML and PDF formats.

There is one significant problem with the on-line manual that you should be aware of: The manual is updated with each Alpha release and doesn't always make clear when features were added to MySQL. So as soon as update occurs, the new features and changes find their way into the manual, and it's often difficult to know if what you're reading is relevant to your installation. You can find yourself attempting to use a command or function that is not available in the version you are using. This can be something of a pain, but there's really no way around it. The best thing you can do is download a copy of the manual and use that local copy whenever possible.

Using Files Included with the MySQL Installation

You may find this somewhat obvious, but many people tend to forget the quick and relatively complete documentation that ships with every MySQL installation. For just about every utility and program that you may wish to run, there are two ways of learning the proper use, with the `--help` flag and the man pages.

Using --help

If you need just a quick listing of the major flags and general usage of a utility you can use the `--help` flag after the command name. The `--help` flag is common in Unix commands, but if you're coming from a Windows background, this may be new to you.

All you need to do is go to the location of the utility or program and enter the name followed by `--help`. For example, the following is the partial output of `--help` on the `mysqldump` utility:

```
shell>/usr/local/mysql/bin/mysqldump --help
./mysqldump  Ver 8.17 Distrib 4.0.0-alpha, for apple-darwin1.4 (powerpc)
By Igor Romanenko, Monty, Jani & Sinisa
This software comes with ABSOLUTELY NO WARRANTY. This is free software,
and you are welcome to modify and redistribute it under the GPL license

Dumping definition and data mysql database or table
Usage: ./mysqldump [OPTIONS] database [tables]
OR     ./mysqldump [OPTIONS] --databases [OPTIONS] DB1 [DB2 DB3...]
OR     ./mysqldump [OPTIONS] --all-databases [OPTIONS]

  -A, --all-databases   Dump all the databases. This will be same as
                        --databases with all databases selected.
  -a, --all             Include all MySQL specific create options.
  -#, --debug=...       Output debug log. Often this is 'd:t:o,filename`.
  --character-sets-dir=...
                        Directory where character sets are
  -?, --help            Display this help message and exit.
```

```
    -B, --databases           To dump several databases. Note the difference in
                              usage; In this case no tables are given. All name
                              arguments are regarded as databasenames.
                              'USE db_name;' will be included in the output
    -c, --complete-insert Use complete insert statements.
    -C, --compress            Use compression in server/client protocol.
    --default-character-set=...
                              Set the default character set
    -e, --extended-insert Allows utilization of the new, much faster
                              INSERT syntax.
    --add-drop-table          Add a 'drop table' before each create.
    --add-locks               Add locks around insert statements.
    --allow-keywords          Allow creation of column names that are keywords.
    --delayed-insert          Insert rows with INSERT DELAYED.
    --master-data             This will cause the master position and filename
to
                              be appended to your output. This will
automagically
                              enable --first-slave.
```

At the top of the listing, you can see the syntax for the command. Following that, you have a listing of flags and their meanings.

Using man pages

On Unix systems, you can get more detailed information from the man pages included with the install. You need to check your installation for the location of your man pages. Usually, these will be in /usr/local/mysql/man. If you want to view these man pages, you can either copy the files to a location where they are automatically read by the man program, or you can indicate the directory for the man page files when running the man program, using the -M flag.

For example, to view the man page for mysqldump, when all the man pages reside in the /usr/local/mysql/man directory, run the following command:

```
shell> man -M/usr/local/mysql/man mysqldump
```

There is a standard man page format used for all Unix programs, and this is replicated with the MySQL man pages. The following is a piece of what you would see for the man page of mysqladmin.

```
shell> man -M/usr/local/mysql/man mysqladmin
man: Formatting manual page...

MYSQLADMIN(1)                                                   MYSQLADMIN(1)

NAME
        mysqladmin [OPTIONS] command command....   - A utility for
        performing administrative operations
```

```
OPTION SYNOPSIS
        mysqladmin [-#|--debug= logfile] [-f|--force]  [-?|--help]
        [--character-sets-dir=directory]            [-C|--compress]
        [-h|--host=[#]] [-p[pwd]]  [--password=[pwd]] [-P|--port=
        pnum]  [-i|--sleep= sec] [-E|--vertical] [-s|--silent]
        [-S|--socket=  #]  [-r|--relative]  [-t|--timeout=  #]
        [-u|--user=     uname]  [-v|--verbose]   [-V|--version]
        [-w|--wait[=retries]]

OPTION DESCRIPTION
        You can get a list of the options your version of mysqlad-
        min supports by executing mysqladmin --help

OPTIONS
        -#|--debug=logfile
                Output debug log. Often this is 'd:t:o,filename`

        -f|--force
                Don't ask  for confirmation on drop database; with
                multiple commands, continue even if an error occurs

        -?|--help
                Display help and exit

        --character-sets-dir=directory
                Set the character set directory
```

Mailing Lists

**20 Min.
To Go**

If, after trying the manual and the man pages, you can't figure out the answers to your questions, you can try a mailing list. If you're new to mailing lists, they work like this: Many people opt to have their e-mail addresses placed on a list, which is held at a central location. Then anybody on the list can send an e-mail to the central location. Everybody on the list receives the e-mail.

A lot of people using open source software tend to be very dedicated to mailing lists. Many of the MySQL core developers, and dozens of expert users, monitor the lists constantly. Most any question you ask will receive an accurate and complete answer in a matter of minutes.

However, before you go posting to any of the MySQL mailing lists, you should be aware of general mailing list etiquette. Mailing list members expect that those posting to the list will have done two things. First, before you post your message, it is expected that you will have Read the Fine Manual. Nothing angers list members more than posts of questions that can be easily answered with a search of the manual. Second, it is expected that you will have researched the question at one of the mailing lists archives. I show ways to best view the mailing list archives in the sections below.

MySQL general mailing list

The MySQL general mailing list is the busiest of the mailing lists and is monitored by dozens, if not hundreds, of experts. Before you subscribe to the mailing list, be aware that this is a very, very busy list. On most days, there are about 100 posts to this list, so be prepared for some tremendous volume if you subscribe. You'll want to set up a rule in your e-mail client that transfers all list mail to a separate mailbox.

You can subscribe to the MySQL general mailing list by sending a blank e-mail to mysql-subscribe@lists.mysql.com. You will then receive a couple of e-mails asking you to confirm your subscription. When you are subscribed, you can send an e-mail to the list by addressing the e-mail to mysql@lists.mysql.com.

When you post, make sure that you give list members the best chance of answering your question quickly. Provide a useful subject line for your e-mail. There's nothing more annoying than looking at mailing list posts and seeing a subject line of "HELP!!," "PLEASE HELP!!," or "NOT WORKING." Instead, try something like "Outer Join Syntax" or "Transactions with InnoDB." Try to include all the relevant information in your post. Many posts don't include the vital information that can help someone solve your problem.

Before posting to the mailing list, do a search of the list archives. There are several archives of the various mailing lists around the Internet. One is kept by mysql.com and can be found at http://lists.mysql.com/cgi-ez/ezmlm-cgi/. This list is searchable, but I find the format difficult to work with and the search results less than ideal. You can also find an archive at Nexial (www.nexial.com/mailinglists/). This archive allows you to search within a specific timeframe.

But my favorite archive is MARC (standing for Mailing list ARCives). This remarkable library is located at http://marc.theaimsgroup.com/. If you call up this URL, you see that there are hundreds of mailing lists that this site archives. You can move to the MySQL general mailing list archive by going to http://marc.theaimsgroup.com/?l=mysql. From there you can run any search that you'd need.

If you're looking to keep sharp on all MySQL-related issues, you may want to consider subscribing to the general mailing list, even if you have no immediate questions. Reading the variety of questions and the quality answers makes you a smarter applications developer and DBA.

Win32 mailing list

If you are using MySQL on a Windows system, such as Windows 98, Windows NT, Windows 2000, or Windows XP, you can post questions to this list. This wouldn't be the best place to ask questions about specific query syntax or use of function (those sort of questions are best asked to the general mailing list). On the Win32 lists, you can raise questions regarding Windows-specific errors, ADO, or DOS-related syntax.

You can subscribe to the list by sending an e-mail to win32-subscribe@lists.mysql.com. After responding to the confirmation e-mails, you can post questions to the lists by sending an e-mail to win32@lists.mysql.com.

Keep MARC in mind even when you're not looking to answer MySQL-related questions. Their extensive mailing list archive is an amazing resource. You can find answers to all sorts of questions on a huge variety of technical subjects.

Other MySQL mailing lists

There are a variety of other mailing lists run by MySQL AB. They cover topics from ODBC to Java and C++. For a complete list, go to `www.mysql.com/documentation/lists.html`.

Web Sites

10 Min.
To Go

If you're looking to increase your MySQL knowledge, there are a variety of Web sites where you can find articles that deal both directly and peripherally with MySQL issues.

O'Reilly's ONLamp.com

O'Reilly, the publisher of technical books, maintains a series of Web sites. This site is dedicated to the LAMP products — Linux, Apache, MySQL, and PHP/Perl/Python. The articles at this site are generally of a high quality and can increase your MySQL knowledge. All of the specific MySQL articles can be found at `www.onlamp.com/onlamp/general/mysql.csp`. Some of the other material at the site will also be of interest to you.

Developer Shed

Found at `www.devshed.com/`, Developer Shed offers articles on all kinds of open source developer tools. Some of their MySQL articles are excellent. You can find a list of these articles at `www.devshed.com/Server_Side/MySQL`.

PHPBuilder

Because so many MySQL users work with PHP, you'll find many MySQL-related articles at many PHP-related sites. PHPBuilder is the perfect example. PHPbuilder, found at `www.phpbuilder.com/`, offers some very good MySQL articles as well as a variety of articles that deal with application development with PHP and MySQL.

Perl.com

This is another site from the O'Reilly network that presents a wealth of information on all things related to Perl. If you are using Perl with MySQL, you'd do well to check in at Perl.com on a regular basis.

weberdev.com

This is another Web developer site that offers a wide range of articles. You can find a complete list of MySQL related articles by going the front door and clicking the link to MySQL.

Buying Support

One oft-voiced complaint states that a problem with open source applications is that there's no one to call at 3:00 a.m. when you have a problem that desperately needs to be fixed. But this is not true of MySQL. MySQL AB, the guys who coded MySQL from the ground up, offer support and training.

Purchasing support from MySQL AB is not only good for your own (and your boss's) piece of mind. It also helps keep development of the MySQL product strong. There are several developers at MySQL AB working full time on the MySQL engine. As it's an open source project, most can use MySQL without spending a dime. If you purchase support, you will see that the developers can make a living on their MySQL development and can continue to improve MySQL on a full-time basis.

You can find out more about commercial support for MySQL from the `mysql.com` Web site, `www.mysql.com/support/index.html`.

Done!

REVIEW

To finish up the book, this session shows some ways you can solve problems and answer questions when they come up. You saw (as was pointed out many times throughout this book) the importance of the MySQL Manual. Following that you learned about some of the mailing lists and Web sites where you can gain even greater MySQL knowledge. Finally, you learned that buying support for MySQL is good for you, your company, and the product.

QUIZ YOURSELF

1. What actions should you take before posting to a mailing list? (See "MySQL general mailing list.")
2. What are the two ways to view usage information for MySQL utilities? (See "Using Files Included with the MySQL Installation.")
3. What do you want to include in a posting to a mailing list? (See "MySQL general mailing list.")
4. What does RTFM stand among those with delicate ears? (See "RTFM.")
5. What company offers MySQL commercial support? (See "Buying Support.")

PART

VI

Sunday Afternoon Part Review

1. What SQL command can you use to check to see if a table is functioning correctly?
2. What keyword can you use with CHECK TABLE to check all rows and indexes in a table?
3. What three SQL commands can be used to repair and optimize tables and indexes?
4. What utility is used to check and repair tables and indexes while a server is running?
5. What utility is used to check and repair tables and indexes while a server is down?
6. What Web-based tool is often used to administer MySQL?
7. What Windows-based tool provides a nice graphic front end for administering MySQL?
8. What Windows protocol is used to connect databases with various clients?
9. Name two clients that can use MySQL as a datasource on Windows.
10. Converting dynamic files to static ones in order to reduce hits on a database sever is known as what?
11. What is the danger of un-normalized data?
12. If there are too many key_reads shown in the SHOW STATUS command, more memory should be allocated to which variable parameter?
13. What hardware change is most likely to improve the performance of MySQL?
14. What utility compresses MyISAM tables, making them smaller and quicker?
15. Before consulting a mailing list, what sources should you use to research your questions?
16. On Unix systems, what are two sources of learning the uses and flags that for all utilities?
17. MySQL commercial support can be purchased from what company?
18. Name three Web sites that offer MySQL-related articles.

Answers to Part Reviews

Friday Evening Part Review Answers

1. PHP, Perl, MySQL command-line client, C, C++, Java, Access
2. MySQL is easier to learn than Oracle. It is also cheaper, easier to install, and doesn't require expensive hardware. Oracle has advanced features MySQL lacks and implements the SQL standard more thoroughly.
3. MySQL AB (www.mysql.com), NuSphere(www.nusphere.com), and Innobase (www.innobase.com)
4. Apache, PHP, and mod_perl
5. Binaries from tarballs, from source, or rpms
6. mysqld_safe
7. The ampersand (&)
8. Depends on the system, usually mysql/var
9. Depends on the system, usually mysql/lib
10. Normalization
11. Primary key
12. Foreign keys
13. It must have a primary key, columns must contain only atomic values, columns must have unique names, no two rows and be identical, and no repeating groups of data are allowed.
14. InnoDB
15. One-to-one, one-to-many, and many-to-many
16. Null
17. Null | Not null and default
18. Set
19. Timestamp
20. Heap

Saturday Morning Part Review Answers

1. SHOW TABLES
2. SHOW DATABASES
3. FIRST
4. When changing the definition of a column
5. ',",\n,\t
6. UPDATE and INSERT
7. IS NULL
8. Remove tables in the file system.
9. LIMIT 5
10. LIMIT 5,5
11. IN
12. ASC and DESC
13. Parentheses
14. When you need to maintain all rows in one of the tables
15. Subselects
16. Union
17. Arguments
18. WHERE restricts the rows used in the grouping, and HAVING restricts the rows returned after the grouping takes place.
19. monthname()
20. %M
21. DATE_MINUTE

Saturday Afternoon Part Review Answers

1. The first is tested to see if it is null. The value of the second argument is returned if the value of the first is null; otherwise, the first argument is returned.
2. The first argument is the condition to be tested; the second is the value to be returned if the condition is true; the third is the value to be returned if the condition is false.
3. md5()
4. There is no such function. md5() is a one-way algorithm and strings cannot be decoded.
5. concat()
6. WHERE 'db1.mydomain.com' LIKE concat('%', url)
7. last_insert_id()
8. Zero or one of the preceding characters

9. `[a-z]` or `[[:lower:]]`
10. `^.*?z`
11. Atomicity, Consistency, Independence, and Durability
12. Read and write
13. Begin work
14. Commit or rollback
15. A two-phase system
16. `SELECT ... FOR UPDATE`
17. Multi-versioning concurrency model
18. By adding the `LOCK IN SHARE MODE` clause
19. `mysql_pconnect()`
20. `mysql_query("...")` or `die(mysql_error())`
21. `error_log()`
22. `magic_quotes_gpc` and `addslashes()`

Saturday Evening Part Review Answers

1. `DBD::mysql`
2. MCPAN
3. `DBI->connect()`
4. `selectall_hashref()`
5. `handle_error()`
6. HTML::Mason
7. By enabling the slow query log
8. `long_query_time`
9. EXPLAIN
10. It takes work to maintain an index. Using unnecessary indexes will slow down your database.
11. `STRAIGHT JOIN`
12. `USE_INDEX(index_name)`
13. Host.
14. The GRANT privilege
15. `INDENTIFIED BY`
16. `GRANT ALL ON my_db.* to john@localhost IDENTIFIED BY 'foo'`
17. `REVOKE`
18. `SHOW GRANTS FOR john@localhost`
19. `FLUSH PRIVILEGES`
20. Yes. Using the syntax GRANT ALL ON (col_name, col_name_two) on `database_name.table_name`.

Sunday Morning Part Review Answers

1. `mysqladmin` shutdown
2. The database would then have authority to operate on any file in the system, introducing a major security risk.
3. `user`
4. Check your distributor's errata page.
5. In the data directory, in the user's home directory, and in `//etc`.
6. `data_dir`
7. The username that will be used to run the MySQL daemon
8. `mysqladmin` ping
9. `mysqladmoin` processlist
10. `mysqladmin` kill
11. `mysqladmin` status
12. `mysqlshow`.
13. `mysqldump`
14. `mysqldump --all-databases`
15. `SELECT INTO OUTFILE`
16. The binary log
17. In case of a disk failure on the disk that stores the databases, you will need the binary log to reconstruct the data.
18. `mysqlbinlog`
19. `LOAD DATA INFILE`
20. `access_to_mysql`
21. Master-slave replication
22. The binary log
23. 1
24. `SHOW SLAVE STATUS`

Sunday Afternoon Part Review Answers

1. `CHECK TABLE`
2. `CHECK TABLE EXTENDED`
3. `ANALYZE TABLE`, `OPTIMIZE TABLE`, and `REPAIR TABLE`
4. `mysqlcheck`
5. `myisamchk`
6. `phpMyAdmin`
7. `mySQLfront`
8. `ODBC`

9. Access, Excel
10. A cache
11. Redundant data that is difficult to maintain
12. `key_buffer_size`
13. Adding RAM
14. `myisampack`
15. The online manual and a mailing list archive
16. The `--help` flag and man pages
17. MySQL AB
18. Onlamp.com, Devshed.com, and Weberdev.com

What's on the CD-ROM?

This appendix provides you with information on the contents of the CD that accompanies this book. (For the latest and greatest information, please refer to the ReadMe file located at the root of the CD.)

Because of potential versioning problems, MySQL software is not included on the CD. You will need to look at Session 2 and the `www.mysqlwcc.com` **Web site in order to install the software.**

Here is what you will find on the CD:

- Author-created materials
- Troubleshooting tips
- The MySQL weekend crash Course Assessment Test
- phpMyAdmin is intended to handle the administration of MySQL over the web.

To install the items from the CD to your hard drive, follow these steps:

1. Insert the CD into your computer's CD-ROM drive.

2. A window appears with the following options. Install, Browse, URLs and Exit.

   Install: Gives you the option to install MySQL Weekend Crash Course Assessment test.

   Browse: Allows you to view the contents of the CD-ROM in its directory structure, including the Author files, located in the Book folder.

   URLs: Launches web page with links from the book.

   Exit: Closes the autorun window.

Author-Created Materials

All author-created material from the book, including code listings and samples, is on the CD in the folder named "book." Within that folder, you'll find a series of subfolders that relate to sessions in the book. For example, a script in Session 6 is found on the CD in the folder /book/session6/. Make sure to see the appropriate session to see how to properly use the file.

The MySQL Weekend Crash Course Assessment Test. This is a self-guided test that covers the majority of topics in this book.

Software

phpMyAdmin is intended to handle the administration of MySQL over the web. With phpMyAdmin you can:

- **Create and drop databases**
- **Create, copy, drop and alter tables**
- **Delete, edit and add fields**
- **Execute any SQL-statement, even batch-queries**
- **Load text files into tables**
- **Create and read dumps of tables**
- **Export data to CSV values**
- **Administer multiple servers and single databases.**

Troubleshooting

If you have difficulty installing or using any of the materials on the companion CD, try the following solutions:

- **Turn off any anti-virus software that you may have running.** Installers sometimes mimic virus activity and can make your computer incorrectly believe that it is being infected by a virus. (Be sure to turn the anti-virus software back on later.)
- **Close all running programs.** The more programs you're running, the less memory is available to other programs. Installers also typically update files and programs; if you keep other programs running, installation may not work properly.
- **Reference the ReadMe.txt:** Please refer to the ReadMe file located at the root of the CD-ROM for the latest product information at the time of publication.

If you still have trouble with the CD, please call the Hungry Minds Customer Care phone number: (800) 762-2974. Outside the United States, call 1 (317) 572-3993. You can also contact Hungry Minds Customer Service by e-mail at techsupdum@wiley.com. Hungry Minds will provide technical support only for installation and other general quality control items; for technical support on the applications themselves, consult the program's vendor or author.

Index

Symbols and Numerics

* (asterisk) special character, 128, 129, 134

| (bar character), 132

^ (caret) special character
  as "must not include," 131
  as "start of string," 129

{} (curly braces), 132

$ (dollar sign) special character, 129

% (percent sign) wildcard character, 286

. (period) special character, 129

+ (plus sign) special character, 129, 134

? (question mark)
  placeholder, 195
  special character, 129

1st normal form. *See also* **normal form**
  data criteria, 30
  shopping cart data in, 31

2nd normal form, 31

3rd normal form. *See also* **normal form**
  shopping cart data in, 32
  transitive dependencies and, 31–32

A

`-a` **flag, 300, 303**

`-A` **flag, 304**

Access (Microsoft)
  data transfer, 276–278
  Jet engine, 11
  System DSN linking from,
    `311access_to_mysql.txt`
  defined, 277
  macro window, 278
  module window, 277
  using, 277–278

ACID properties
  BDB tables and, 144
  defined, 138
  Gemini tables and, 147
  InnoDB tables and, 147
  list of, 138
  MyISAM tables and, 139

`acos()` **function, 100**

`--add-drop-table` **flag, 266**

`--add-locks` **flag, 266**

aggregate function. *See also* **functions**
  defined, 97
  `GROUP BY` clause, 97
  `HAVING` predicate, 99

alias
  creating, 92
  defined, 96
  referencing, 96
  specification, 93

`ALTER STATEMENT` **command**
  column addition syntax, 59
  column definition change syntax, 61
  column drop syntax, 60
  defined, 58
  index addition syntax, 60
  index drop syntax, 60
  table name change syntax, 59

`ANALYZE TABLE` **command, 299**

`AND` **keyword, 66**

anomaly
  defined, 27
  delete, 28
  fix through normalization, 29
  insert, 29
  update, 27–28
Apache Web server
  documentation, 278
  Linux/Unix installation, 158–159
  log files, importing, 278–281
  mod_log_mysql, 281
  mod_perl, 198, 199
  Perl with, 198–204
  starting, 161
applications
  client, 253–261
  creation purpose, 7
  data storage, 26
  data transfer, 276–278
  developing, 5–6, 11–12
  lock use in, 140–141
  post-installation review, 20–22
  restarting, 236
argument. See also functions
  defined, 95
  examples, 95–96
array
  retrieving, 191
  two-dimensional, retrieving, 192
asin() *function, 101*
ASP (Microsoft), 11
atan() *function, 101*
atomicity, 138
AUTOCOMMIT *mode, 143, 152*
autohandlers. See also HTML::Mason
  defined, 202
  example, 202–203
--auto-repair *flag, 301*
avg() *function, 98*

B

-B *flag, 303*
backup
  with BACKUP TABLE command, 268–269
  before myisampack utility, 322
  good practices, 271
  maintaining, 304
  with mysqldump, 263–267
  with SELECT INTO OUTFILE, 267–268

BACKUP TABLE *command*
  limitations, 269
  syntax, 268
BDB tables. See also tables
  ACID properties, 144
  configuring, 144–145
  creating, 142
  locks, 144
  MyISAM table conversion to, 142
  transaction application, 142–144
  variables, 144
  working with, 142–144
BEGIN WORK *keyword, 142*
best practices
  database/table creation, 54–55
  Perl, 195–204
  PHP, 169–178
bigint *column type, 42*
binary log
  defined, 270
  deleting, 290
  listing, 290
  replication and, 286
  starting, 270
  using, 269–271
bind values, 195
binding, 195
blocking errors, 257
Boolean search, 134
buying support, 330–331

C

-c *flag, 266, 300, 302*
-C *flag, 301, 302*
cache
  creating, 316–318
  defined, 317
  maintaining, 317–318
  scripts, 317–318
cascading deletes, 34
CD
  author-created materials, 339
  contents, 339–340
  sample database loading, 46–47
  troubleshooting, 339–340
ceiling() *function, 102–103*
CGI. See Common Gateway Interface scripts
cgi-bin directory, 188
CHANGE *command, 61*

CHANGE MASTER TO **command, 291**
char **column type, 39, 40**
character class. *See also* **regular expressions**
    brackets, 130
    character assignment, 130
    defined, 129
    list, 130
characters
    grouping, 132–133
    special, 128–129
    wildcard, 78–79
CHECK TABLE **command**
    form, 297
    options, 298
    response, 298
    use, 298
client applications
    defined, 253
    mysqladmin, 253–258
    mysqlshow, 258–259
    shell script, 259–261
.cnf **files, 320**
ColdFusion, 11
columns. *See also* **tables**
    adding, 59
    date and time types, 43–44
    db table, 220
    definitions, 61
    dropping, 60
    grouping by, 98
    indexes and, 44–45
    mathematical operations on, 99–103
    names of, 38
    numeric types, 41–43
    order, 59
    primary key and, 30, 44
    retrieval order, 79
    SELECT statement specification, 76
    showing, 56–57
    text types, 39–41
    user table, 219
columns_priv **table, 218, 220**
command-line client
    configuring, 248–250
    starting, 250–251
command-line clients start-up options
    complete list of, 248
    listing, 249
    for parsing query results, 250

commands
    ALTER STATEMENT, 58–61
    ANALYZE TABLE, 299
    CHANGE, 61
    CHANGE MASTER TO, 291
    CHECK TABLE, 297–298
    COMMIT, 142, 143
    CREATE DATABASE, 37, 38
    CREATE TABLE, 38–46
    DELETE, 68, 76–77
    DROP, 254
    EXPLAIN, 210–215
    GRANT, 222
    INSERT, 63–64, 106
    LOAD DATA INFILE, 273–275
    LOAD TABLE FROM MASTER, 291
    MODIFY, 61
    mysqlbinlog, 270, 271
    mysqld_safe, 21, 38
    mysqldump, 264–267, 271, 277
    OPTIMIZE TABLE, 299
    Perl shell, 185
    PURGE MASTER LOGS TO, 290
    REPAIR TABLE, 299
    REPLACE, 67–68
    replication, 289, 290–292
    RESET MASTER, 290
    RESET SLAVE, 291
    REVOKE, 224
    ROLLBACK, 142, 143
    SELECT, 75–76, 79–80, 151, 208–209, 223–224
    SELECT DISTINCT, 80–81
    SELECT INTO OUTFILE, 267–268
    SET SQL_LOG_BIN, 290
    SET SQL_SLAVE_SKIP_COUNTER, 291
    SET TIMESTAMP, 270
    SHOW COLUMNS, 56–57, 209
    SHOW CREATE TABLE, 58
    SHOW DATABASES, 55, 217–218
    SHOW GRANTS, 225
    SHOW INDEX, 57, 209–210
    SHOW MASTER LOGS, 290
    SHOW MASTER STATUS, 290
    SHOW PROCESS LIST, 256
    SHOW SLAVE STATUS, 291, 292
    SHOW STATUS, 320
    SHOW TABLE STATUS, 57–58
    SHOW TABLES, 56

Continued

commands *(continued)*
  SHOW VARIABLES, 257, 321
  SLAVE START, 290
  SLAVE STOP, 291
  UPDATE, 67, 76, 147–148
  USE, 38, 56
COMMIT **command, 142, 143**
Common Gateway Interface scripts. *See also* **Perl**
  defined, 183
  Perl scripts conversion, 188–190
comparison operators, 65
concat() **function**
  arguments, 122
  defined, 109
  example, 122
  wildcards and, 123
CONCURRENT **keyword, 274**
configurable variables. *See also* **start-up options**
  binlog_cache_size, 246
  complete list, 246
  connect_timeout, 246
  flush_time, 246
  interactive_timeout, 246
  join_buffer_size, 246
  key_buffer_size, 247
  long_query_time, 247
  lower_case_table_names, 247
  max_allowed_packet, 247
  max_binlog_cache_size, 247
  max_binlog_size, 247
  max_connections, 248
  max_user_connects, 247
  net_buffer_length, 248
  query_buffer_size, 248
  sort_buffer, 248
  table_cache, 248
configuration
  examining, 320–321
  my.cnf choices, 243
  options, 243–248
  PHP connection, 175–176
  slave options, 187–189
configuration file. *See* my.cnf **file**
connect() **method, 187**
connection function
  creating, 174–175
  defined, 174
  final, 175
consistency, 138
--correct-checksum **flag, 303**
cos() **function, 100**

cot() **function, 101**
CPAN module, 186, 188
CREATE DATABASE **statement**
  syntax, 37
  use example, 38
CREATE TABLE **command**
  column types, 39–44
  foreign key constraint creation, 46
  index creation, 44–45
  syntax, 38
  table types, 44
cryptographic functions, 119–121

Ⓓ

-d **flag, 266, 303**
-D **flag, 303**
data. *See also* **tables; user data**
  backing up, 263–271
  deleting, 68
  exporting, 263–271
  importing, 273–281
  inserting, 63–64, 193–194
  retrieving, 75–81, 83–93, 191
  selecting, 192–193
  transferring, 276–278
  un-normalizing, 318–320
  updating, 67
Data Definition Language (DDL), 37
data transfer
  Access, 276–278
  Excel, 276
Database Design for Mere Mortals: A Hands-On
      Guide to Relational Database Design, 25
--database **flag, 265**
database() **function, 123**
database handle, 187
database server. *See* **SQL server**
databases
  adding, 218
  choosing, 162
  concept, 33–34
  creating, 37–47
  creation best practices, 54–55
  creation principles, 25–34
  dropping, 218, 254
  files, copying, 269
  loading, 46–47
  multiple copies of, 284
  names, returning, 123
  newly created, 38

post-installation review, 22
relational, 28
showing, 55
uses of, 13
viewing, 53–54
working with, 56
date
formats, 105
formatting, 106–111
inserting, 105–106
ranges, calculating, 111–113
selecting, 106
date *column type, 43, 106*
date_add() *function operators, 111, 112*
date_format() *function*
calculations with, 113
defined, 109
specifiers, 109–110
datetime *column type, 43*
dayname() *function, 107, 108*
dayofmonth() *function, 107*
dayofweek() *function, 107*
dayofyear() *function, 107*
db *table. See also* GRANT *tables*
columns list, 220
defined, 218
permissions, 220
DBD::mysql module. See also Perl; Perl modules
defined, 185, 186
installing, 186
DBI module. See also Perl; Perl modules
connect() method, 187
do() method, 193–194
documentation, 192
installation determination, 185–186
installing, 186
quote() method, 191, 194
selectall_arrayref() method, 192
selectall_hashref() method, 192–193
selectrow_array() method, 191
send/receive methods, 190–194
DDL. See Data Definition Language
decimal *column type, 42–43*
decode() *function, 121*
--defaults-extra-file *flag, 251*
--defaults-file *flag, 251*
--delayed *flag, 266*
delete anomaly, 28
DELETE *statement*
defined, 68
syntax, 68
WHERE clause, 76–77

dependency
defined, 31
transitive, 31–32
Developer Shed, 330
directory ownership, changing, 235–236
do() *method. See also DBI module*
defined, 193
use, 194
double *column type, 42*
DROP *command, 254*
durability, 138

E

-e *flag, 266, 301, 302, 303*
embperl, 198
encode() *function, 120–121*
enum *column type, 41*
eperl, 198
equi-join. See also join
defined, 84
INNER JOIN syntax, 85–86
STRAIGHT JOIN syntax, 215
error_log() *function, 173, 175*
escaping string
defined, 169
PHP and, 170–171
Excel data transfer, 276
exclusive lock. See also locks
application, 150
defined, 150
in SELECT statement, 151
EXPLAIN *command*
defined, 210
Extra item, 212
with index availability for joins, 214
output, 215
query results, 213–214
row item, 215
running, 211, 212
type values, 211
exporting data, 263–271

F

-f *flag, 254, 301, 302, 303*
-F *flag, 302*
--fields-enclosed-by *flag, 275*
--fields-terminated-by *flag, 275*
filename, table type and, 54
file system, case-sensitive and, 54

files
    deleting, 54
    list, 22
    log, 144, 257, 270, 278–281
    moving, 54
    my.cnf, 208, 241–243, 250–251
    with MySQL installation, 326–328
    ownership, changing, 235–236
    post-installation review, 22
    renaming, 54
    unzipping, 17
flags
    -a, 300, 303
    -A, 304
    --add-drop-table, 266
    --add-locks, 266
    --auto-repair, 301
    -B, 303
    -c, 266, 300, 302
    -C, 301, 302
    --correct-checksum, 303
    -d, 266, 303
    -D, 303
    --database, 265
    --defaults-extra-file, 251
    --defaults-file, 251
    --delayed, 266
    -e, 266, 301, 302, 303
    -f, 254, 301, 302, 303
    -F, 302
    --fields-enclosed-by, 275
    --fields-terminated-by, 275
    --flush-logs, 267, 271
    --force, 254, 275
    --help, 264, 271, 326–327
    --host, 275
    -i, 259
    -I, 302
    --ignore, 275
    -j, 271
    -k, 259, 303
    --lines-terminated-by, 275
    listing, 253
    --local, 275
    --lock-tables, 275
    --log-bin, 270
    -m, 301, 302
    mysqlcheck utility, 300
    mysqlimport utility, 275
    -o, 300, 303
    --position, 271

    -q, 267, 301
    -r, 300, 303
    -R, 304
    --replace, 275
    --result-file, 265
    -s, 301, 302
    -S, 304
    -t, 266, 303
    -T, 302
    -u, 303
    -U, 302
    -v, 258, 259, 302
    -V, 302
    -w, 267, 302
float *column type, 42*
flow control functions, 117–119
flush *commands, 257–258*
--flush-logs *flag, 267, 271*
--force *flag, 254, 275*
foreign key
    constraints, 34, 46
    defined, 30
    in relationship maintenance, 34
FOREIGN KEY *keyword, 46*
FreeBSD, 237
FROM *clause, 84, 92*
FULLTEXT *indexes, 133*
functions
    acos(), 100
    aggregate, 97–99
    arguments, 95–96
    asin(), 101
    atan(), 101
    avg(), 98
    ceiling(), 102–103
    concat(), 109, 122–123
    connection, 174–175
    cos(), 100
    cot(), 101
    count(), 97–98
    cryptographic, 119–121
    database(), 123
    date, 105–113
    date_format(), 106, 109–111
    dayname(), 107, 108
    dayofmonth(), 107
    dayofweek(), 107
    dayofyear(), 107
    decode(), 121
    defined, 95
    encode(), 120–121

error_log(), 173, 175
floor(), 102
flow control, 117–119
handle_error(), 197
handle_query(), 173–174
hour(), 108
htmlspecialchars(), 196
if(), 119
ifnull(), 90–91, 118
ini_get(), 170
last_insert_id(), 124–125
lcase(), 121
left(), 96, 121–122
ltrim(), 123
max(), 99
md5(), 120, 177
min(), 99
minute(), 108
month(), 107
monthname(), 107
mysql_affected_rows(), 165
mysql_connect(), 162, 175, 176
mysql_create_db(), 164
mysql_error(), 165, 172
mysql_fetch_array(), 163
mysql_fetch_assoc(), 163
mysql_insert_id(), 165
mysql_list_dbs(), 164
mysql_pconnect(), 162, 175, 176
mysql_query(), 162–163, 172
nested, 102
now(), 111
parentheses, 95
password(), 120, 177
phpinfo(), 170
quarter(), 107
rand(), 125
recursive, 170
remove_html(), 196
right(), 121–122
round(), 101–102
rounding, 101–103
rtrim(), 123
scrub_data(), 171, 172
second(), 108
sin(), 100
string, 121–123
strip_tags(), 172, 196
sum(), 98
system information, 123–124
tan(), 100
trigonometric, 100–101

trim(), 123
truncate(), 103
ucase(), 95–96, 121
user(), 124
version(), 124
week(), 107
weekday(), 107
year(), 108
yearweek(), 108

G

Gemini tables. See also tables
available for use, 148
default locking mechanisms, 152
exclusive lock, 150–151
installing, 148
locks, 151–152
share lock, 149–150
transactions, 149
two-phase transaction system, 149
using, 148–152
GNU Public License (GPL), 150
GRANT *statement*
defined, 222
IDENTIFIED BY, 222
privileges, 222
SELECT privileges, 223–224
user table options, 222
using, 222–224
GRANT *tables*
columns_priv, 218, 220–221
db, 218, 220
defined, 217
flushing, 257
reloading, 225, 257
replication and, 285–286
tables_priv, 218, 220–221
understanding, 217–221
user, 218, 219–220
viewing, 225
GROUP BY *clause*
aggregate functions with, 97
datename() function with, 108
date/time formatting functions in, 108
HAVING predicate, 99
groups
creating on Unix/Linux, 233
creating on Mac OS X, 233–234
directory ownership, 235

H

handle_error() *function,* 197
handle_query() *function,* 173–174
handler.pl *file,* 199–201
hardware, upgrading, 322
HAVING *predicate,* 99
--help *flag*
    defined, 326
    with mysqlbinlog, 271
    with mysqldump, 264, 326–327
    output example, 326–327
    using, 326–327
--host *flag,* 275
hour() *function,* 108
HTML::Mason
    advantages, 198
    %ARGS hash, 201
    autohandlers, 202–204
    component example, 203
    configuring, 199
    defined, 198
    file creation, 201
    footer example, 204
    header example, 203
    index.html file example, 204
    installing, 199
    sample file rendering, 204
    syntax tricks, 201
    variable display, 201
HTML
    file components, 201
    parsing functions, 196
    unwanted, removing, 172, 196
HTML page
    code embedded in, 201
    different parameters request, 9
    user data request, 9
    user preference gathering, 8
htmlspecialchars() *function,* 196
httpd.conf *file,* 278
Hungry Minds Customer Care, 340
Hypertext Transfer Protocol (HTTP), 7

I

-i *flag,* 259
-I *flag,* 302
if() *function,* 119

ifnull() *function*
    arguments, 118
    defined, 118
    return value, 90–91
    when to use, 119
--ignore *flag,* 275
IGNORE *keyword,* 275
IIS. *See* **Internet Information Server (Microsoft)**
importing data
    Apache log files, 278–281
    application, 276–278
    with LOAD DATA INFILE statement, 273–275
    with mysqlimport utility, 275
IN *predicate,* 77–78, 87–88
indexes
    adding, 60
    applying, 209–215
    creating, 44–45
    defined, 34
    details, viewing, 209–210
    dropping, 60
    examining, 209
    FULLTEXT, 133
    on joins, 212–215
    left to right, 211
    list, 57
    location, 34
    multi-column, 209–212
    multiple-row, 45
    names, finding, 60
    proper use of, 45, 208
    RAM usage, 320
    resource requirement, 209
    SELECT with, 208–209
    slow querying and, 208
    testing, 209–215
    use methods, 215
ini_get() *function,* 170
INNER JOIN *syntax. See also* **equi-join**
    defined, 85
    joining order, 85–86
InnoDB tables. *See also* **tables**
    advantages, 152
    foreign key constraints support, 46
    locks, 154–155
    multi-versioning transaction model and, 155
    SELECT statement and, 154
    transaction model, 153–154
insert anomaly, 29
INSERT *command*
    date statements, 106
    double quotes, 64

single quotes, 63, 64
syntax, 63
installation
  file links, 16
  Linux, 16–17
  methods, 15
  NuSphere, 16, 19, 20, 152, 326
  post-installation review, 20–23
  from source, 18–19
  Unix/MacOS X, 17–18
  Windows, 17
Internet Information Server (Microsoft), 7, 157
int/integer *column type, 41–42*
INTO OUTFILE *clause, 267–268*
isolation, 138

J

-j *flag, 271*
join
  equi-join, 84–85
  indexes on, 212–215
  inner, 85–86
  outer, 86–87
  self, 91–93

K

-k *flag, 259, 303*
keywords
  AND, 66
  BEGIN WORK, 142
  COMMIT, 142, 143
  CONCURRENT, 274
  EXPLAIN, 210
  FOREIGN KEY, 46
  IGNORE, 275
  LOCAL, 274
  LOW_PRIORITY, 274
  OR, 66
  REFERENCES, 46
  REGEXP, 128
  REPLACE, 275
  ROLLBACK, 142, 143
  UNION, 89

L

last_insert_id() *function*
  defined, 124
  example, 124

in PHP, 124
  thread-specific characteristic, 125
lcase() *function, 121*
left() *function, 96, 121–122*
library, 22
LIKE *predicate, wildcard characters,*
  78, 127
LIMIT *clause*
  defined, 80
  first number in, 80
  results starting point, 80
  uses, 81
--lines-terminated-by *flag, 275*
Linux
  environment, examining, 236–238
  installation from RPMs, 17
  installation from tarballs, 16–17
  my.cnf file, 242
  MySQL start-up configuration, 23
  Perl installation on, 184–185
  PHP/Apache installation on, 158–159
  process initiation at startup, 237–238
  security, 231, 236
  stability, 231
  use recommendation, 231
  user/group creation, 233
Linuxconf, 237
LOAD DATA INFILE *statement*
  clauses, 273
  CONCURRENT, 274
  defined, 273
  example, 274
  IGNORE, 275
  LOCAL, 274
  LOW_PRIORITY, 274
  optional keywords, 274–275
  REPLACE, 275
  security and, 274
LOAD TABLE FROM MASTER *command, 291*
—local *flag, 275*
LOCAL *keyword, 274*
locks
  BDB table, 144
  exclusive, 150–151
  Gemini table, 151–152
  InnoDB table, 154–155
  MyISAM table, 139–141, 144
  page improvement with, 143
  READ, 139–140
  row-level, 147–148
  share, 149–150, 154–155

Continued

locks *(continued)*
  use in applications, 140–141
  WRITE, 140, 141
--lock-tables *flag, 275*
log file
  Apache, importing, 278–281
  cleaning, 271
  closing/re-opening, 257
  contents examination, 270
  placement, 144
  running mysqlbinlog against, 270
--log-bin *flag, 270*
logging in, 225
longtext *column type, 41*
LOW_PRIORITY *keyword, 274*
ltrim() *function, 123*

Ⓜ

-m *flag, 301, 302*
Mac OS X
  Developer Tools CD, 159, 185
  installation on, 18
  Perl installation on, 184–185
  PHP installation on, 159–160
  user/group creation, 233–234
MacSQL
  connections screen, 312
  defined, 312
  options for, 313
  starting, 312
magic quotes, 170
mailing list
  defined, 328
  etiquette, 328
  list of, 330
  MySQL general, 328–329
  topics, 330
  Win32, 329
Mailing list ARCives (MARC), 329
man pages
  example, 327–328
  location, 327
  viewing, 327
Mandrake Linux, 237
manual
  NuSphere install, 326
  on-line, 326
  reading, 325–326
many-to-many relationship, 33

master. See also replication
  parameters, changing, 291
  replication commands, 290
  setting up, 285–286
MATCH...AGAINST *syntax, 133–134*
mathematical operations, 99–103
max() *function, 99*
md5() *function, 120, 177*
mediumint *column type, 42*
mediumtext *column type, 40*
methods. See also DBI module
  connect(), 187
  do(), 193–194
  quote(), 191, 194
  selectall_arrayref(), 192
  selectall_hashref(), 192–193
  selectrow_array(), 191
middleware
  application logic, 10–11
  defined, 7
  example use, 8
  importance, 8
  types, 11
min() *function, 99*
minute() *function, 108*
MODIFY *command, 61*
mod_log_mysql, *281*
mod_perl, *281*
month() *function, 107*
monthname() *function, 107*
multi-column index, 209–212
multi-versioning concurrency model
  defined, 153
  InnoDB tables and, 155
my.cnf *file*
  configuration choices, 243
  defined, 241
  example, 241–242
  locations, 242
  ownership, 250
  permissions, 251
  sections, 243
  set-variable value, 321
  slave, 286
  specifying, 251
  understanding, 241–243
  on Unix/Linux systems, 242
  useful, creating, 250–251
MyISAM tables. See also tables
  ACID transactions and, 139
  BACKUP TABLE command and, 269
  choosing, 141

conversion to BDB tables, 142
as default, 44
defined, 44
errors, 298
file extensions, 269
locking abilities, 139, 144
log analysis and, 278
order processing code, 140–141
packing, 322–323
READ lock, 139–140
SELECT speed, 141
status, checking, 297–298
working with, 139–141
WRITE lock, 140, 141
myisamchk *utility*
  basic format, 301
  defined, 299, 301
  flags, 301–304
  running, 301
  uses, 301
myisampack *utility*
  back up before running, 322
  defined, 322
  using, 322–323
MyODBC, 310
MySQL
  advantages, 12–14
  clients at startup, 242
  commercial support, 331
  competition comparison, 12–14
  configuration options, 13
  dangers, 137–138
  disadvantages, 14
  ease of use, 13
  installation, 15–20
  ODBC with, 310–312
  open source, 13–14
  optimizing, 315–323
  parts, 37
  with Perl, 183–194
  popularity, 13
  post-installation review, 20–23
  speed, 12–13
  status information, 255–256
  transaction support, 13
  version, 88, 124
MySQL AB, 331
MySQL daemon
  configuring, 243–248
  file ownership, 235
  running as mysqlusr, 236
  running as root user, 233

  shutting down, 232
  starting, 236
  at startup, 242
  testing, 232–233
mysql *database*
  defined, 217
  running query on, 218
MySQL general mailing list. See also mailing list
  defined, 328
  MARC archive, 329
  posting to, 329
  subscribing, 329
MySQL server
  configuration options, 243–248
  database availability, 22
  interacting with, 21–22
  slowdown, 320
  starting, 21
mysqladmin *utility*
  administrative functions, 254
  defined, 253
  extended-status, 256
  flush-hosts, 257
  flush-logs, 257
  flush-privileges, 257
  flush-tables, 258
  kill, 257
  man page example, 327–328
  MySQL daemon shutdown with, 232
  password changing with, 254
  ping, 254–255
  processlist, 256
  status, 255–256
  status information commands, 254–257
  use advantages, 254
  variables, 257
  version, 255
mysql_affected_rows() *function, 165*
mysqlbinlog *command, 270, 271*
mysqlcheck *utility*
  copies, 300
  defined, 299, 300
  flags, 300
  options, 301
  on Unix systems, 300
mysql_connect() *function, 162, 175, 176*
mysql_create_db() *function, 164*
mysqld_safe *command, 21, 38*
mysqldump *command*
  --add-drop-table, 266
  --add-locks, 266

Continued

`mysqldump` *command* *(continued)*
  `-c`, 266
  `-d`, 266
  `--database`, 265
  defined, 264
  `--delayed`, 266
  on DOS, 265
  `-e`, 266
  export content, 264
  `--flush-logs`, 267, 271
  format, 265
  `--help`, 264
  mimic applications, 277
  options, 264
  `-q`, 267
  `--result-file`, 265
  `-t`, 266
  on Unix systems, 265
  `-w`, 267
`mysql_error()` *function, 165, 172*
`mysql_fetch_array()` *function, 163*
`mysql_fetch_assoc()` *function, 163*
`mysqlFront`
  column view, 309
  defined, 308
  server connection through, 308
  support for, 309
  table view, 309
MysqlGUI
  defined, 309–310
  download/installation, 310
  uses, 310
  view of, 310
`mysqlhotcopy` *utility, 269*
`mysqlimport` *utility*
  defined, 273, 275
  example, 275
  flags, 275
`mysql_insert_id()` *function, 165*
`mysql_list_dbs()` *function, 164*
`mysql_pconnect()` *function, 162, 175, 176*
MySQL/PHP Database Applications, 169
`mysql_query()` *function*
  arguments, 163
  defined, 162
  error messages, 172
`mysqlshow` *utility*
  defined, 258
  flag combinations, 259
  `-i` flag, 259
  `-k` flag, 259
  output, 258
  `-v` flag, 258, 259

N

natural language search
  defined, 133
  `MATCH...AGAINST` syntax, 133–134
  running, 133–134
normal form
  1st, 30–31
  2nd, 31
  3rd, 31–32
  defined, 30
normalization
  anomaly fixes through, 29–32
  defined, 29
  normal forms, 30–32
  process, 30
`NOT IN` *predicate, 78*
`now()` *function, 111*
null
  defined, 34
  values, 66
  working with, 66
numeric column types. See also columns
  `bigint`, 42
  `decimal`, 42–43
  defined, 41
  `double`, 42
  `float`, 42
  `int/integer`, 41–42
  `mediumint`, 42
  `tinyint`, 42
NuSphere installation. See also installation
  defined, 16, 19
  documentation, 152
  manual, 326
  on Windows, 20

O

`-o` *flag, 300, 303*
one-to-many relationship, 33
one-to-one relationship, 33
one-way algorithm, 120
online shopping cart
  in 1st normal form, 31
  in 3rd normal form, 32
  data storage, 26

sample data, 27
in tables, 29
Open Database Connectivity (ODBC)
defined, 310
linking to MySQL through, 312
using, 310–311
open-source languages, 14
OPTIMIZE TABLE *command, 299*
OR *keyword, 66*
ORDER BY *clause, 79*
order of precedence, 77
O'Reilly's ONLamp.com, 330
OUTER JOIN. *See also* **join**
defined, 86
sample, 86–87
support, 87
syntax, 86, 87

P

packing tables, 322–323
Paradox (Microsoft), 11
part review answers
Friday evening, 333
Saturday afternoon, 334–335
Saturday evening, 335
Saturday morning, 334
Sunday afternoon, 336–337
Sunday morning, 336
passing by reference
example, 170–171
indication, 171
password() *function, 120, 177*
passwords
changing, 254
entering, 232
policies, 237
root user, 232
percentage sign (%) wildcard character, 78, 79
Perl. See also **Common Gateway Interface scripts**
with Apache, 198–204
array retrieval, 191
best practices, 195–204
compiling and installing, 185–186
data insertion, 193–194
data retrieval, 191
data selection, 192–193
defaults, 185
distribution download, 184
embedded, 198
error handling, 196–197
HTML removal, 196

installation testing, 187–188
installing, 183–187
Linux installation, 184–185
Mac OS X installation, 184–185
scalar retrieval, 191
shell commands, 185
tainted variables protection, 191
two-dimensional array retrieval, 192
Unix installation, 184–185
uses, 183
Windows installation, 187
Perl.com, 330
Perl modules
Apache:DBI, 198
CPAN, 186, 188
DBD::mysql, 186–187
DBI, 185–186
Perl script
conversion into CGI script, 188–190
DBI connect() method demonstration, 187–188
MySQL connect, 189–190
row display, 193
PERLDOC utility, 269
permissions. See also **security**
assigning, 233–236
daemon, 235
data file, 235–236
db table, 220
granting, 218
levels, 222
my.cnf file, 251
removing, 224
SELECT, 223–224
tables_priv table, 221
user table, 219
Personal Web Server (PWS), 157
PHP
authentication script, 177–178
best practices, 169–178
code organization, 176–178
configuring, 159
connection configurations, 175–176
connections, establishing, 174–176
connections to server, 162
defined, 157
display table script, 163–164
escaping strings and, 170–171
information page, 161
installation testing, 161
installing, 158–160
last_insert_id() function, 124

Continued

PHP *(continued)*
    Linux/Unix installation, 158–159
    Mac OS X installation, 159–160
    magic quotes, 170
    MySQL functions, 162–167
    port/socket file locations, 175–176
    script using MySQL functions, 165–167
    table manipulation application, 68–72
    Web servers, 157
    Windows installation, 160
php.ini *file, 175*
PHPBuilder, 330
phpinfo() *function, 170*
phpMyAdmin
    database view from, 307
    defined, 305–306
    Documentation.html page, 306
    installing, 306
    running, 306
    table view from, 307
phpWizard.net, 305
placeholders, 195
ports
    MySQL default, 238
    scanning, 238
    testing, 255
--position *flag, 271*
post-installation review. *See also* ***installation***
    databases and files, 22
    libraries, 22
    scripts and applications, 20–22
primary key
    declaration, 44–45
    defined, 30
    multi-column, 31
    in relationship maintenance, 34
processes
    at startup, 237–238
    turning on/off, 238
    unnecessary, 237–238
PURGE MASTER LOGS TO *command, 290*
PWS. *See* ***Personal Web Server***

Q

-q *flag, 267, 301*
quarter() *function, 107*
queries
    efficient, 198
    handling, 172–174
    inefficient, 198
    optimization, 207–215

    optimization for Web, 197–198
    per second average, 256
    results, writing, 267
    slow, logging, 207–208
quote() *method, 191, 194*

R

-r *flag, 300, 303*
-R *flag, 304*
RAM
    importance, 322
    index use of, 320
    open table storage amount, 321
    server slowdown and, 320
    upgrading, 322
rand() *function, 125*
READ *lock, 139–140*
Read the Fine Manual (RTFM), 325–326
recursive functions, 170
Red Hat Package Manager
    errata page, 237
    installation from, 17
    Perl installation via, 184
REFERENCES *keyword, 46*
referential integrity
    benefits, 46
    defined, 34
    MySQL support for, 34
REGEXP *keyword, 128*
regular expressions
    basics for, 128
    character classes, 129–130
    defined, 128
    pattern matching, 128
    resource, 133
    special characters, 128–129
    using, 127–133
relational database. *See also* ***databases***
    defined, 28
    null, 34
Relational Database Management System
        (RDBMS). *See* ***SQL server***
relationship
    maintenance, 34
    many-to-many, 33
    one-to-many, 33
    one-to-one, 33
remove_html() *function, 196*
REPAIR TABLE *command, 299*
--replace *flag, 275*

REPLACE *keyword, 275*
REPLACE *statement*
  defined, 67
  syntax, 67
  uses, 67–68
replication
  applying, to online store, 285
  binary log changes and, 286
  defined, 283
  logs, deleting, 290
  master setup, 285–286
  master-slave system, 284
  setting up, 285–289
  slave setup, 286–289
replication commands
  defined, 289
  master, 290
  slave, 291–292
reserved word list, 38
RESET MASTER *command, 290*
RESET SLAVE *command, 291*
resource identifier, 162
--result-file *flag, 265*
REVOKE *statement, 224*
right() *function, 121–122*
ROLLBACK *command, 142, 143*
round() *function*
  arguments, 102
  defined, 101
  nesting, 102
rounding functions, 101–103
row-level locking, 147–148
rows. See also tables
  for completing join, 215
  deleting, 68
  inserting, 64
  multiple, indexes, 45
  number determination, 97
  retrieval order, 79
  specification in WHERE clause, 65
  two-dimensional array of, 192
  updating, 67
RPM. See Red Hat Package Manager
RTFM, 325–326
rtrim() *function, 123*

Ⓢ

-s *flag, 301, 302*
-S *flag, 304*
script
  mysql.server, 23
  post-installation review, 20–22

scrub_data() *function, 171, 172*
search
  Boolean, 134
  natural language, 133–134
second() *function, 108*
security. See also permissions
  alerts, 237
  Linux, 231, 236
  Unix, 231, 236
SELECT DISTINCT *statement*
  against multiple columns, 81
  defined, 80–81
  syntax, 81
SELECT INTO OUTFILE *statement*
  defined, 267
  ENCLOSED BY clause, 268
  FIELDS TERMINATED BY clause, 267
  LINES TERMINATED BY clause, 268
  OPTIONALLY ENCLOSED BY clause, 268
SELECT *statement*
  basic, 75–76
  defined, 75
  exclusive lock in, 151
  granting, 223–224
  with indexes, 208–209
  InnoDB tables and, 154
  LIMIT clause, 80
  ORDER BY clause, 79
  queries, 75
  results, 76
  for specified columns, 76
  syntax, 75
  WHERE clause, 76–79
selectall_arrayref() *method, 192*
selectall_hashref() *method. See also*
    DBI module
  defined, 192
  use, 193
selectrow_array() *method, 191*
self join, 91
set *column type, 41*
SET SQL_LOG_BIN *command, 290*
SET SQL_SLAVE_SKIP_COUNTER *command, 291*
SET TIMESTAMP *statement, 270*
share lock, 149–150
shell script
  actions, 259–260
  administrative sample, 260–261
  creating, 259–260
SHOW COLUMNS *command*
  results, 56–57, 209
  syntax, 56

SHOW CREATE TABLE *command, 58*
SHOW DATABASES *command, 55, 217–218*
SHOW GRANTS *statement, 225*
SHOW INDEX *command, 57, 209–210*
SHOW MASTER LOGS *command, 290*
SHOW MASTER STATUS *command, 290*
SHOW PROCESSLIST *command, 256*
SHOW SLAVE STATUS *command, 291, 292*
SHOW STATUS *command, 320*
SHOW TABLE STATUS *command, 57–58*
SHOW TABLES *command, 56*
SHOW VARIABLES *command*
  key_buffer_size, 321
  listing, 257
  table_cache, 321
sin() *function, 100*
slave. See also replication
  my.cnf file, 286
  replication commands, 291–292
  setting up, 286–289
  thread, starting/stopping, 291
slave configuration options
  log-slave-updates, 289
  master-connect-retry, 287
  master-info-file, 287
  replicate-do-db=database_name, 289
  replicate-do-
     table=db_name.table_name, 287
  replicate-ignore-db=database_name, 288
  replicate-ignore-
     table=db_name.table_name, 287
  replicate-rewrite-db=from_name-
     >to_name, 289
  replicate-wild-do-
     table=db_name.table_name, 288
  replicate-wild-ignore-
     table=db_name.table_name, 288
  skip-slave-start, 289
  slave_read_timeout=#, 289
SLAVE START *command, 290*
SLAVE STOP *command, 291*
Slow Query log
  defined, 207
  query slowness, 208
source installation. See also installation
  flag settings, 19
  process requirements, 18
  steps, 18–19
special characters. See also regular expressions
  * (asterisk), 128, 129, 134
  ^ (caret), 129, 131
  $ (dollar sign), 129

. (period), 129
+ (plus sign), 129, 134
? (question mark), 129
  combinations, 129
  defined, 128
  list, 129
SQL. See Structured Query Language
SQL server
  in applications development process, 12
  benchmarks, 13
  defined, 5
  in development process, 5–12
  functions, 7
  query function, 7
  statistical information function, 7
start-up options. See also configurable variables
  base-dir, 243
  bind-address, 243
  complete list of, 243
  data-dir, 243
  default-character-set, 244
  default-table-type, 244
  language, 244
  Log, 244
  Log-bin, 244
  Log-slow-queries, 244
  myisam-recover, 244
  port, 244
  --safe-show-database, 245
  skip-grant-tables, 245
  skip-networking, 244
  socket, 245
  tmpdir, 245
  user, 245
status information, 255–256
straight join. See equi-join
string
  concatenation, 122–123
  escaping, 169–171
  functions, 121–123
  lowercase/uppercase conversion, 121
  matching, 128
  parsing, 128
  spaces, removing, 123
strip_tags() *function, 172, 196*
Structured Query Language (SQL). See also
     SQL server
  defined, 6
  implementations, 6–7
subselects, 88
sum() *function, 98*
SuSE, 237

System DSN, 311
system information functions, 123–124

T

-t *flag, 266, 303*
-T *flag, 302*
table manipulation application
  code, 68–71
  defined, 68
  illustrated, 71
  logic, 72
tables. See also columns; data; rows
  alterations, 58–61
  analyzing, 299
  BDB, 142–145
  checking, 297–298
  creation best practices, 54–55
  creation information, 58
  defined, 26
  definition replication, 91
  foreign key, 30
  Gemini, 148–152
  information, 57–58
  InnoDB, 152–155
  joins, 84–87
  MyISAM, 44, 139–141
  names, 38
  names, changing, 59
  online shopping cart data, 29
  open, closing, 258
  optimizing, 299
  packing, 322–323
  primary key, 30
  problems, 27–29
  relationships, 33
  repairing, 299
  temporary, 89
  types, 44
  viewing, 56
tables_priv *table. See also* GRANT *tables*
  columns listing, 221
  defined, 218
  permissions, 221
tan() *function, 100*
tarballs
  defined, 16
  installing from, 16–17
TCP Wrappers, 238
temporary table
  creating, 89
  inserting in, 90

text *column type, 40*
text column types. See also columns
  char, 39, 40
  enum, 41
  longtext, 41
  mediumtext, 40
  set, 41
  text, 40
  tinytext, 40
  varchar, 39, 40
threads
  active, viewing, 256
  slave, starting/stopping, 291
time *column type, 43–44*
timestamp *column type, 43*
tinyint *column type, 42*
tinytext *column type, 40*
transactions
  ACID support, 138–139
  application, 142–143
  code rewriting with, 143–144
  defined, 138
  Gemini table, 149
  MySQL support, 13
  properties of, 138–139
transitive dependency, 31–32
trigonometric functions, 100–101
trim() *function, 123*
troubleshooting CD, 339–340
truncate() *function, 103*

U

-u *flag, 303*
-U *flag, 302*
ucase() *function*
  argument, 95–96
  defined, 95, 121
underscore (_) wildcard character, 78, 79
union
  defined, 89
  example, 89
  mimicking full outer join, 90
  workaround, 89
UNION *keyword, 89*
Unix
  environment, examining, 236–238
  installing on, 17–18
  my.cnf file, 242
  MySQL start-up configuration, 23
  mysqlcheck on, 300

Continued

Unix *(continued)*
mysqldump on, 265
Perl compilation, 184–185
Perl installation on, 184–185
PHP/Apache installation on, 158–159
security, 231, 236
stability, 231
use recommendation, 231
user/group creation, 233
un-normalizing data
dangers, 318
defined, 318
example, 318
when to use, 318–319
update anomaly. *See also* ***anomaly***
defined, 27
solving, 28
UPDATE ***statement***
defined, 67
row-level locking, 147–148
syntax, 67
WHERE clause, 76
upgrading hardware, 322
USE ***command, 38, 56***
user data
cleaning, 169–172
handling, 195–196
HTML page request, 9
--user ***flag, 241***
user() ***function, 124***
user ***table.*** *See also* GRANT ***tables***
administrative rights columns, 219–220
columns listing, 219
defined, 218
users
creating, on Unix/Linux, 233
creating, on Mac OS X, 233–234
login form, 177, 178

V

-v ***flag, 258, 259, 302***
-V ***flag, 302***
varchar ***column type, 39, 40***
variables
BDB table, 144
configurable, 246–248
tainted, protection, 191
viewing, 257
version() ***function, 124***

W

-w ***flag, 267, 302***
Web applications. *See* ***applications***
Web development tools, 6
Web form
code, 68–71
creating, 68–72
illustrated, 71
logic, 72
Web server
Apache, 7, 157–159, 278–281
function, 7
with PHP, 157
types, 7
Web sites, 330
weberdev.com, 330
week() ***function, 107***
weekday() ***function, 107***
WHERE ***clause***
comparison operators, 65
conditions, 65
data/time formatting functions in, 107–108
defined, 65
DELETE statement, 76–77
grouping portions of, 77
IN predicate, 77–78
LIKE predicate, 78–79
multiple conditions, 66
NOT IN predicate, 78
SELECT statement, 76–79
UPDATE statement, 76–77
wildcard characters
LIKE predicate, 78, 127
percentage sign (%), 78, 79
searching for, 79
underscore (_), 78, 79
Win32 mailing list, 329
Windows
installation on, 17
NuSphere installation on, 20
Perl installation on, 187
PHP installation on, 160
WinZip, 17
WRITE ***lock, 140, 141***

Y

year() ***function, 108***
year ***column type, 44***
yearweek() ***function, 108***

Hungry Minds, Inc.
End-User License Agreement

READ THIS. You should carefully read these terms and conditions before opening the software packet(s) included with this book ("Book"). This is a license agreement ("Agreement") between you and Hungry Minds, Inc. ("HMI"). By opening the accompanying software packet(s), you acknowledge that you have read and accept the following terms and conditions. If you do not agree and do not want to be bound by such terms and conditions, promptly return the Book and the unopened software packet(s) to the place you obtained them for a full refund.

1. **License Grant.** HMI grants to you (either an individual or entity) a nonexclusive license to use one copy of the enclosed software program(s) (collectively, the "Software") solely for your own personal or business purposes on a single computer (whether a standard computer or a workstation component of a multi-user network). The Software is in use on a computer when it is loaded into temporary memory (RAM) or installed into permanent memory (hard disk, CD-ROM, or other storage device). HMI reserves all rights not expressly granted herein.

2. **Ownership.** HMI is the owner of all right, title, and interest, including copyright, in and to the compilation of the Software recorded on the disk(s) or CD-ROM ("Software Media"). Copyright to the individual programs recorded on the Software Media is owned by the author or other authorized copyright owner of each program. Ownership of the Software and all proprietary rights relating thereto remain with HMI and its licensers.

3. **Restrictions on Use and Transfer.**

   (a) You may only (i) make one copy of the Software for backup or archival purposes, or (ii) transfer the Software to a single hard disk, provided that you keep the original for backup or archival purposes. You may not (i) rent or lease the Software, (ii) copy or reproduce the Software through a LAN or other network system or through any computer subscriber system or bulletin-board system, or (iii) modify, adapt, or create derivative works based on the Software.

   (b) You may not reverse engineer, decompile, or disassemble the Software. You may transfer the Software and user documentation on a permanent basis, provided that the transferee agrees to accept the terms and conditions of this Agreement and you retain no copies. If the Software is an update or has been updated, any transfer must include the most recent update and all prior versions.

4. **Restrictions on Use of Individual Programs.** You must follow the individual requirements and restrictions detailed for each individual program in Appendix B of this Book. These limitations are also contained in the individual license agreements recorded on the Software Media. These limitations may include a requirement that after using the program for a specified period of time, the user must pay a registration fee or discontinue use. By opening the Software packet(s), you will be agreeing to abide by the licenses and restrictions for these individual programs that are detailed in Appendix B and on the Software Media. None of the material on this Software Media or listed in this Book may ever be redistributed, in original or modified form, for commercial purposes.

5. Limited Warranty.

(a) HMI warrants that the Software and Software Media are free from defects in materials and workmanship under normal use for a period of sixty (60) days from the date of purchase of this Book. If HMI receives notification within the warranty period of defects in materials or workmanship, HMI will replace the defective Software Media.

(b) HMI AND THE AUTHOR OF THE BOOK DISCLAIM ALL OTHER WARRANTIES, EXPRESS OR IMPLIED, INCLUDING WITHOUT LIMITATION IMPLIED WARRANTIES OF MERCHANTABILITY AND FITNESS FOR A PARTICULAR PURPOSE, WITH RESPECT TO THE SOFTWARE, THE PROGRAMS, THE SOURCE CODE CONTAINED THEREIN, AND/OR THE TECHNIQUES DESCRIBED IN THIS BOOK. HMI DOES NOT WARRANT THAT THE FUNCTIONS CONTAINED IN THE SOFTWARE WILL MEET YOUR REQUIREMENTS OR THAT THE OPERATION OF THE SOFTWARE WILL BE ERROR FREE.

(c) This limited warranty gives you specific legal rights, and you may have other rights that vary from jurisdiction to jurisdiction.

6. Remedies.

(a) HMI's entire liability and your exclusive remedy for defects in materials and workmanship shall be limited to replacement of the Software Media, which may be returned to HMI with a copy of your receipt at the following address: Software Media Fulfillment Department, Attn.: *MySQL Weekend Crash Course*™, Hungry Minds, Inc., 10475 Crosspoint Blvd., Indianapolis, IN 46256, or call 1-800-762-2974. Please allow four to six weeks for delivery. This Limited Warranty is void if failure of the Software Media has resulted from accident, abuse, or misapplication. Any replacement Software Media will be warranted for the remainder of the original warranty period or thirty (30) days, whichever is longer.

(b) In no event shall HMI or the author be liable for any damages whatsoever (including without limitation damages for loss of business profits, business interruption, loss of business information, or any other pecuniary loss) arising from the use of or inability to use the Book or the Software, even if HMI has been advised of the possibility of such damages.

(c) Because some jurisdictions do not allow the exclusion or limitation of liability for consequential or incidental damages, the above limitation or exclusion may not apply to you.

7. U.S. Government Restricted Rights. Use, duplication, or disclosure of the Software for or on behalf of the United States of America, its agencies and/or instrumentalities (the "U.S. Government") is subject to restrictions as stated in paragraph (c)(1)(ii) of the Rights in Technical Data and Computer Software clause of DFARS 252.227-7013, or subparagraphs (c) (1) and (2) of the Commercial Computer Software - Restricted Rights clause at FAR 52.227-19, and in similar clauses in the NASA FAR supplement, as applicable.

8. General. This Agreement constitutes the entire understanding of the parties and revokes and supersedes all prior agreements, oral or written, between them and may not be modified or amended except in a writing signed by both parties hereto that specifically refers to this Agreement. This Agreement shall take precedence over any other documents that may be in conflict herewith. If any one or more provisions contained in this Agreement are held by any court or tribunal to be invalid, illegal, or otherwise unenforceable, each and every other provision shall remain in full force and effect.

CD-ROM Installation Instructions

The CD that accompanies this book includes the following:

- Author-created materials
- Troubleshooting tips

See Appendix B for details on installing items from the CD.